THE OAKWOOD LIBRARY

THE MANCHESTER & MILFORD RAILWAY

JOHN S. HOLDEN

THE OAKWOOD PRESS
1979

BIBLIOGRAPHICAL NOTE ON THE 'OAKWOOD LIBRARY' SERIES

For the benefit of present and future collectors of this series, the following notes on publications over the past forty years are given:

The series was started with the first edition of The North London Railway *in September 1937; this was in wire-stitched format, but thereafter flat-back binding was used, and up to No. 17 there was a limited cloth-bound edition published at the same time as the paper-back. In 1952 a new series was started bound in boards with quarter-cloth and of a larger page-size; these were numbered from 51 to distinguish them, but after No. 59 was published in 1959, this style was given up and later issues were in flat-back paper binding and numbered on from the earlier series; this explains why for instance No. 52 is dated 1952 (first edition) while No. 41 is dated 1977. The gap of seven years between Nos. 2 and 3 is accounted for by the fact that both editors were in the Army. The editor for issues No. 1 to 17 was R. Michael Robbins and for later issues R.W. Kidner. Most of this series have been reprinted, some more than once; No. 1 is now in its eighth reprint. In recent years, owing to the high cost of thread-sewn binding, some of the reprints or new issues of the smaller titles have been in wire-stitched format. The above notes are provided because this series, devised to record the history of Britain's smaller railways, is the longest-running so far in the history of railway publishing. It should be noted that the series has on the whole been confined to lines of a fairly substantial nature; the history of many of the really small companies, some of narrow gauge, has been covered in a companion series "Locomotion Papers", started in 1946.*

ISBN 0 85361 244 7

CHAPTER 1

"THE NEAREST AND BEST COMMUNICATION", 1845-1860

By 1845, railways were an accepted part of the landscape. The lessons from the early years of cautious experiment had been learnt. Confidence in the money-earning potential of the new form of travel ran high, unchecked by the disappointments and failures to come. There was, so it appeared, nothing but a want of enterprise to prevent those major towns and cities not yet endowed with rail communication from being linked.

Thus it was that the first scheme to connect Manchester with Milford Haven was conceived. Manchester was a thriving manufacturing centre, its wares sought all over the country and beyond. At Milford, there was a natural harbour with obvious potential as a port, being better situated than Liverpool to serve the growing commerce with North America. Another factor may also have influenced the promoters of the Manchester and Milford Haven Railway in 1845. If it were built, Manchester would have an alternative to the stranglehold of the Port of Liverpool and of the erstwhile Liverpool and Manchester Railway.

The real motives of the promoters will have to remain conjecture, for few details of the 1845 scheme have survived. The line was, however, expected to cost about £2.6 million, and was reputed to have been engineered by Rastrick. It also boasted no fewer than 86 directors! The route would have started at Crewe and proceeded by way of Whitchurch and Oswestry to Welshpool, following the course of the River Severn from there to Newton and Llanidloes. A branch to Aberystwyth was planned from near Devil's Bridge, the main line descending to the River Teifi which it would have followed by way of Tregaron and Lampeter to Newcastle Emyln. A short branch to Cardigan was intended to start here. Milford was to be reached finally by way of Haverfordwest.

In the event, this grandiose scheme came to nothing, in common with so many others from the years of the Railway Mania.

Another contemporary plan merits passing mention, as it anticipated the route from Carmarthen to Aberystwyth — all that was eventually built of the ambitious "Manchester and Milford" concept — by more than 20 years. Known as the Great North and South Wales and Worcester Railway, it was in fact to continue beyond Aberystwyth along the cliffs to Borth, thence to Machynlleth. Its total

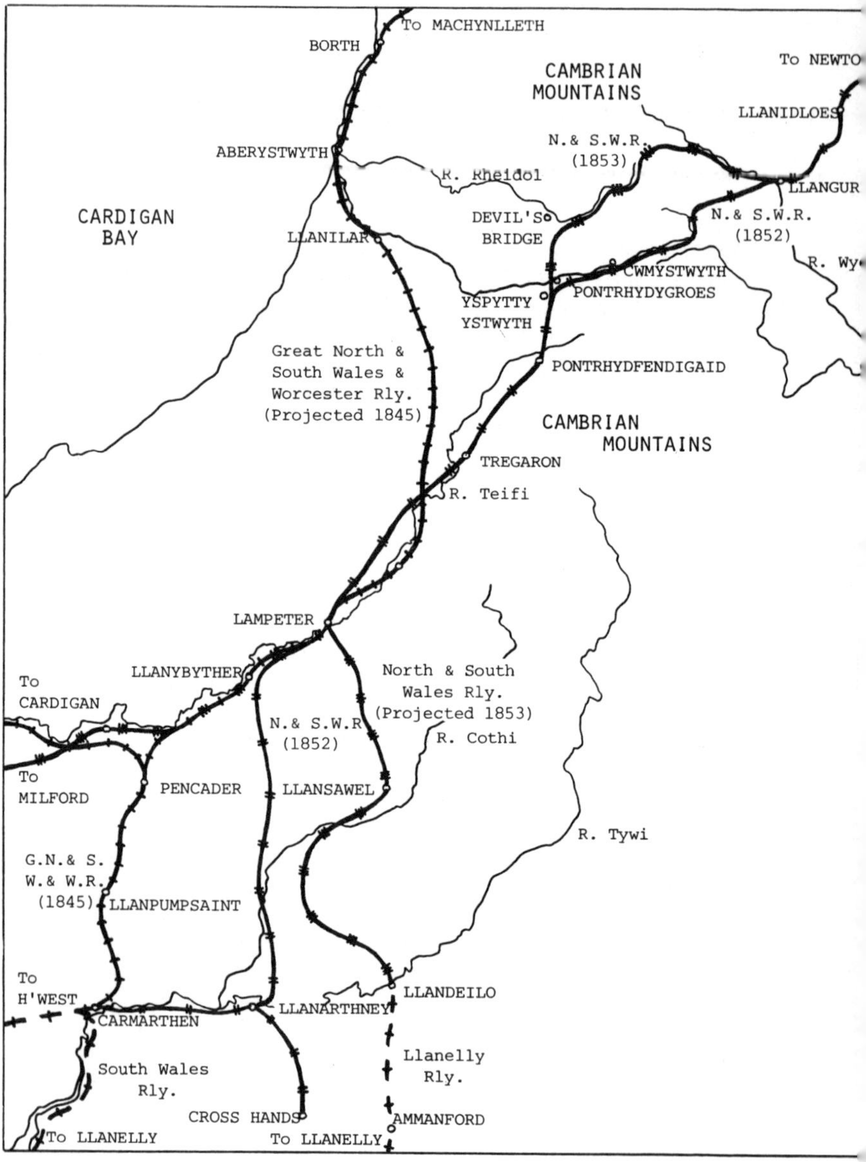

1845 - 1853. Antecedents of the Manchester and Milford Railway.

length of 66½ miles included no less than 10½ miles in tunnel, so it is scarcely surprising that this scheme also failed to progress any further.

Seven years were to elapse before the idea of a rail link between the industrial North of England and a port at Milford Haven was resurrected. This new proposal, like its predecessor, was destined not to materialise. The North and South Wales Railway of 1852 was to commence by a junction north of the River Tywi and just west of Carmarthen, with the South Wales Railway. The South Wales company's line at that time ran no further towards Pembrokeshire, although plans were well advanced to extend its authorised but as yet unbuilt branch to Haverfordwest, onwards towards Neyland on the north shore of Milford Haven. So the North and South Wales Railway's backers might feel reasonably confident that their ultimate goal could soon be reached over South Wales metals.

The plans show a line heading east from the junction, across the Tywi just beyond Carmarthen, and on to Llanarthney, nine miles distant. From here, a branch was planned to Cross Hands, a mining town and outpost of the Llanelly Railway. The main line was to turn north, over the Rivers Tywi and Cothi and through three miles of tunnel to emerge at Llanybyther on the River Teifi, which was to be followed to Pontrhydfendigaid.

Then, however, came the obstacle of the Cambrian Mountains, dividing West Wales from the valleys of the Upper Severn and Wye, the Midland Plain and beyond. The problems of driving a railway through this barrier were to prove the downfall of the Manchester and Milford Railway, as will be seen. The question facing the promoters of all the various schemes which set out to cross the mountains in this vicinity was, which route to adopt? Both Pontrhydfendigaid to the west and Llanidloes to the east are at much the same height above sea level, but in between a climb of at least 700 feet would be unavoidable. Two obvious alternatives presented themselves. The first, from the area of Devil's Bridge, would have been to head north-east, up under the slopes of Plynlimon, to about 1,300 feet above datum, before descending to join the Wye Valley down to Llangurig and Llanidloes. This is very much the course of the present-day main road inland from Aberystwyth. The other, further to the south, would have been to follow the old mountain road beside the River Ystwyth to its summit, also about 1,300 feet above sea level. It would then have been necessary to strike off north-east in the direction of Llangurig if a very devious route was to be avoided.

In engineering terms, there can have been little to choose between the two, since no clear preference ever emerged. Both would have involved severe gradients and a long summit tunnel. The second of the two routes described was perhaps just to be preferred, because it avoided a major viaduct over the Ystwyth Gorge near Pontrydygroes.

The 1852 scheme opted for this southern route, along the Ystwyth into the marshy uplands between Ystwyth and Elan. There it was to curve sharply to follow a tributary, the Diluw, deeper into the hills, before entering a tunnel, almost two miles long and up to 650 feet below the mountainside. The line would then have descended on a virtually straight course for the remaining three miles to Llangurig. Penpontbren, 64 miles from the start and later the site of the Manchester and Milford Railway's junction with the Mid Wales Railway, would have been passed on the way to Llanidloes. Beyond Llanidloes, the River Severn was to be crossed and recrossed before the line terminated at Newtown, 77 miles from Carmarthen. Newtown was not in 1852 connected by railway to any other part of the country, but there were good prospects that it soon would be.

The North and South Wales Railway was launched afresh in the next year, retaining the same title. The route was, however, modified at both ends to take account of developments involving neighbouring companies, and of the undoubted attraction of an independent route to Milford; the line's role in "connecting Manchester and the North with Milford Town and Haven" was much emphasised. The prospectus for the revised scheme provides an excellent example of the thinking of those who sought to promote railways through this sparsely populated and mountainous area, and demonstrates the way in which it was hoped both to attract the investing public, and to make the line a paying proposition.

"The centre of the Principality of Wales is" — so the prospectus ran — "entirely destitute of railway accommodation, although perhaps there is no part of the Kingdom where greater advantages would arise from (its) establishment . . . The district contains many important towns . . . abounds in water power, and is exceedingly rich in various minerals, comprising at its southern limits the most extensive anthracite coal field in the Kingdom. While at the present time it supplies the neighbouring manufacturing districts with (much) agricultural produce, its capability would be greatly augmented by the facility afforded by railway communication of obtaining valuable manures, and especially lime, to be distributed throughout the country at a moderate cost . . . A railway in such a district must undoubtedly prove a remunerative project having reference solely to the local traffic, but when it is borne in mind that the entire line carried through Cardiganshire will also complete the link of communication from Manchester and the North by the shortest route to Milford, it becomes evident that the prospects . . . will be of the very first order. The advantages of the roadstead at Milford . . . cannot be overstated, whilst it is most favourably situated for vessels trading to the greater part of the world . . . An Act of Parliament and Admiralty sanction for the construction of docks of great magnitude at Milford have already been obtained, and railway communication is alone required to make it the first outport in the Kingdom.

"A Royal Charter has lately been granted to a company for establishing a direct steam navigation with Australia, the directors of which have decided that Milford Haven shall be the port of departure . . . In respect of pleasure traffic . . . thousands of tourists are prevented every year from visiting the romantic scenery of South Wales, owing to the absence of access by railway to various beauty spots situate on its western coast.

"The entire line may be thus described. It will commence by a junction at Llanidloes with the railway to that town sanctioned by Parliament, and will be continued by Llangurig, Yspytty Ystwyth and Tregaron to Lampeter . . . down the valley of the Teifi . . . and on by the most favourable route to Milford. A line will branch off near Lampeter, pass by Llansawel and the Valley of the Cothi to Llandeilo, where it will form a junction with the railway from Llanelly, and thus secure . . . cheap distribution of coal and lime throughout the counties of Carmarthen and Cardigan at a cost which will be less than the amount now paid for tolls alone on the present turnpike roads. It has been decided not to undertake at the outset branches to Cardigan, Aberystwyth and Carmarthen, all which however, when the formation of the trunk line is secured will receive the earliest attention of the directors.

"The line is promoted by the landed interest throughout its course" — it was dubbed a "landholders' line". "Friendly negotiations have been entered into with the Llanelly and Llandeilo Railway Company . . . the Llanidloes and Newtown Railway, and also with the proprietor of the proposed docks at Milford . . . The line's advantages may be briefly summed up as follows — it will meet the wants of the large population of several counties . . . and open the most direct communication from Manchester and the North to Milford Haven. The undertaking has already received public approbation and extensive local support from the nobility, magistrates, clergy and owners and occupiers of land throughout the counties of Carmarthen, Pembroke, Cardigan and Montgomery" — the prospectus in fact began with a list of 96 such local notables including the Earl of Lisburne at Crosswood, or Trawscoed, and the Dean of St David's — "and all the great proprietors on the line have stated their willingness to meet the company in the most liberal manner. The promoters are in possession of accurate statistics as to the traffic, and after a very careful estimate . . . it may be fairly stated that . . . a remunerative dividend will be secured. It will be difficult to estimate the enormous addition through traffic from the north which must come upon the line when once open to Milford Haven, and which must be taken into consideration as a source of future increase of revenue."

Having thus raised expectations with vistas of a great traffic artery, the promoters were forced to conclude tamely that "in consequence of the continued unsettled state of the money market, the company have determined to confine their present application to Parliament for power to construct the northern section only . . . between Llanidloes and Lampeter" 40,000 shares of £12 10s. each were deemed sufficient for this purpose, 40% of the expected outlay on the entire line.

It might be thought that in these circumstances, the adoption of a more ambitious route at the southern end was of academic interest. However, the appeal of Milford as the ultimate terminus was probably necessary to "sell" the scheme, even in truncated form. The Extension of the South Wales Railway to the west was in any case not proceeding at the hoped-for speed. Its line was also broad gauge, so could not be used for through running: hence the desire to establish direct access to Milford and, via Llandeilo, to the South Wales industrial region. It should be noted, though, that despite the wording of the prospectus, the Llanelly Railway's extension to Llandeilo was not then built, being opened in 1857.

At the other end, the publication of proposals for the Llanidloes and Newtown Railway late in 1852 meant that there was now little purpose in projecting the North and South Wales Railway beyond Llanidloes. The course adopted for the mountain section was revised at the same time in favour of the northern alternative. Onwards from Yspytty Ystwyth, the new route would have crossed the Ystwyth on a substantial viaduct, tunnelling just south of Devil's Bridge to join the course of the Mynach and then the Myherin. At Blaen Myherin, a lonely farmhouse deep in the hills, there was to be another tunnel, over a mile long, before the line emerged into the valley of the Wye.

The money market was obviously more unsettled than the promoters gave credit for, so nothing further was heard of the North and South Wales Railway. For the next stage in the evolution of the "Manchester and Milford" concept, we must turn to a company with ostensibly much more limited horizons, the Carmarthen and Cardigan Railway.

In 1854, an Act was obtained for the construction of a line from Carmarthen to Newcastle Emlyn, the intention being to secure powers subsequently to extend to Cardigan. Unlike the other projects considered so far, this was essentially a local concern, acting as a feeder to the broad gauge South Wales Railway. It was therefore only to be expected that it too would be built with the wider 7-foot gauge to obviate a break at Carmarthen; and this was in fact specified in the company's Act.

The Carmarthen and Cardigan was a most valuable stepping stone for those who sought a north-south link through Central Wales, but who found the means eluded them. Reliance on part of the line to

Newcastle Emlyn would usefully reduce the total length of railway needed to complete the link and tap the lucrative North-of-England traffic. Through running was obviously of the essence if this purpose was to be served. With both the South Wales Railway and the Carmarthen and Cardigan built to the broad gauge, there was thus a certain logic in the north-south link also having this gauge.

Just such an arrangement was proposed in the Direct Manchester and Milford Haven Junction Railway scheme of 1854. This line was to commence at a junction with the Carmarthen and Cardigan near Pencader, from which point running powers were sought to Carmarthen. At the northern end, conversion of the Llanidloes and Newtown Railway was envisaged. A new broad gauge line was proposed between Oswestry and Newtown, anticipating the standard gauge railway of that name by a year. Finally, at Oswestry, there was to be a connection with the Oswestry branch of the Shrewsbury and Chester Railway. Quite how it was intended to cope with the break of gauge here does not emerge.

From Pencader, the line was projected north to the River Teifi which was to be followed by way of Llanybyther to Lampeter. After bridging the river here, the railway would have continued north-east before recrossing the Teifi just before Tregaron. A route was then planned alongside the Bog of Tregaron, Cors Goch Glanteifi, and on to Pontrhydfendigaid and Yspytty Ystywth, where a viaduct of some 17 arches, each of 60 feet span, was called for; two centre arches being 200 feet above the level of the Ystwyth. Thereafter, the northern or Blaen Myherin — Pant Mawr alignment was adopted. At Llanidloes, an end-on junction with the Llanidloes and Newtown Railway was spurned, probably to ease the gradients from Llangurig. A trailing connection about 1½ miles out towards Newtown was planned instead. This meant an unnecessarily longer line and either independent traffic facilities or reversal into Llanidloes (L. & N.) station.

The Direct Manchester and Milford Haven Junction Railway would have been well-endowed with tunnels, no doubt because contemporary thinking demanded easy curves and gradients if the advantages of the broad gauge were to be exploited. The first was to be at Pont Llanio; an alternative to the two substantial viaducts over a loop in the Teifi which were ultimately built. Others were called for near Yspytty Ystwyth, at Devil's Bridge, where a particularly sharp bend in the line would otherwise have been required, at the summit between Myherin and Pant Mawr on the River Wye, and at Penpontbren; all told, some 4 miles.

The fortunes of this particular scheme were clearly intertwined with those of the Carmarthen and Cardigan Railway. Yet about all the C. &. C. did successfully was to obtain its Act of Incorporation.

Thereafter, it ran into numerous problems, culminating in bankruptcy. Along the way, there was much delay in the construction of the line and an unsuccessful application to Parliament for a change of gauge. With such an unreliable neighbour, the broad gauge Direct Manchester and Milford Haven Junction predictably fared no better than its predecessors.

Despite its own parlous financial state, the Carmarthen and Cardigan was not averse to encouraging new lines. At the beginning of 1857, we find Robert Bower of the C. & C. writing to one William Chambers regarding the "Manchester and Milford" project, and claiming that he had been at personal expense in having surveys and Parliamentary plans made. Bower had also visited Manchester with a view to raising finance, but without success. In his view, efforts would have to be concentrated on Cardiganshire instead, and support canvassed from the landed proprietors there who, with the notable exception of the Earl of Lisburne, "were undecided as to which of the possible lines they should fall in with". For, according to Bower, "unless a spirited attempt is made this year to link Pencader and Llanidloes, the intervening district will be excluded from railway communication . . . as the projected line between Llandovery and Llanidloes via St Harmon will entirely supercede the route from Yspytty Ystwyth to Llangurig, and would certainly be easier and cheaper in construction."

William Chambers was active during much of 1858 with just such a "spirited attempt" to get a Pencader-Llanidloes link under way. Solicitors and Parliamentary agents were found, meetings convened with local landowners, and a good deal of lobbying undertaken to muster support. Henry Jones, a local M.P., wrote to Chambers in favour of the project, his only reservation being "the ranges of high ground between Llanidloes and Cwmystwyth . . . a formidable obstacle in a purely local line". The Llanidloes and Newtown Railway was also amenable, as well it might be in view of the prospects of additional traffic: the L. & N. had actually contemplated a scheme of its own for a line south from Llanidloes.

An 1858 report described the gradients beyond the Ystwyth valley as good, and indicated that no heavy works were required apart from the tunnel and a viaduct near Llangurig: at this stage, the "southern" route over the hills was proposed. Mention was also made of the many lead, silver and copper mines within easy reach of the line's course, and of the prospects for through traffic to Milford with an 80 mile advantage over the route via Gloucester: the line which was being advocated would cut the total distance from Manchester to about 210 miles. Finally, the break of gauge at Pencader was noted with the suggestion "that the share holders will soon see the necessity of dispensing with it by continuing the line on direct to Milford Haven at an early period", a view which was indeed advanced by some local landowners.

A meeting was held on the 6th July 1859 at the Mariners' Hotel, Haverfordwest, to consider the best means of promoting the new "Manchester and Milford" scheme. Hamilton Fulton's survey of the route was approved, and it was agreed to seek the co-operation of the London and North Western and South Wales Railways. The Carmarthen and Cardigan was a notable absentee from this list. Its opposition could be assumed from the floating of a nominally independent, but in fact C. & C.-dominated, company to build a rival line from Pencader to Lampeter.

By 1860, the Manchester and Milford concern was taking shape. A contractor had been found, Frederick Beeston, who would construct the whole line for £447,000 exclusive of land purchase. Arrangements had been made to borrow the Parliamentary deposit from the Union Bank. One Alfred Beeston was appointed Secretary, a post he had previously held for the N. & S. Wales Rly. scheme, and four provisional directors were named: William Chambers, Frederick Harrison, Colonel William Thomas Rowland Powell M.P., and C. Locock Webb.

The Manchester and Milford's Bill was through its Committee Stage in May, so the directors could give their approval to the prospectus with some confidence. The prospectus reveals two extra provisional directors: John Barrow, later to be the major influence in the affairs of the Manchester and Milford Railway, and the Hon. Robert Fulke Greville of Castle Hall, Milford Haven.

Capital of £555,000 in £10 shares was proposed for the stated purpose of "promoting a railway to complete the nearest and best communication between Manchester and Milford Haven, and to accommodate the agricultural and mineral interests of Cardiganshire". This was to be achieved with a line from Llanidloes, accessible from the north via either the Great Western or the London and North Western Railway, which "after passing through the heart of the lead mining district" was to follow the Teifi for most of the remaining distance to the Carmarthen and Cardigan Railway at Pencader: a route virtually identical to that proposed in the 1854 broad gauge scheme. Access to Milford would be via the South Wales Railway from Carmarthen.

The prospectus then went on to cite the familiar justification for the line, stressing the difficulties of carting coal and limestone in the area, and the limitations placed on a lead mining industry forced to rely on water power. Tourist traffic was not forgotten; nor was the depressed state of agriculture, a result of primitive communications. Much play was made of an agreement with major landowners along the route, whereby payment for land would be in shares. An optimistic picture was painted for through traffic based on the expansion of Milford as a port. One shipping line, it was stated, was already operating from there to Portugal and Brazil, and there were daily sailings to Southern Ireland.

The prospectus concluded with some dubious cost and profit estimates. If the cost of construction were in line with a "national average", the total outlay on almost 52 miles of railway would be just under £700,000, of which £125,000 would be for land and £40,000, Parliamentary costs. The Manchester and Milford's directors believed however, that they could manage on respectively £30,000 and £10,000, reducing the total needed to around £575,000. Leafing through the statistics, they were also able to discover that railways were, according to another "national average", earning £1,400 net per mile in 1858. For the Manchester and Milford, therefore, this would equate to more than £70,000 p.a. net profit; enough to pay 5% interest on loans and 6½% on shares twice over: so much for an objective assessment of the line's earning capacity!

Whatever the deficiencies of the prospectus, the Manchester and Milford's Bill cleared its Parliamentary hurdles where all before had failed. The Royal Assent was received on July 23rd 1860, much to the surprise of certain parties. Chambers wrote to the company's solicitors, "that we have succeeded in obtaining an Act and that so quickly seems to have excited as much surprise in the County as you say it has in London".

Share capital was set in the Act at £555,000, and a further £185,000 could be borrowed with the usual precondition that all shares should first be subscribed. Of relevance to the railway's subsequent history was clause 9, authorising the appointment of a receiver should arrears exceed £15,000. Three years were allowed for purchase of land, and powers were to lapse in the normal way if the line was not completed within five. An omission was any provision for mixing the gauge of the Carmarthen and Cardigan Railway to allow running powers to Carmarthen. The M. & M. was empowered to construct a junction with the C. & C. at Pencader and no more. There were also to be junctions with the Llanidloes and Newtown and Mid Wales Railways, but again no running powers.

The Act divided the line into five sections: the first from Pencader to Pencarreg, about four miles short of Lampeter; the next, on to Tregaron, and the third to Yspytty Ystwyth. The fourth was the difficult one, crossing the mountains by the "northern" route via Devil's Bridge, to Pant Mawr in the Wye valley. The final section would take the railway to its junction at Llanidloes. Although the proposed route was similar to that already described for the Direct Manchester and Milford Haven scheme, it was about 1½ miles longer, and this despite a saving of almost a mile from the adoption of an end-on junction with the Llanidloes and Newtown. The extra distance appears to be the result of adopting a more circuitous alignment to minimise engineering works. At Pont Llanio and Devil's Bridge, for example, a less direct route was chosen to avoid tunnels foreseen in the earlier broad gauge project. Then a broader more easterly sweep was taken just before Llanidloes: this was soon to exacerbate friction with the Mid Wales Railway whose line was likewise to approach Llanidloes from the south. A deviation was also planned at Cross Inn (New Quay Road) station, although a short tunnel was in fact substituted when this part of the line was built.

The gradients and works over the northern part can only be described as fearsome for a railway with modest capital which nonetheless saw itself as an important intermediary for through traffic. North of Pontrhydfendigaid, there was to be a mile at 1 in 50 up towards Llangurig, followed by a similar distance down at 1 in 45, partly in tunnel, to the Ystwyth viaduct. This was now planned to have one arch of 80 feet span, 90 feet high, and a second of 170 feet, 240 feet above the river. There was then to be over 4½ miles up at 1 in 43 or 1 in 50, easing only as the mile-long summit tunnel was approached at Blaen Myherin. The summit, 650 feet above rail level at the Ystwyth viaduct, came at the Llangurig end of the tunnel. Thereafter, it would have been slightly easier down to the junction with the Llanidloes and Newtown, with about 4 miles at 1 in 50 or 1 in 54 as the worst encountered.

The Manchester and Milford Railway had at last been authorised after a delay of 15 years. Now all that was needed was to build the line.

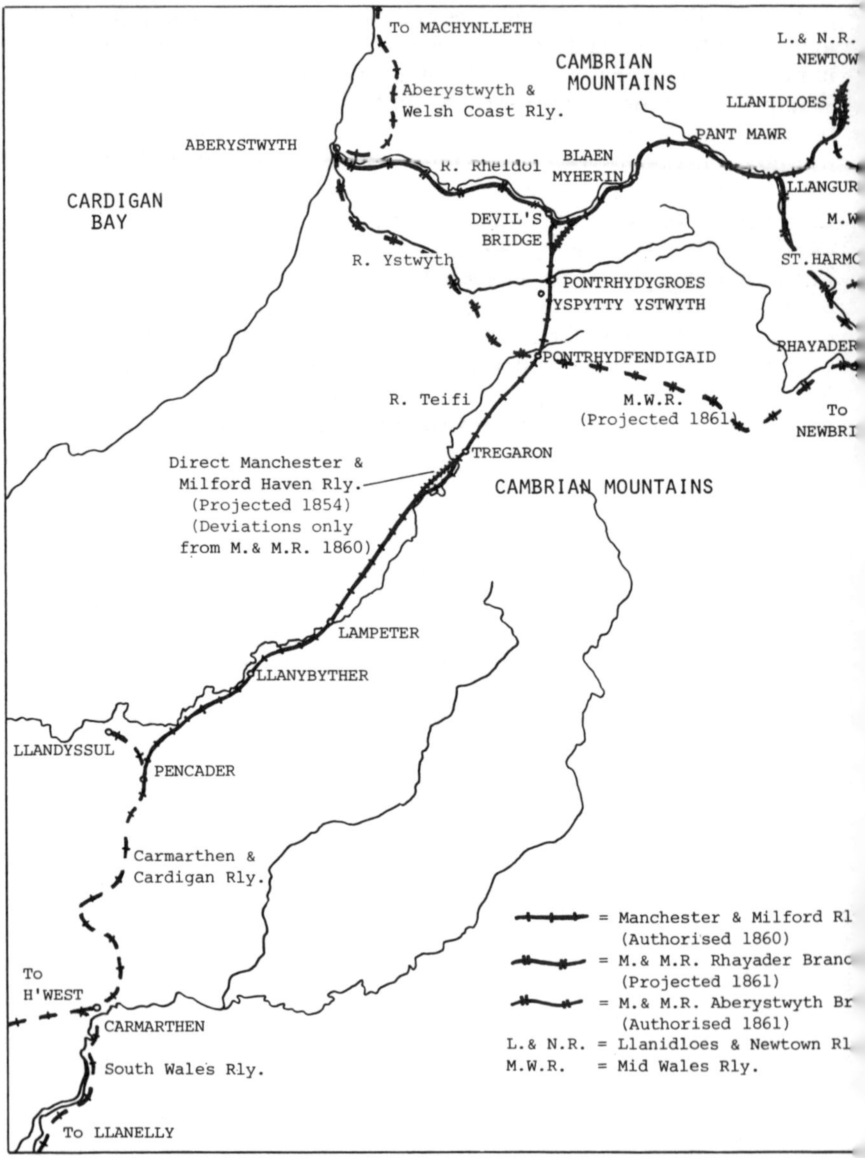
To MACHYNLLETH
L.& N.R.
NEWTOW
CAMBRIAN MOUNTAINS
Aberystwyth & Welsh Coast Rly.
LLANIDLOES
ABERYSTWYTH
PANT MAWR
R. Rheidol
BLAEN MYHERIN
LLANGUR
CARDIGAN BAY
DEVIL'S BRIDGE
M.W
R. Ystwyth
ST.HARMO
PONTRHYDYGROES
YSPYTTY YSTWYTH
RHAYADER
PONTRHYDFENDIGAID
R. Teifi
M.W.R. (Projected 1861)
To NEWBRI
TREGARON
Direct Manchester & Milford Haven Rly. (Projected 1854) (Deviations only from M.& M.R. 1860)
CAMBRIAN MOUNTAINS
LAMPETER
LLANYBYTHER
LLANDYSSUL
PENCADER
Carmarthen & Cardigan Rly.
= Manchester & Milford Rl (Authorised 1860)
= M.& M.R. Rhayader Branc (Projected 1861)
= M.& M.R. Aberystwyth Br (Authorised 1861)
L.& N.R. = Llanidloes & Newtown Rl
M.W.R. = Mid Wales Rly.
To H'WEST
CARMARTHEN
South Wales Rly.
To LLANELLY

1860 - 1861. The Manchester and Milford reaches the Statute Book.

CHAPTER 2

CONSTRUCTION, 1860-1867

The Manchester and Milford Railway began its fractious career by provoking a dispute with its contractor. Money, or rather the lack of it, was the root of the trouble. Investors were being slow to promise subscriptions and the directors were hard-pressed to find the funds needed to ensure progress. Even before the company obtained its Act, it was intimated to Chambers that the well-known contractors, David Davies and his partner at that time, Thomas Savin, would take up shares in return for an agreement that they should build part of the line. Davies and Savin were then the dominant force in railway construction in Central Wales, and their finance and expertise would have been valuable. It was proposed that Beeston should meet Savin with a view to Savin having a contract for nine miles at the northern end of the line, but Beeston would have none of it. His exclusive contract for the works was sufficient — for the time being — to thwart this initiative.

Company and contractor were soon distracted with other difficulties. The Mid Wales Railway had secured an Act in 1859 for a line from Newbridge-on-Wye to Llanidloes, and Parliament, in sanctioning the Manchester and Milford's plans in the subsequent Session, omitted to notice that both companies were being authorised to build over much the same territory immediately south of Llanidloes. The Manchester and Milford's reaction to this situation was to seek as early a start as possible on construction work over the disputed territory. The directors were anxious "to anticipate the operations of a rival company which had simultaneous Parliamentary powers to acquire the land over which this line is designed to pass", and approached Frederick Beeston with a view to making a specific arrangement covering the last few miles into Llanidloes within the framework of the overall contract.

Beeston's proposal, which amounted to £30,000 cash and £10,000 in paid-up shares for a line from Llanidloes to Llangurig, was quickly accepted. There was, however, no imminent prospect of raising even this relatively modest sum, and the contractor agreeed instead to a down-payment with the balance of £28,000 cash and £5,000 in shares in monthly instalments. He was also prepared to have paid-up shares substituted for cash at the rate of £30 in shares for each £20 so dealt with. Beeston reckoned to be able to complete the line as far as

Llangurig in not much more than a year.

By early 1861, therefore, he was in a position to begin preparatory work, and only waiting for the M. & M. to purchase the land needed before starting actual construction. It was at this stage, according to evidence presented at a court hearing some years later, that the rival workforces of the Manchester and Milford's and the Mid Wales' contractors began to interfere physically with each other's progress. While Frederick Beeston bemoaned the delays, there was nothing for it but for the M. & M. to attempt to come to terms with the M.W.R. over the disputed section.

A minute of the M.W.R.'s board from March 1861 recorded that they were anxious to help the M. & M. and were thus prepared to offer the use of their own earthworks, on which the M. & M. could lay a line. Alternatively, double track could be laid from Llanidloes to the point of divergence, with the M. & M. paying rent for its use. On the face of it, this seemed a reasonable offer, but Chambers apparently thought otherwise. A month later, he wrote that it was not the Manchester and Milford's intention to interfere with the alignment for the M.W.R. which had been sanctioned by Parliament. Rather, the M. & M. wanted to offer its neighbour every facility. Chambers proposed that the Mid Wales should join the Pencader-Llanidloes route at either Penpontbren or Llangurig, and that the construction of the relevent portion of the M.W.R.'s line by the M. & M., or the accommodation of Mid Wales traffic on M. & M. metals, should be negotiated.

From these diametrically opposed positions, with each company vying to retain the advantage, matters deteriorated so much that, before long, law suits were being tossed back and forth. The Manchester and Milford asserted, among other things, that the Mid Wales had deviated from its authorised course, with the result that the M. & M.'s line would actually have to cross to the east of the Mid Wales Railway on the approach to Llanidloes.

The difficulty was finally overcome by the novel expedient of inviting a third company, the Llanidloes and Newtown Railway, to build the line as far as the divergence at Penpontbren. The idea seems to have originated with a Mr Lefaux, a director of the L. & N., who wrote to Chambers in September 1861 suggesting that the L. & N. should take over the land and works of the two warring companies and complete the undertaking. The arrangement was formalised between the three companies in October, in time for a Bill to be put before Parliament in the following Session: the L. & N. could not, of course, carry out the works without Parliamentary sanction.

The Llanidloes and Newtown's 1862 Act provided for the construction of a double line, 1½ miles long, from Llanidloes to Penpontbren for the sole use of the M.W.R. and the M. & M. The L. & N. was to have no rights over this section. From opening, the two companies were to pay, jointly, interest at 5% p.a. on the Llanidloes and Newtown's construction costs, plus the costs incurred by the L. & N. for maintenance. There was also to be a joint station at Llanidloes for the use of all three companies, with running costs and interest at 5% shared equally between the three prospective users. The fact that the Manchester and Milford was never to be a user, but was still required to pay its third, soon proved to be a sore burden on its limited resources, and gave rise to conflict with the Cambrian Railways, as successor to the L. & N., which persisted until the Manchester and Milford was leased by the Great Western Railway. The M. & M.'s own powers to build the Penpontbren to Llanidloes section were repealed by the Act.

The Llanidloes joint station and line were completed in February 1864, whereupon the L. & N. transferred to the new facilities and the original terminus was demoted to non-passenger duties: its site could still be readily identified in 1976. The L. & N. was thus the only occupier of the joint station until the Mid Wales' line was ready for opening in September 1864. 1872 appears in a number of sources as the year in which the works covered by the L. & N.'s Act came into use, but this probably relates to the laying in of a physical junction at Penpontbren.

While the dispute and negotiations with the Mid Wales Railway ran their course, Beeston was saddled with a contract for the northernmost section which he was in no position to fulfil. Why he was not then set to work elsewhere, once the objective of beating the Mid Wales into Llanidloes had been thwarted, is not clear. The headings for the tunnel had been defined before the end of 1860, so operations could presumably have been commenced there. "Southern" shareholders were also pressing for a start to be made at Pencader.

By July 1861, Beeston considered that his position had become sufficiently difficult to justify abandonment of the subsidiary contract, and advised the Manchester and Milford directors accordingly. They, in turn, had little choice but to acquiesce and promised to compensate him generously for the costs he had incurred. However, the sums involved at that time amounted to less than £1,000, and the contractor was understandably becoming exasperated with a situation where he could make little progress, owing to a want of funds and direction. He therefore proposed that, without prejudicing his right to the contract for the remainder of the line, responsibility for the first section to Llangurig should be deputed to his son. Frederick Beeston Jnr. was prepared to undertake the work for £31,500 cash and £10,500 in shares, his father agreeing to transfer the £2,000 cash and £5,000 in shares already received as part of this sum. Negotiations with the M.W.R. and the L. & N. over the approach to Llanidloes were not concluded until October 1861 — after the new contract was signed — so specifically excluded the cost of any bridge over the Mid Wales Railway which might prove necessary.

A year later, the directors were able to report that considerable progress had been made towards Llangurig, and that this part of the line should be ready for traffic by Christmas. There was, however, no mention of difficulties over possession and access to land along the line's course, which were still delaying the contractor. The directors also noted that arrangements had been made to continue construction as far as the tunnel near Pant Mawr. £34,000 was agreed for "contract 2", a single line 5½ miles long, westwards from the termination of "contract 1" at Llangurig, through Pant Mawr to the tunnel approach, located about 11 miles from Llanidloes. The work was to be completed by May 1863, or within eight months of Beeston being put in possession of the land.

Meanwhile, Chambers was once again looking elsewhere for someone to begin work on other parts of the route, in prospective violation of the original January 1860 agreement with Beeston. Chambers proposed to let as much of the tunnel works "as would be taken by a contractor with payment in shares", while Alfred Beeston, the Manchester and Milford's secretary, wrote in reply to a disgruntled shareholder suggesting that if the complainant could find a contractor to start at Pencader on the right terms, the company would take him on. Chambers was soon in negotiations with Savin covering the whole of the Manchester and Milford's authorised line south from Pant Mawr, and a preliminary agreement was reached just four days before Beeston's contract for the Llangurig-Pant Mawr section was sealed in mid-October 1862.

The motives for involving Savin and risking a confrontation with Beeston were primarily financial. The deal with Savin involved his discharging existing Manchester and Milford liabilities, financing the costs of land purchase, and completing the line within the time limit laid down; no mean task as a third of the five years allotted had by then been wasted. Savin was, however, to get £100,000 cash, but all the remaining payments were to be in shares.

Beeston quickly got wind of the arrangement. In December, Beeston's lawyer wrote to the M. & M.'s solicitors, mentioning "rumours" that Savin was to have the contract for the remainder of the line, and assuming that "as legal advisers to the Manchester and Milford (they would) deny these negotiations . . . which would involve all the parties in an immediate Chancery suit". To Savin, he indicated that F. Beeston Snr. had the whole contract except between Llangurig and Penpontbren which was let to his son, and that if Savin continued to negotiate with the M. & M., litigation would ensue.

By the end of 1862, work on "contract 1" amounted to £25,000.

The annual accounts imply expenditure of some £16,000 on "contract 2", but it seems likely that this is overstated. Certainly, construction never proceeded very far beyond the end of "contract 1" at Llangurig. Beeston appears to have done some work near the tunnel, for which he had the greatest difficulty obtaining payment. However, this could only have been of a very modest nature, and no trace can be found today.

It might be thought that, as the Manchester and Milford was making such heavy weather of its authorised line, the company would not be anxious to divert its energies elsewhere. Such was not the case. The directors' thoughts were soon turning towards the construction of a branch line to Aberystwyth. Chambers had written in September 1859, "There was the idea at one time to carry a branch on to Aberystwyth, but that has been abandoned and we reserve all our strength for the main line." A year later, however, the engineer, Fulton, had begun to survey a route to Aberystwyth with a view to depositing plans for a Bill in the next Session.

The M. & M.'s intention was partly defensive. The Mid Wales Railway had a strong interest in securing access to Aberystwyth, and had a Bill before Parliament in November 1861 for this purpose. Their proposed line was to start from a triangular junction just south of Rhayader, follow the Rivers Elan and Caerwen into the mountains south of Llyn Teifi, and continue via Pontryhdfendigaid to Ystrad Meurig, following the River Ystwyth thence to Aberystwyth. The ruling gradients were not as severe as might be expected: 1 in 60 in both directions. But there was to be a tunnel a mile long between points 13 and 14 miles distant from Rhayader, and a 300 yard viaduct, 150 feet above the River Teifi. The total length of the scheme would have been 33½ miles. This, and the difficult nature of the country, was enough to deter the Mid Wales, and the Bill was withdrawn.

The Manchester and Milford's branch was to begin at Devil's Bridge, and to keep south of the Rheidol all the way to a terminus by the river bridge at Aberystwyth. The route would not be easy, as anyone who has travelled over the Vale of Rheidol Light Railway can testify, but it was a more realistic project than the Mid Wales scheme. It is interesting to speculate that if the M. & M. had managed to build its line as originally authorised, there would probably be no Vale of Rheidol narrow-gauge line today to delight the railway enthusiast and tourist alike.

The company was successful in its application to Parliament. The Act, dated July 1861, allowed an additional £111,000 of share capital to be raised for the purposes of either the previously authorised line or the Aberystwyth branch. A further £37,000 in loans could be created once all shares were subscribed and half paid up. The Llanidloes and

Newton could subscribe £20,000 towards the scheme, raising this sum — if the shareholders agreed — by a new issue of shares. The M. & M. was also empowered to make agreements for traffic working with an unlikely-sounding selection of railways, the Great Western, London and North Western, and the Oswestry and Newtown, subject to safeguards aimed at that Victorian bogey, monopoly power and its abuse.

Flushed with success, the M. & M. then went on in November 1861 to propose a short 6½ mile line from Llangurig along the River Wye to Aber Marteg, at the confluence of the Marteg and Wye near St. Harmon, where there was to be a junction with the Mid Wales Railway. The scheme was styled the "Rhayader branch" and mutual running powers between the Mid Wales and M. & M. were proposed. A dual purpose could be discerned. The line would increase the utility of the Aberystwyth branch by providing a better outlet to South Wales, and would contain and pre-empt the Mid Wales company's aspirations on Aberystwyth.

The first objective had a particular significance, because the M. & M. had been unsuccessful in opposing the Act incorporating the Aberystwyth and Welsh Coast Railway, later a part of the Cambrian system, in the 1861 Session. The best it could do was to have a "simultaneous" clause inserted, which bound the A. & W.C. not to build the line from Machynlleth to Aberystwyth before that to Barmouth. It is noteworthy that, on the evidence of petitions passed to local M.P.s Colonel Powell, who was also a M. & M. director, and Captain Pryce, the townsfolk of Aberystwyth regarded the A. & W.C. as providing their outlet to the north, and the M. & M., to the south.

The Manchester and Milford's Rhayader branch was hastily conceived, and almost as quickly dropped. Other considerations aside, there was no possibility of raising the funds locally with which to build the line, and the general state of the company's finances would hardly permit the extravagance. The Mid Wales put forward a similar scheme the next year, differing mainly by favouring the west bank of the Wye and by omitting the Llangurig triangle. An Act was obtained for the construction of this line, but it too was abandoned — in favour of more ambitious plans.

The Manchester and Milford and the Aberystwyth and Welsh Coast Railways were at loggerheads in the Parliamentary Session of 1863. Both had plans for a branch to Aberystwyth Harbour and for a connection between their respective termini in Aberystwyth. The M. & M.'s harbour scheme involved a tramway half a mile long curving sharply to the north and west of the proposed station site. The line to the A. & W.C.'s station would have been a mile long, with junctions arranged so that M. & M. trains, but not its rival's, could proceed without reversal to either terminus. As the two stations were to be on opposite sides of the River Rheidol, a substantial bridge would have been necessary in this link. Once again, the M. & M.'s plans came to nothing. The Welsh Coast concern obtained its Act but, being beset by financial problems, never built its harbour line, and never needed the link to an independent M. & M. station.

We must now return to the Manchester and Milford's internal affairs, and to the conflict which quickly developed between the two major characters on the board of directors, William Chambers and John Barrow. Chambers, the chairman and a local landowner, had been a leading figure in developing railway communication across Cardiganshire for some time, and may perhaps take most credit for the Act of 1860. Barrow, on the other hand, had come more recently to the company, and from quite a different background. His early career had been spent trading with Spain and Portugal in partnership with an elder brother, Richard. Both brothers then augmented sizeable fortunes from this activity by being among the first to open up commerce with China, allowing Richard to take over the Staveley Coal and Iron Works, and John to retire to farm his land at Normanton Hall, Southwell, in Nottinghamshire. Just why he should, at the age of 70, become involved in the affairs of the Manchester and Milford Railway is a mystery. But whatever the reason, Chambers was able to write of Barrow in March 1861 that he had taken up a strong interest in the line, and guaranteed £70,000.

The need was pressing, as the M. & M. had been desperately impoverished from the outset. Even the Parliamentary deposit for the original Act had to be raised by means of a bank loan. Financial support from Manchester was sought repeatedly but unsuccessfully, and most of the few shares subscribed came from farmers along the line. Early in 1861, therefore, when the company had no more than a few hundred pounds in the bank, a loan of £10,000 was obtained on the personal sureties of Chambers and Barrow jointly. The money was to be spent on forestalling creditors, paying the contractor, and so on. The two directors accordingly signed the promissory note supported by a resolution of their fellow directors authorising them to do so "on behalf of the company".

The M. & M. continued its hand-to-mouth existence until a general meeting in February 1863, when all the original directors with the exception of Chambers and Barrow were suddenly voted off. John Barrow's son and three others, all of whom appear to have been Barrow nominees, were elected instead. Beeston was dismissed as secretary, and steps were taken to replace Marriott and Jordan, the company solicitors. There had not, however, been a quorum when these changes were steam-rollered through by the Barrow faction, a state of affairs which Marriott and Jordan were quick to spot. In March, they circulated a letter warning that the meeting had no proper legal standing and that the new directors should not assume that they had been properly elected.

Barrow was not present when the directors next gathered. Chambers was there, together with Frederick Harrison. Powell and Locock Webb resigned, and no doubt considered themselves well out of it, and two new men replaced them, George Glover and Philip Firmin. The meeting heard how Barrow had, through the "new" M. & M. solicitor, a Mr Forster, purported to withdraw the company's opposition to the Aberystwyth and Welsh Coast Railway's Bill. The Bill was, however, still being fought in Parliament by counsel briefed by Marriott and Jordan, who were instructed to put Forster "straight" and then to oppose the A. & W.C. Bill in the Lords in every way possible.

A petition, signed by John Barrow, Frederick Beeston, and about 50 others, was presented to the directors towards the end of March, seeking an extra-ordinary general meeting to question the removal of the company books and seal from the company's office, where Barrow could get at them, and to consider the disputed election of directors and the accounts, which had never yet been properly audited. The other directors would have nothing to do with the petition, so Barrow, styling himself "chairman", called a special meeting anyway. The board countered with a notice to shareholders warning that Barrow's meeting was illegal, and resolving that he should not use the company's offices for the purpose. It was nonetheless held, for Chambers reported that, as a result of being misinformed of the starting time, Barrow was already in the chair when he arrived! Yet Barrow was still unable to sway those present to his way of thinking, and for the time being his bid for power was lost.

He did have one more card to play, though. The Union Bank had been pressing for repayment of the £10,000 loan, and Barrow had reimbursed the whole sum, suing Chambers for his share of the joint promissory note. Chambers then turned to the company, for it was of course for company purposes that the loan was first obtained. The M. & M. was entirely willing to take the responsibility, but needless to say, lacked the cash.

While the company cast around for means of raising Chambers' half of the £10,000, some alleged sharp practice on Barrow's part came to light. It appeared that Barrow had, quite legitimately, been financing Frederick Beeston and taking over the contractor's share entitlement in return as payments for construction work accrued. Barrow was, however, obtaining Beeston's shares at a discount and thus, according to the other directors, "participating in the profits of the contract". It was reckoned that the sums which might be reclaimed exceeded Chambers' liability, although this seems unlikely. A counter-claim was nevertheless begun against Barrow, and Chambers also sought an injunction to stop him proceeding with his disruptive activities. The sum owed to Barrow was raised by the issue of "Lloyds" bonds, a form of security which was the normal means of raising money for a company whose capital had not been fully subscribed or had proved insufficient, and whose borrowing powers could not be resorted to or had been exhausted. Bonds to the value of £7,000 were issued to Chambers who used them to raise a mortgage for £5,000 plus interest and commission, the £5,000 going to pay Barrow.

By mid-1863, William Chambers' days at the helm of the Manchester and Milford Board were numbered. The minutes are tantalisingly silent about what actually transpired, but we know there was a meeting in August at which Chambers, Harrison, Glover and Firmin were present, that the company was suddenly awash with funds, and that it was therefore proposed to redeem the Lloyds bonds which had been issued to enable Chambers to settle his debt to Barrow. Barrow was absent on this occasion, as indeed he had been since the abortive takeover in February, but he was present with Chambers and Harrison when the meeting reconvened the next day. Glover and Firmin thereupon resigned, and two of Barrow's nominations from February, John Barry and Henry Downing, were elected instead. Alfred Beeston also resigned, and was replaced as secretary by Barrow's legal representative, Forster. The takeover was soon complete. Chambers took no further part in board meetings, and the new directors quickly agreed that "all resolutions of the alleged board since February last are to be submitted . . . for consideration and approval". Marriott and Jordan were instructed to give up their papers to Forster, and the resolution relating to Barrow's alleged profits from company contracts was rescinded.

Barrow also prevented the Lloyds bonds from being redeemed, so Chambers had no option but to sue in order to extricate himself. In the event, the ousted chairman was unsuccessful with his action, for although the original loan had been taken out by Chambers and Barrow, the resolution of the board authorising them to do so on behalf of the company turned it into "illegal" company borrowing. All the subsequent activity was thereby also tainted with illegality, so the bonds' redemption was unenforceable. This was rather hard on Chambers, but he was able to derive some consolation by being instrumental in defeating Barrow's 1864 Deviation Bill.

The general meeting in February 1864 marked a changed and — if the new emphasis on construction of the southern part of the line is a fair indication — a more realistic era. John Barrow brought his son, John James, onto the board to join Barry and Downing. The remaining directors were John Hardy and George E. Forster, who was replaced as secretary by Joseph Butler.

The directors were able to state "that the line between Llanidloes and Penpontbren has been completed by the Llanidloes and Newtown company . . . and that the portion between Penpontbren and Llangurig has been completed by the contractor, and only awaits the sanction of the Government Inspector . . . should it be thought desirable to do more at present than to open it for goods traffic . . . Arrangements were in progress . . . to carry on the works from Llangurig to a point near the proposed tunnel at Pant Mawr, but this involved the question as to the expediency of making that portion of the original line lying between Pant Mawr and Pontrhydfendigaid, in which are comprised the formidable works of a viaduct, to be carried on piers 280 feet high, and of two tunnels measuring together 1½ miles. The directors have had such serious representations made to them upon the inadvisability of carrying out these works that . . . they have determined to recommend the abandonment of that portion (and) about 5½ miles of line between Llangurig and Pant Mawr, and have made application to Parliament for powers to take another, shorter, course between Llangurig and Pontrhydfendigaid, which will involve the abandonment of the authorised branch to Aberystwyth, and the substitution of another line to that town, commencing at a point near Pontrhydfendigaid."

Meanwhile, work would not be proceeded with beyond the point, just beyond Llangurig, where the newly-proposed line would deviate from the original scheme. The directors had, however, "entered into a contract with David Davies and Frederick Beeston for the (27 miles) from Pencader to Pontrhydfendigaid", and took the view that "in the current state of the money market . . . the Manchester and Milford may be considered fortunate in this engagement with two gentlemen, one of whom is so well-known in the principality" and that "the experience which the directors have had of their contractor Mr Beeston gives every reason for confidence". It is interesting to note that while Chambers had flirted with Savin as a potential contractor for the Manchester and Milford's line, Barrow opted for Savin's one-time partner, but now fierce rival, David Davies.

"Referring to the accounts, the directors regret that certain differences of opinion have hitherto prevented their being properly audited. The directors, however, lay upon the table the accounts to June 1863 in the handwriting of the former secretary, upon which they offer no opinion." The auditors in turn called attention to the fact that expenditure greatly exceeded receipts: more than £20,000 had been advanced by Barrow, who had incurred further outlay which had not yet been brought into the accounts. The auditors also found that £1,400 had been paid to Chambers for expenses which were not properly accounted for. The boot was now firmly on the other foot! They concluded that the future prospects of the company would depend on outstanding claims being settled as quickly as possible, and arrears on shares being paid up. Calls on shares had by then reached their full face value.

There had long been doubts over the choice of route between Llangurig and Pontrhydfendigaid, Barrow for one being of the view that the "northern" route via Devil's Bridge and Pant Mawr was unnecessarily arduous, and that the "southern" alternative was greatly to be preferred. This much was clear from the report of the February general meeting. A Bill had accordingly been assembled in some haste for the 1864 Session. The line now proposed took a more southerly course from Llangurig, following a stream called the Nant Troedyresgair into the hills, before tunnelling through to the River Diluw, and following this river and the south bank of the Ystwyth down to Yspytty Ystwyth.

Shorter the line might have been, but the gradients were the most formidable yet proposed for this area; 3½ miles up from Llangurig at 1 in 30 to the summit, then 8 miles down, 5 miles of it at 1 in 45 or worse. At Yspytty Ystwyth, 14 miles from Llangurig, the gradients would once more have been against Pencader-bound trains, with another summit reached a mile beyond. The line would then have descended towards the Marchnant river and the level of the Teifi, crossing to the west of the 1860 route and rejoining it at Alltddu, a farmhouse at the edge of the Bog of Tregaron. This spot, almost 25 miles from Pencader, was in later years to be graced with a halt. The distance from Llangurig would have been 19½ miles, reducing the total between Pencader and Llanidloes by around two miles compared with the line in the 1860 Act.

North from Alltddu, the deviation was to be taken across the Bog of Tregaron, with a triangular junction near Ystrad Meurig giving access to a revised Aberystwyth branch: a new route to Aberystwyth was essential now that Devil's Bridge was no longer on the main line. Jumping briefly a few years ahead, the "branch" to the coast was built, much as envisaged in 1864, but the mountain line was not; hence the line's course directly across the bog when the best route to Aberystwyth lay to the west, and the sharp curve at Strata Florida, originally intended as the south to west arm of the Ystrad Meurig triangle.

Approaching Aberystwyth, the M. & M.'s new branch would have made a junction with the Aberystwyth and Welsh Coast Railway's proposed harbour extension. There would then have been a short link, completing another triangle between the harbour line and the A. & W.C.'s main line into Aberystwyth station. The Bill included running powers over the A. & W.C. into the terminus, and provided for the building of a joint station. The A. & W.C. was to be empowered to invest £50,000 in the Manchester and Milford if it so wished, entitling it to elect two directors. There was still no mention of running powers over

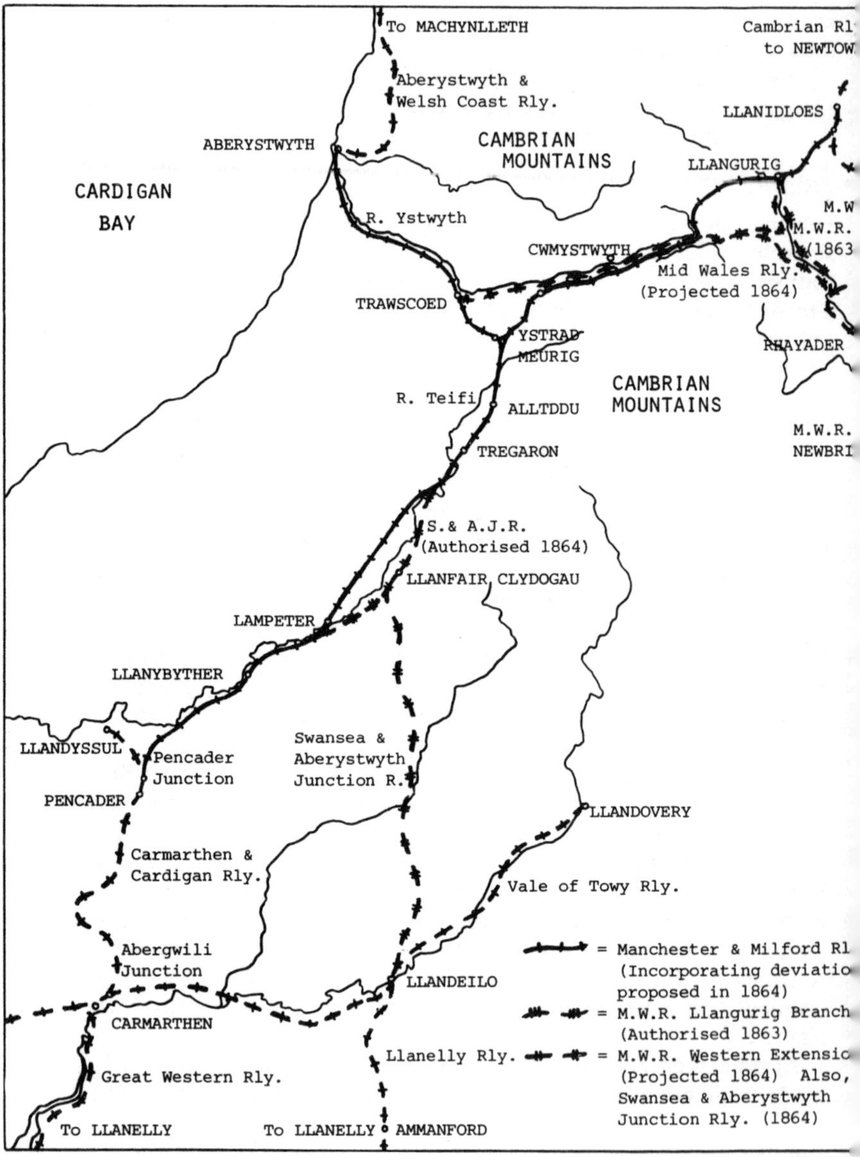

1863 - 1864. Confrontation in the Mountains.

the Carmarthen and Cardigan Railway, although the M. & M. had been negotiating for the laying down of a third rail between Pencader and Carmarthen since 1860.

The M. & M.'s Deviation Bill was defeated, apparently through William Chambers' efforts, and withdrawn. The directors professed not to be unduly concerned. "The delay of one Session does not interfere with the prosecution of the works on the unaltered portions, while it has given an opportunity for a thorough examination of the country to get the best line practicable." Construction of the southern part of the line was already making good progress now that Davies' undoubted organisational capability had been brought to bear. The M. & M. and Beeston had agreed to arbitration over differences concerning the works around Llangurig, and both parties promised not to sue each other pending the outcome! A contract with Davies and Beeston jointly for the line from Pencader had been drawn up in April 1864. By the date of the next general meeting in August, £75,000 in progress payments had been made to the contractors.

The directors were on this occasion able to report that the company's prospects had greatly improved. The heavy works between Pencader and Lampeter, including the Bryn Teifi tunnel, had been all but finished, and opening to Lampeter was forecast within four months. Most land purchases had now been agreed, so work was in progress over the whole distance via Tregaron to near Pontrhyd-fendigaid. Llanidloes to Llangurig remained unopened.

Supervision of the works was vested from mid-1864 in James Weekes Szlumper, who came from a notable "railway" family. The former engineer and last representative of the old order, Hamilton Fulton, was sacked and died not long afterwards. Szlumper had been Fulton's assistant from the days when the route was surveyed for the 1860 Act, so he was well placed to succeed, particularly as he was able to meet with Davies' approval. This was to be his making. To quote Davies, "Some contractors stipulate that they shall have their own engineer, but when I saw Mr Szlumper, I said to myself, he has got a jolly good-natured face, and as far as I can see he looks right enough . . . I said we will try him, we will risk it."

James, with his brother Arthur Weekes assisting him, later engineered the Barry Railway, and then several other lines in South Wales, together with two of London's tube lines. Knighted in 1894, High Sheriff of Cardigan in 1898 and three times Mayor of Richmond, Surrey, he died — respected but not rich — at the age of 92 in 1926. Arthur Weekes Szlumper went on to be chief engineer of the London and South Western Railway and the Southern, where his son, Gilbert, in turn became general manager. James' own son, Charles David, succeeded him on the Manchester and Milford.

Davies and Beeston were employing about 700 men between

Pencader and Lampeter at this time, despite the scarcity of labour in that part of the country. They also had around 150 wagons and a large number of horses: the use of steam locomotive power was not recorded until the following year. The permanent way comprised 70 lb./yard double headed iron rails of 18, 21 and 24 feet lengths rolled by the Ebbw Vale company, and carried in 28 lb. cast iron chairs which were secured to sleepers with iron spikes. The sleepers were half round, 10 inches wide and 5 deep, varied in length between 8ft. 9in. and 9ft., and were laid at three feet centres. Some were from larch trees in the vicinity, but most came from abroad. In accordance with custom on many Welsh railways, no creosote was used.

The first of two new threats to the Manchester and Milford's territorial hegemony west of the Cambrian mountains came from a little-known concern entitled the Llandeilo and Teiffi (sic) Valley Railway. This company had succeeded in obtaining an Act in the 1864 Session for a railway from Llandeilo to the M. & M.'s line just north of Pont Llanio, with the junction arranged for through running towards Aberystwyth. A second line was authorised, leaving the Llandeilo-Pont Llanio route at Llanfair Clydogau, and ending at a junction with the M. & M. just south of Lampeter. As this link was projected in such a way that a journey from Llandeilo to Lampeter would have required two reversals of direction, it is difficult to see what purpose it would have served.

The Llandeilo and Teiffi Valley was not content to rest there. First, it acquired a new title, rivalling the Manchester and Milford's in its pretentiousness. In the 1864 Act, the company became the Swansea and Aberystwyth Junction Railway: misleading, but probably a better indication of its aspirations. Some of the anomolies of the authorised route were to be eliminated in a new Bill, which sought a connecting link to Llandovery and a north-to-east curve to give direct access to Lampeter. But the worst feature from the M. & M.'s viewpoint was the suggestion of an independent line to Aberystwyth or running powers as far as Llanidloes and Aberystwyth.

The second, and probably more urgent threat — because it came from an established albeit struggling concern — was that of the Mid Wales Railway. It too was casting its eyes on Aberystwyth, and was out prospecting a route which proved to have much in common with the M. & M.'s revised 1864 scheme. The Mid Wales proposed to build from a junction at Aber Marteg, near St Harmon, along the west bank of the Wye for three miles and into the hills along the valley of the Nant-y-Dernol. After a substantial tunnel at the head of the valley, some 6 miles from the junction, the line would have deviated south of Glan Fedwen and then followed the road and river down to Yspytty Ystwyth. From here, the route lay along the river's south bank to a junction with the M. & M. at Trawscoed, with through running from there to Aberystwyth. A second, and for the later turn of events, most important line was also proposed. This would have left the first just east of the tunnel, and taken the other side of the Nant-y-Dernol valley down to the Wye, where it would have turned north to Llangurig.

The ruling gradients would have been somewhat less severe than those of the M. & M.'s 1864 scheme. The first three miles' climb from St Harmon would have been at 1 in 50, followed by 1 in 45 and 1 in 55 to the summit just beyond the tunnel. From Llangurig, only the last two miles to the junction were particularly heavily graded, mostly at 1 in 40. West from the tunnel, the line would have descended sharply for nearly 12 miles, much at between 1 in 45 and 1 in 55.

What happened next depends on who is to be believed. The Manchester and Milford claimed it saw the folly of building competing lines in arduous territory, where the local traffic would scarcely justify one, and considered that some form of agreement was therefore essential. From the Mid Wales viewpoint, it was reckoned that the M. & M. was incapable of building its authorised line, or any other that might be substituted. It was accordingly an act of friendship to volunteer the use of the Mid Wales' "Western Extensions" so that the M. & M. would not be entirely shut out from its line to Llangurig.

Anyway, an agreement was reached in October 1864 between the three companies; the Manchester and Milford, the Mid Wales and the Swansea and Aberystwyth Junction. According to this agreement, the Mid Wales was to seek an Act to build the two lines described above, and to abandon its existing powers for a Llangurig branch. The Swansea and Aberystwyth was to drop its threat of an independent line to Aberystwyth, and to be satisfied with running powers from Pont Llanio to Aberystwyth over the M. & M., and to Llanidloes over both the M. & M. and Mid Wales. Finally, the Manchester and Milford was to forget its plans for a revised course for the main line to Llangurig, and instead build from the same starting point at Ystrad Meurig only as far as was necessary to connect with the Mid Wales Railway's new line in the vicinity of Yspytty Ystwyth. The company was then to get running powers over both M.W.R. lines, to St Harmon and to Llangurig, and also from St Harmon to Rhayader. In return, the M. & M. was to grant similar facilities over the lines from Ystrad Meurig to Aberystwyth and to Yspytty Ystwyth, and also over the line south as far as the S. &. A.J. Railway's proposed junction at Pont Llanio. None of the Mid Wales or the S. & A.J.'s running powers was, however, to apply until the M.W.R. had fulfilled its part of the bargain, by building the mountain line as far

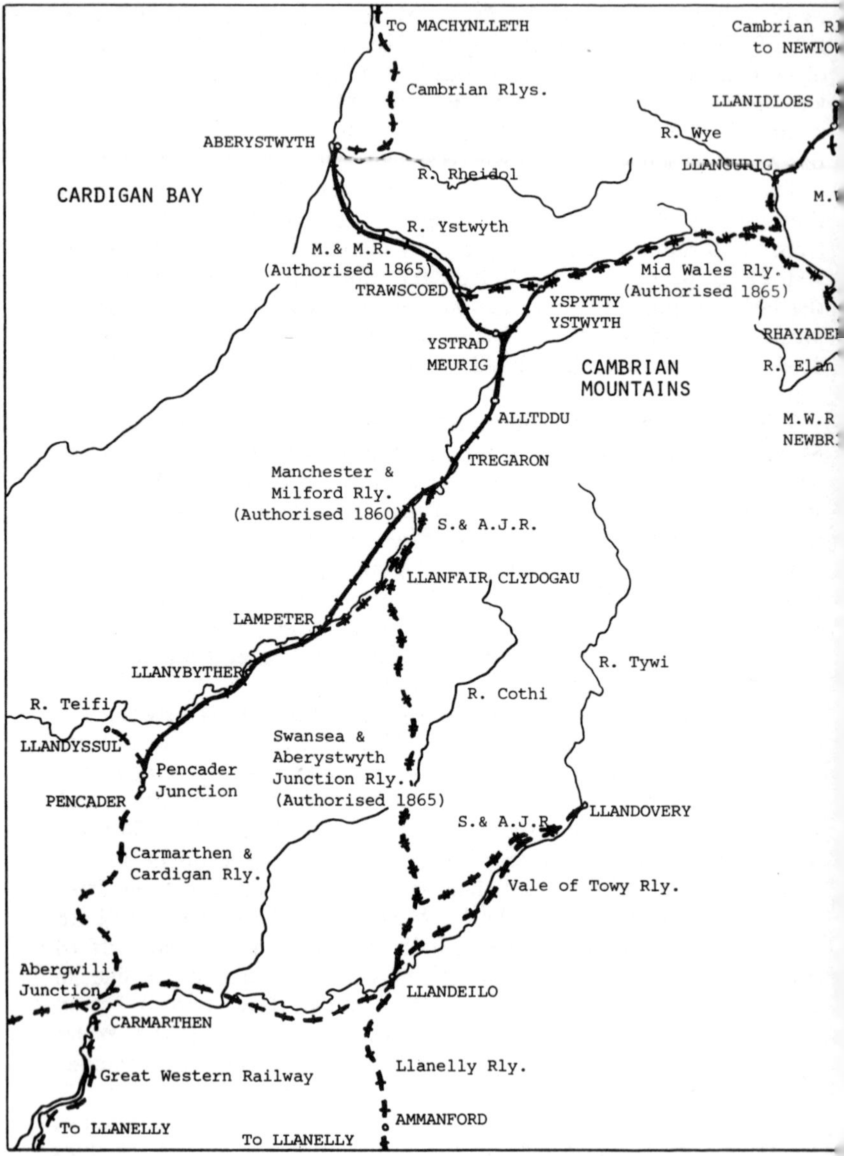

To MACHYNLLETH
Cambrian Rlys.
LLANIDLOES
R. Wye
ABERYSTWYTH
R. Rheidol
CARDIGAN BAY
R. Ystwyth
M.& M.R.
(Authorised 1865)
TRAWSCOED
Mid Wales Rly.
(Authorised 1865)
YSPYTTY
YSTWYTH
YSTRAD
MEURIG
CAMBRIAN
MOUNTAINS
ALLTDDU
TREGARON
Manchester &
Milford Rly.
(Authorised 1860)
S.& A.J.R.
LLANFAIR CLYDOGAU
LAMPETER
LLANYBYTHER
R. Tywi
R. Teifi
R. Cothi
LLANDYSSUL
Pencader
Junction
PENCADER
Swansea &
Aberystwyth
Junction Rly.
(Authorised 1865)
LLANDOVERY
S.& A.J.R.
Carmarthen &
Cardigan Rly.
Vale of Towy Rly.
Abergwili
Junction
LLANDEILO
CARMARTHEN
Llanelly Rly.
Great Western Railway
AMMANFORD
To LLANELLY
To LLANELLY

1865. The M. & M. R. Relinquishes its Mountain Line.

as Yspytty Ystwyth. Bills to give effect to the agreement were to be put forward by all three companies in 1865, and if unsuccessful, to be presented anew in 1866, the agreement stipulating that the other company or companies involved were not then to oppose the re-introduction of such a Bill.

All three duly obtained their Acts. The Swansea and Aberystwyth Junction, however, faded from the scene and will detain us no further. The M. & M.'s Bill did not go forward entirely free of opposition. At the Wharncliffe meeting called to obtain shareholder approval to proposed legislation of this sort, a counter-amendment was tabled by the former engineer, Fulton, defending to the last his own original route.

The Mid Wales (Western Extensions) Act authorised construction from the existing M.W.R. at Aber Marteg to Trawscoed and from the M. & M. at Llangurig to the Aber Marteg-Trawscoed line, together with an extra £380,000 of share capital and £126,500 of loans. All but the most optimistic would regard the raising of this sum, an increase of almost 50% over the Mid Wales' existing powers, as being beyond the capability of that company. Three years were allowed for compulsory purchase of land, and four years to complete the line. An interesting provision was that for the protection of the Hafod Estate, once described by George Borrow as "a truly fairy place . . . beautiful but fantastic", and then in the ownership of William Chambers, the former M. & M. chairman. Chambers retained rights to plant and fell timber on the railway's slopes, and to extract minerals, the Mid Wales being obliged to pay for any minerals which had to be left unexploited so that the line should not be undermined. The Mid Wales was allowed to abandon its previously authorised Llangurig Branch, and the M. & M.'s running powers over the new lines were confirmed.

The Manchester and Milford's Act also confirmed the arrangements made in the 1864 tri-partite agreement in all respects. Railway 1, as set out in the Act, began at Alltddu and terminated 2½ miles beyond at Ystrad Meurig, and Railway 2 covered the 7 miles from there to the junction with the newly authorised Mid Wales line near Yspytty Ystwyth. Railway 4 — for some reason there was no Railway 3 — commenced with a junction with Railway 2 at Ystrad Meurig and ended at the Aberystwyth and Welsh Coast company's Aberystwyth Harbour branch. Railway 5 completed the Ystrad Meurig triangle and Railway 6, that between the two A. & W.C. lines.

The redundant stretch of the 1860 route from Alltddu to Llangurig was to be abandoned, together with the previously authorised branch to Aberystwyth and the powers in the 1861 Act to raise money. Instead, the Manchester and Milford was allowed to cancel up to £175,000 of shares which had either been forfeited or were unissued, and to reissue them as preference stock. Entirely new capital was limited by the Act to the curious sum of £15,300 with a further £5,100 as loans. It was reasonably to be expected that the money saved by not building the mountain line would be sufficient for the lighter task embraced by the 1865 Act.

The time given in the M. & M.'s 1860 Act of Incorporation had run out: five years had been allowed to build the line. The 1865 Act therefore permitted another year for compulsory purchase between Pencader and Alltddu, and two years for completion of this portion. Three years and four years respectively were allowed for the new works. The M. & M. was able to improve its standing in relation to the Carmarthen and Cardigan Railway, no doubt because by this time the broad gauge was regarded as a general irritant by the Legislature. The C. & C. was obliged to grant the M. & M. running powers to Carmarthen and use of both Carmarthen and Pencader stations, and to lay in mixed gauge — but at the Manchester and Milford's expense. Failing compliance, the M. & M. was entitled to lay the third rail for itself. At the other end of the line, the company was empowered to build that part of the A. & W.C.'s harbour line which was necessary for access to the existing Aberystwyth terminus, subject to elaborate provisions for the A. & W.C.'s protection. A contemporary, but incomplete, plan shows the M. & M.'s Railway 6 heading right through the site of a carriage or loco shed, and across several running lines, so the A. & W.C.'s power of veto is perhaps a little more understandable.

The lines finally authorised in 1865 were by no means easily graded. Railway 1 from Alltddu to Ystrad Meurig was all but level, but there was then a two mile ascent along Railway 2, beginning at 1 in 55, before the summit of this short line, and a further two miles down at 1 in 41½ to the junction with the Mid Wales Railway. The line to Aberystwyth began with a sharp climb of nearly a mile at 1 in 45 in order to cross into the Ystwyth Valley: it would not be possible to get a run at this gradient, because of the sharp curve and junctions at Ystrad Meurig. Then followed the long descent of Trawscoed bank, down to the level of the Ystwyth. Its three miles at 1 in 43 and one at 1 in 52 were later to cause the company a number of headaches through runaways, trains frequently being unable to stop at Trawscoed station. The total length of Railway 4 from its junction at Ystrad Meurig to the A. &. W.C. Railway's harbour branch amounted to 13½ miles.

Thus revitalised, and with a line which it had real prospects of being able to complete, the Manchester and Milford set about construction with some speed. At the general meeting in February 1865, the directors were able to anticipate opening from Pencader to

Lampeter in the spring, with completion to Ystrad Meurig before year-end. A month later, the contract with Davies and Beeston for the Aberystwyth line was finalised. Needless to say, the directors' forecasts proved optimistic. In August they were still awaiting Board of Trade inspection of the twelve miles to Lampeter. They had, however, made provision for the engines and rolling stock needed for this section, and the builders were finishing off the extra stock needed for the next section to Ystrad Meurig.

Another notable landmark at this time was official recognition that all capital had been subscribed and half paid up, as required before loans could be raised. It must of course be borne in mind that "subscribed" included shares forfeited through non-payment, and that very little money as such had actually come from shares. Most were issued paid-up to the contractor and others for services and land. Nonetheless, the ability to raise up to £190,000 in loans greatly eased the company's immediate quest for cash, although its longer-term effects were far from beneficial.

The line from Pencader to Lampeter was duly opened on January 1st 1866. Through running over the Carmarthen and Cardigan Railway from Carmarthen was as yet not possible, as the C. & C. had neglected to lay the third rail. Davies and Beeston were therefore authorised to proceed with the work instead. At the next general meeting, the opening of a further 15 miles to Ystrad Meurig, for goods only, and the rapid progress towards Aberystwyth were noted. By the end of August 1866, the line was open to Strata Florida, as Ystrad Meurig had now become — despite the opposition of the Earl of Lisburne, the headmaster of Ystrad Meurig grammar school, and sundry others who had petitioned the M. & M. against the change. The company was not, however, to be deterred from naming the station after a ruined abbey some three miles distant, which was in any case known locally by its Welsh name. The railway lovers' heritage would perhaps be the poorer without this little eccentricity.

The laying of standard gauge rails over the C. & C. was also complete by August 1866, the contractors receiving £20,000 in shares for the work. The Carmarthen and Cardigan appeared very much aggrieved by this imposition, and sought running powers to Aberystwyth. Fortunately for the M. & M., its neighbour's 1867 Bill was rejected by Parliament.

By February 1867, a workforce of 450 was being employed to complete the line to Aberystwyth. Only 2½ miles of permanent way remained to be laid, although some embankment had yet to be built, together with a number of bridges and signalling. Six months later, all was ready. The entire route of rather more than 41 miles to Aberystwyth had met with Board of Trade approval by early August, and the line was opened to traffic on the 12th. Up to that date, payments for work between Pencader and Aberystwyth amounted to £460,000. Ultimately, the total excluding land and legal costs amounted to around £700,000 of which £75,000 was on the Llangurig section. No money was ever spent on the authorised line between Ystrad Mcurig (Strata Florida) and Yspytty Ystwyth.

The birth had been too long and painful for anything very elaborate in the way of a celebration to be expected, although David Davies did give a banquet at the Belle Vue Hotel in Aberystwyth. The occasion was one of some sadness for Davies, for he had himself had to fund much of his work on the M. & M. once the financial panic following the well-known collapse of the bankers Overend, Gurney and Co. eliminated any possibility of raising capital elsewhere. He was at least luckier or wiser than some other contractors, who went bankrupt. Having his capital tied up in the M. & M. until the Barrow family bought him out brought the realisation that he would never have the funds to build another line, although he did build the insignificant Van Railway four years later.

At the banquet, he said that he "felt very anxious, after paying up a great deal of money and opening all the way to Lampeter and Strata Florida . . . You can imagine how I looked around to see how that great cutting at Tanycraig — between Ystrad Meurig and Trawscoed — was to be brought about . . . But to find the money in the midst of this panic, that was the difficulty; and if we had not had it in our pockets we should not have had it at all . . . I feel, when I am riding up through the cutting, that these old rocks will tell a tale of Mr Beeston and me when we are gone". Moving on to the actual opening, "we had the honour of having one of the oldest and most strict inspectors of the day, I mean Colonel Yolland. I am told that he rarely does pass a railway on the first examination. However, he has passed this, and I think I have won a new hat by it this time, for I wagered a new hat with Mr Szlumper that he would pass the railway the first time".

The next day, there was a dinner for the navvies, at which they presented Davies with a £40 clock, and no doubt chided him on not going on with the mountain section, for he replied, "You must not think that I am hard with you because I will not go on to finish the old railway over the hills to Llanidloes. You say it wants finishing; so it does, but we must see our way where to get the money from because, perhaps, if it was done it would not pay, and then where would be the result to you and me?" Privately, Davies is reputed to have stated in 1869 that "he would not put a farthing of his own money on the line".

CHAPTER 3

THE DEVELOPING CRISIS, 1867-1875

The train services in the first months of operation were worked by the contractors on behalf of the Manchester and Milford Railway with three engines supplied by Sharp Stewart. All were to Sharp Stewart standard designs, and very similar engines were to be found on the Furness, Cambrian, and Pembroke and Tenby Railways. "General Wood" was a six-coupled goods engine, and "Carmarthen" and "Lady Elizabeth" were four-coupled passenger engines. All three were subsequently taken over by the company, and performed valuable service over a number of years, although only "Lady Elizabeth" lasted to the end of the M. & M.'s independent career.

A small saddle-tank locomotive to one of Manning Wardle's standard designs also saw service on the line in 1867. This engine was purchased by John Barrow, but was not really suitable, and was part-exchanged with the makers for a much larger six-coupled goods engine. The new engine, named "Aberystwyth", was also Barrow's property and was hired to the M. & M. at £10 per week. A final addition in this period was "No. 5", another goods tender engine from Sharp Stewart, identical to "General Wood". No. 5, which never carried a name, was likewise on hire from Barrow at £10 a week, and started work in mid-1870. Both "Aberystwyth" and No. 5 carried plates from some time after June 1871 recording their true ownership.

The company's first timetable was published on January 12th 1866, under the signature of Edward Hamer, the traffic manager and locomotive superintendent. Wisely — in view of the appalling reputation for timekeeping which the M. & M. soon gained — the timetable proclaimed that no guarantee could be given of schedules being kept to, or of trains arriving in time for the nominally corresponding train or coach. The service comprised three mixed trains each way, with provision for passengers travelling 1st, 2nd and 3rd class, timed as follows:

Up	*a.m.*	*a.m.*	*p.m.*	*Down*	*a.m.*	*p.m.*	*p.m.*
Lampeter	6.30	10.50	3.15	Pencader	9.00	2.20	6.45
Llanybyther	6.50	11.05	3.32	Pencader J.	9.05	2.22	6.49
Maesycrugiau	7.02	11.15	3.42	Maesycrugiau	9.20	2.34	7.00
Pencader J.	7.13	11.30	3.53	Llanybyther	9.30	2.45	7.15
Pencader	7.15	11.35	3.55	Lampeter	9.45	3.00	7.30

It appears that trains made a stop at Pencader Junction itself in the early years, and one minute was allowed between arrival and departure times. Quite what form the facilities took is unclear, but the station is recorded as being closed in May 1880: no evidence of its site remains.

To establish the Manchester and Milford's claim to "trunk" status, an elaborate series of connections was shown by which a hardy traveller might reach Milford from the North of England and vice versa. By leaving Liverpool at 7.30 a.m. or Manchester at 7.50, it was possible to arrive at Whitchurch in time for the Cambrian's 1.15 p.m departure, which reached Aberystwyth at 5.55. Alternatively, LNWR departures from the North between 3.15 p.m. and 4.15 p.m. would allow the late afternoon Cambrian train to be caught, and this arrived in Aberystwyth at 10.35 p.m. Intermediate times for both trains were given for Oswestry, Welshpool, Montgomery, Newtown, Moat Lane Junction, Machynlleth, Ynyslas and Borth. An overnight stop to sample the sea air at Aberystwyth was obligatory before departing by stagecoach at 9.30 the following morning, to reach Lampeter by way of Aberayron at 1.15. There was then time for a leisurely luncheon at the Black Lion before catching the last train of the day for Pencader, where the Carmarthen and Cardigan Railway considerately provided departures 5-10 minutes after the scheduled arrival of each of the M. & M.'s three trains.

Our traveller would thus have found himself in Carmarthen Town at 5 p.m. when he could, if everything was running to time, make the 5.05 connection offered by the Llanelly Railway to Carmarthen Junction station. Here, there was a 15 minute breathing space before the Great Western Railway, as successor to the South Wales Railway, provided a train at 5.24 p.m., arriving at New Milford as it was then called, 1 hour and 34 minutes later. A first or second class ticket would have been necessary for this part of the journey. The GWR took a rather snooty attitude to third class passengers, and the 5.24 was only for the upper orders. The alternative offered was not until 9.21 the next morning, implying almost 48 hours on the journey altogether.

In the reverse direction, a train from New Milford at 11.20 a.m. reached Pencader in time for the Manchester and Milford's 2.20 p.m. departure. An overnight stop in Lampeter was then required, the coach leaving at ten the next morning and reaching Aberystwyth in mid-afternoon. The timetable then implied that the Cambrian's 5.30 p.m. departure for Oswestry would allow Manchester or Liverpool to be reached at around eleven at night: it was in fact necessary to catch the 4 p.m. Whitchurch train. A first class return between Pencader and Lampeter cost 3s. 9d. when the line opened, and a second class return was 2s. 6d. Single fares were two-thirds of return rates. A third class single ticket between these two stations was 1s. 1d., the cheapest intermediate distance being that between

Pencader and Maesycrugiau at 4d.

A new public timetable came into force in September 1866 following the line's opening to Strata Florida. Much the same connections were indicated with the Cambrian and the LNWR, but an earlier start was required from Aberystwyth. The coach arrived at Strata Florida in time for the first train of the day at 10 a.m., which must have been rather too late in the morning for the convenience of most of the local population. Other departures were at 1.30 p.m. and 4.30 p.m., with arrivals at Pencader, almost 28 miles from Strata Florida, at 11.42 a.m., 4.02 p.m. and 6.10 p.m. Stops were shown at Tregaron, Pont Llanio, Bettws, Lampeter, Llanybyther, Maesycrugiau and Pencader Junction. Good connections were provided by the Carmarthen and Cardigan, Llanelly, and Great Western Railways for the first two trains, by which it was possible to reach New Milford at 2.24 and 6.45 p.m.

The Manchester and Milford had close relations for a number of years with the Pembroke and Tenby Railway, and was at pains to promote its standard gauge ally's ferry service between Milford and Pembroke Dock, and the connecting P. & T. departures at 3 p.m. and 7.30 p.m. for Tenby, reached forty minutes later. The P. & T.'s extension to the Great Western at Whitland was not opened until after the timetable's appearance; hence the roundabout route. In the Down direction — in M. & M. terms — there was just one connection leaving Tenby at 10 a.m., Milford at 11.15, Carmarthen Town at 1.20 p.m., and arriving at Pencader at 2 o'clock. M. & M. departures were 10.05 a.m., 2.05 p.m., and 6.30 p.m., arriving at Strata Florida at 12.30, 3.40, and 8.20 p.m. The stagecoach connection was also with the middle train of the day, so the journey from "coast-to-coast" became a reasonable proposition, taking 7 to 8 hours. Arrival at Aberystwyth was, however, too late to allow departure the same day for the north.

The standard gauge over the Carmarthen and Cardigan was complete, as noted, in August 1866, and through running for goods trains began on November 1st. It has been stated that the passenger service was extended to Carmarthen one year later, but the directors were in fact still awaiting Board of Trade inspection between Pencader and Carmarthen in February 1868. In the meantime, guards of M. & M. Up trains were instructed to put off carriages at Pencader and work through with goods and empties only, re-attaching carriages on the return trip.

The working timetables of this period showed trains crossing at Llanybyther and Lampeter. The line was in five sections, with a different colour of train staff for each: orange for Strata Florida to Tregaron, white for Tregaron to Lampeter, blue from there to Llanybyther, red to Pencader Junction, and yellow between the junction and Pencader station. Immediately after opening, there was just one section between Lampeter and Pencader Junction, and the original train staff was inscribed "Go on to Lampeter" on one side and "Go on to Pencader Junction" on the other. Approaching the junction, M. & M. trains were to give two whistles and have a red light on the buffer beam at night to distinguish them from C. & C. trains giving one whistle and showing a white light. Similar arrangements applied at Abergwili Junction to distinguish Llanelly Railway trains. Speed was not to exceed 5 m.p.h. through stations or 10 m.p.h. on sharp curves, and engine drivers were not to make up lost time. With maximum speeds of 15 m.p.h. for goods trains, 20 m.p.h. for light engines, and 25 m.p.h. for passenger trains, there was unlikely to be any exciting running! Loads were limited to 15 laden or 30 empty wagons; less in wet or slippery weather.

Firemen were to sign on 45 minutes before starting time, and drivers 30 minutes. The fireman was responsible for keeping the accounts of miles run and fuel and materials used, and both were to receive premiums for economical running. Guards also had to sign on 30 minutes beforehand. As well as their traditional responsibility for timekeeping, they were to deliver luggage and parcels, collect excess fares, lock carriage doors on the "far" side, and call out at junctions the places for which passengers must change trains! Had there been any "M. & M." junctions, the guards would have been rivalled by the stationmasters, whose job it was to call out the station's name when trains arrived.

Shortly after the opening of the line throughout to Aberystwyth in August 1867, a new timetable was published under the proud boast, "Forming the shortest and most direct route between Swansea, Milford, Tenby, Carmarthen and Liverpool, Manchester, Chester and the North". The service remained three mixed trains each way:

Up	*a.m.*	*p.m.*	*p.m.*	*Down*	*a.m.*	*p.m.*	*p.m.*	*Miles*
Aberystwyth	7.00	2.30	6.10	Carmarthen	7.30	1.30	6.40	
Llanrhystyd Rd.	7.09	2.38	6.20	Pencader arr.	8.30	2.28	7.30	14¼
Llanilar	7.18	2.46	6.32	Pencader dep.	8.31	2.30	7.31	
Trawscoed	7.25	2.54	6.42	Pencader Junc.	8.33	2.32	7.33	14¾
Strata Florida	7.50	3.10	7.10	Maesycrugiau	8.47	2.45	7.46	18¼
Tregaron	8.03	3.23	7.30	Llanybyther	9.12	2.56	8.00	22
Pont Llanio	8.12	3.33	7.43	Lampeter arr.	9.27	3.08	8.12	27
Bettws	8.25	3.46	7.50	Lampeter dep.	9.40	3.12	8.15	
Lampeter arr.	8.30	3.52	8.03	Bettws	9.50	3.20	8.25	29¼
Lampeter dep.	8.40	3.55	8.10	Pont Llanio	10.10	3.38	8.42	34¼
Llanbyther	8.55	4.10	8.30	Tregaron	10.25	3.50	8.52	36¼
Maesycrugiau	9.10	4.18	8.45	Strata Florida	10.40	4.05	9.07	41¾
Pencader Junc.	9.22	4.29	8.56	Trawscoed	11.00	4.23	9.26	46¾
Pencader arr.	9.23	4.30	8.58	Llanilar	11.10	4.32	9.34	49¾
Pencader dep.	9.25	4.35	9.00	Llanrhystyd Rd.	11.20	4.42	9.43	52¾
Carmarthen	10.23	5.24	9.50	Aberystwyth	11.30	4.50	9.50	55¾

Mileages were now shown from Carmarthen in anticipation of Board of Trade sanction for through running by standard gauge passenger trains. The Manchester and Milford advertised refreshment rooms at Pencader and Strata Florida stations, which would doubtless have provided some relief from the grinding monotony of a journey over the line. By the middle of 1868, it was necessary to set off from Carmarthen at 6.00 a.m. to be at Aberystwyth at 11.10 a.m., in time for a connection with trains reaching Lancashire the same day. This represented a miserable 11 m.p.h. average over the M. & M.

Another mixed train was added to the timetable early in 1869, leaving Aberystwyth at 9.10 a.m. and terminating at Pencader at 1.05 p.m. The return working departed from Pencader at 6.30 p.m., and was overtaken en route at Lampeter by the 6.40 from Carmarthen, before arriving back at Aberystwyth at 10.30 p.m. The last train Up and the first Down were also mixed, but the remaining two trains each way no longer took goods wagons, with some modest benefit to the journey times. The 2.35 p.m. from Aberystwyth then managed a creditable 2 hours and 35 minutes to Carmarthen, and was shown with connections via Whitland and Tenby to Pembroke Dock: Milford had now disappeared from the published connections in favour of the Pembroke and Tenby's line.

Passenger traffic was not, however, developing sufficiently to justify four trains each way daily, so the timetable soon reverted to three. Aberystwyth departures at the end of 1869 were 8.30 a.m., 2.30 and 6.15 p.m., and trains left Carmarthen at 6.20 a.m., 1.15 and 6.40 p.m. The 6.15 mixed Up working was allowed 3 hours 45 minutes for the trip and the first Down train, no less than 4 hours 25 minutes: the others managed the journey in around 3 hours. Although speeds were thus back to their pedestrian norm, the Manchester and Milford sought to improve the service by running through carriages in conjunction with the Pembroke and Tenby Railway to Pembroke Dock. This was made possible by the laying of standard gauge between Whitland and Carmarthen for the P. & T.'s use, and by the construction of a north-to-west curve — the "P. & T. loop" — which by-passed the Great Western's Carmarthen Junction station and led without reversal to the C. &. C.'s Town station. The new line was opened for goods traffic, mainly lime, in June 1868 and for passenger trains in August 1869. Through running did not, however, last long. Three months after conversion of the gauge in West Wales in May 1872, the Pembroke and Tenby was forced to cease running beyond Whitland.

New stations at Llangybi — for market and fair days only — and at Cross Inn (Llanfihangel) were introduced into the timetable in 1869. Cross Inn was renamed New Quay Road in July 1874, and

Bettws became Derry Ormond at about the same time. The passenger service of three trains each way daily excluding Sundays remained the pattern for the next few years, with just minor changes in the departure and arrival times. The number of people carried was still not great: in 1871, for example, the following tickets were issued:

	Return			*Single*			
Train	*1st*	*2nd*	*Market*	*1st*	*2nd*	*3rd*	*Parliamentary*
First up	129	430	6,492	495	990	192	17,734
Second up	67	320	35	407	1,115	9,676	—
Third up	3	—	—	110	220	—	8,919
	199	750	6,527	1,012	2,325	9,868	26,653
First down	202	501	9,567	424	718	3,871	17,044
Second down	44	150	—	452	804	14,617	—
Third down	1	14	—	195	250	417	7,409
	247	665	9,567	1,071	1,772	18,905	24,453

Of the total of 120,000, an average of 65 on each train, barely more than 2% were first class and 5% second. There were also around 300 round trips by holiday excursion, and over 400 people booked to travel with special goods trains. Tickets, in later years at least, were a colourful assortment. The predominant colours seem to have been yellow for first class, deep pink or buff for second, pale pink or yellow ochre for third, and green for Parliamentary. Return tickets were generally banded with other colours; first class and Parliamentary with white, second class with light blue, third with mauve. The record may well be held by some second class returns with no less that ten stripes on a normal-sized ticket in pink, blue and white. Two colours and white were also the rule on 14-day returns. Oddities included those stamped "Voter's through ticket", market returns in deep blue, and excursion returns overprinted with six thin blue or red stripes.

By late 1872, the company was casting round for economies and as a result all trains once more became mixed, much to the detriment of journey times. Connections were again shown to New Milford following the cessation of the Pembroke and Tenby's through service. Trains leaving New Milford at 10.25 a.m. and 4.25 p.m. connected with the M. & M.'s middle and last down services, but it was still not possible to reach Manchester the same day. The Cambrian's Whitchurch train left several hours before the M. & M.'s arrived at Aberystwyth at 5, although in later years the Cambrian did run a 6 o'clock train by which Manchester could be reached in the small hours. Coming south the situation was rather better. A departure from Manchester around 7 a.m. allowed the 9.45 Cambrian train from Whitchurch to be caught. This connected with the M. & M.'s 2.30 departure, whose passengers reached Carmarthen Town at 5.30 p.m. There then followed the renewed irritant of the four minute trip to the Junction for the GWR's 6.15 Milford train, which reached its destination at 7.45 p.m., just over twelve hours after leaving Lancashire.

The inconvenience at Carmarthen caused by the revised traffic arrangements imposed on the P. & T. was not the only one to afflict passengers. A similar agreement was apparently pressed on Hamer by his equivalent on the Carmarthen and Cardigan, with the effect of curtailing use of the M. & M.'s running powers. The timetables of the period are strangely mute on the change. Not until 1876 is it quite clear from this source that M. & M. trains were no longer running beyond Pencader, and by then the cut-back would have been forced as much by dire economic necessity as by anything else. The mileage statements showed a reduction in other companies' lines worked from 14¼ — the distance from Carmarthen Town to Pencader Junction — to nil as from mid-1873.

For a brief period from the beginning of 1874 until the onset of the financial crisis the next year, an additional Mondays-only train was run for the benefit of the farming community, and in response to requests. It began at Pont Llanio, of all unlikely places, at 8.45 a.m. and terminated at Aberystwyth at 10.30: the balancing movement was not advertised in the public timetables. The company set about developing the limited traffic potential of the area in other ways too. An omnibus service from Aberayron to Lampeter was organised to connect with trains on Tuesdays, Thursdays and Saturdays, and there was a daily run with a covered van between Newquay and New Quay Road station.

Most of the available ways of developing the traffic inevitably required the outlay of capital, which was in precious short supply. Many things were, as might be expected, incomplete when the line opened, and a great deal had to be done towards providing quite basic facilities. Nor was the company helped by the forces of nature when, in October 1867, not-yet-consolidated embankment alongside the Ystwyth was washed away when the river flooded, and abutments to the girder bridge over the river were damaged. Work in hand in 1868 included sidings for the Aberystwyth Harbour Trustees — the Aberystwyth and Welsh Coast Railway having entirely failed to build its line to the harbour. A siding for agricultural trade at the level crossing between Llanybyther and Maesycrugiau was requested, but not in fact laid. Barrow asked for platform sheds and a locomotive repair shop and smithy at Aberystwyth. Weighing machines were to be erected. A second, wooden, platform was to be built at Strata Florida, another was to be provided at Pont Llanio, and the goods shed at Tregaron was to be completed. In the following years, the board sanctioned the construction of stone goods sheds at Strata Florida and Pont Llanio, that at Pont Llanio still standing a hundred years later. Cattle pens were erected at Lampeter, and new sidings provided at New Quay Road, together with interlocking at Aberystwyth Harbour and the Corporation's quarry near Ystrad Meurig.

Important though they may have been in developing the traffic, these items were trivial in comparison with what the company should have been spending its money on; namely the extension to meet the Mid Wales at Yspytty Ystwyth. Yet while the Mid Wales showed no signs of building its line, a failing which the M. & M.'s directors remarked on as early as 1868, there was little point. The Manchester and Milford soon acquired an alternative scheme on which to dissipate its expansionist ambitions in the shape of a branch to Devil's Bridge. Quite why anyone should want to build a railway to that charming hamlet is a mystery, as the traffic potential in the immediate area was negligible. Devil's Bridge was, though, a reasonable concentration centre for the mining industry further into the hills, and this was no doubt the aim. The directors decided to support a semi-independent scheme late in 1871, and a year later had reached agreement on a Bill in the next Session, which would also include compulsory purchase powers for land for a new station at Aberystwyth.

By this time, the direction of the company was in new hands. John Barrow died "in harness" in July 1871, leaving his son and Forster as the only active members of the board. Some strengthening of the ranks was clearly essential, and William Felix Poole was elected a director in October, followed in May 1872 by George Deans and A.C. Sherriff, M.P., who was no doubt expected to prove useful when the Devil's Bridge Bill came before Parliament. It was J.J. Barrow in his new role as chairman who advanced the Parliamentary deposit for the scheme. This he was well able to do as principal beneficiary from the estate left by his father — somewhat depleted by the ravages of the M. & M. — and also from that of his uncle Richard, who had died in 1865. When John James died in 1903, aged 78, his effects amounted to not far short of £½ million, making him perhaps one of the richest commoners of his era. J.J. Barrow, like his grandfather before him, had a large family comprising four sons and two daughters by his first wife, and one son, Charles Deans Barrow, and two daughters by his second. All but one of the male children were involved at one time or another in the affairs of the M. & M. The eldest, John Burton Barrow, became a director in 1876 and succeeded John James as chairman from 1903 until the end of the company's existence in 1911. Copner Walton was the least involved, serving on the board only in 1880/1 and 1894/5. Leonard Norman Barrow became a director in 1893 and Charles Deans Barrow in 1904, both participating actively until the absorption of the M. & M. by the GWR.

Returning to 1873, the Devil's Bridge Branch Bill passed successfully through Parliamentary committee in April, despite opposition from the Cambrian and the Aberystwyth School Board, whose land was to be purchased for the new station. The Act empowered the company to build a seven mile long light railway from a junction about 1 mile from Trawscoed and 2 miles from Llanilar station. The River Ystwyth was to be crossed immediately beyond the junction, the route then following the valleys east and north before terminating besides the Devil's Bridge to Cwmystwyth road, not far from the later terminus of the Vale of Rheidol Light Railway. To pay for all this, new shares to a total of £40,000 were authorised, and these were to be kept strictly separate from the remainder of the M. & M.'s capital. Branch shareholders were to receive a fixed dividend of 5% from branch income, and only then could remaining profits go towards the gross reciepts of the company. Three years were allowed for compulsory purchase, and five to complete the line.

As with so many other of the Manchester and Milford's schemes, the Devil's Bridge branch was never to be built. The most immediate reason was the financial crisis that erupted in 1875. An extension of time was obtained in 1876, but by December 1879 there had still been no money raised from the issue of branch shares, and compulsory purchase powers were about to run out. So in order to recover the Parliamentary deposit, an Act was obtained in 1880 authorising abandonment.

As a prelude to the financial failure of the Manchester and Milford in 1875, it is necessary to consider the hostile relations that grew up with the Cambrian Railways, as successors to the Aberystwyth and Welsh Coast Railway at Aberystwyth, and to the Llanidloes and Newtown at Llanidloes. The M. & M. had complained in 1868 that it was paying too much for station facilities at Aberystwyth, and managed to have the payments provided for in the A. & W.C.'s 1863 Act revised in its favour. The situation at Llanidloes was yet more irksome, because here the company was expected to pay for something it had no means of using. Furthermore, the L. & N. had taken the opportunity presented by the cost-sharing agreement and the Act of 1862 to build itself an unnecessarily extravagent station, whose main building stands to this day, a gaunt reminder dominating the outskirts of the town. So while the joint line cost £16,000, outlay on the station amounted to more than £20,000.

Now it is by no means clear that the M. & M. ever began paying for the Llanidloes joint line and station, relying on a strict interpretation of the term "from the time of opening" and on the fact that they had never "opened" the line to Llangurig. As far as is known, only contractor's traffic ever used it, although a trial goods train was recorded in February 1864: the M. & M. was certainly reluctant to do so, and even turned down a request from a Mr Owen who wanted to run some wagons of his own. The Cambrian therefore provoked a confrontation by, it appears, taking some unilateral action in relation to the trackwork at Penpontbren Junction. Whatever precisely was involved, it had the desired effect. J.J. Barrow and A.C. Sherriff departed hot-foot to Penpontbren, the matter came to court, and was decided in the Cambrian's favour, whereupon the line was "officially" declared open as of August 1st 1872.

Promptly in February 1873, the Cambrian slapped in its bill for the half-year since "opening", the Manchester and Milford predictably neglected to pay, and the Cambrian — equally predictably — sued. The price for the M. & M. was high: costs of £220 had to be paid as well as the £550 bill. Nonetheless, the M. & M. continued to default on its share of the Llanidloes outgoings, and another action was brought at the end of 1874 for the three half-yearly payments then due, amounting to almost £1,500. The Cambrian obtained judgment in January 1875. In the following July, the M. & M.'s manager at Aberystwyth telegraphed the directors to say that the Cambrian had put in execution on the company's rolling stock. Since the train service could hardly be operated with the rolling stock impounded, the secretary was hastily despatched to Aberystwyth with the necessary cash. The Cambrian had by this time embarked on yet a third law suit! Not only had the Manchester and Milford failed to pay the £560 owing for Llanidloes facilities for the half-year to January 1875, but it had also stopped payments in mid-1874 for the use of Aberystwyth. By July 1875, the sum outstanding was over £1,700. On this occasion, however, the Cambrian was unable to obtain satisfaction, as a receiver had been appointed over the M. & M.'s affairs.

For the Cambrian was not alone in having claims outstanding against the company. Nor was it simply a question of sheer cussedness on the part of the M. & M., although the company no doubt felt that it had some moral right in resisting the Llanidloes charges. Much the biggest creditors were the executors of the late John Barrow, to whom the M. & M. had good reason to feel grateful. The truth was that the company had been unable to build its line employing only shareholders' funds, and that the receipts from traffic were insufficient to pay interest on loans or rent charges — the preferential payments to landholders who had sold land without demanding cash or, on the other hand, being prepared to accept shares in lieu — or the various user charges of neighbouring railways. So it was that the Manchester and Milford was in almost constant need of cash injection, most of which was provided by John Barrow.

We have already seen that John Barrow became much the biggest shareholder, largely by subsidising the contractors during the line's construction and taking over their share entitlement. From the time of the line's opening, the company minutes are sprinkled with references to money advanced by him. In mid-1875, John Barrow's executors finally felt obliged to set the late chairman's affairs in order, and placed a writ on the company for just short of £39,000. The amount was not in dispute, but the company had of course no means of finding the money. A petition was therefore entered for the appointment of a Receiver; more in sorrow than in anger as it was proposed that the Secretary should undertake the task, and head an inquiry into whom was owed what, with which priority. The Secretary was accordingly summoned to appear before Vice Chancellor Hall of the Court of Chancery, and was appointed to the position on July 23rd 1875, fifteen years to the day from the Manchester and Milford's Act of Incorporation.

Investigation of the company's debts and liabilities revealed that, at that date, debenture loans amounted to almost £164,000, on which arrears of interest were accruing at 5% p.a. Other liabilities came to £46,000, this figure including the £1,700 judgment debt to the Cambrian and the £39,000 to John Barrow's executors. None of this should have come as any surprise, however. A similar position was evident from the published accounts which revealed that £11,500 in arrears of interest was already owing at the end of 1868, and that this sum had been increasing at around £8,000 p.a. to reach £62,500 by mid-1875. Much the same was occurring with rent charges, although at a more modest rate. Only the extent of "temporary loans" could have been unexpected, since these were not fully recorded in the accounts until the executors' writ in July 1875. In simple cost-and-revenue terms, the line was operating at a profit — even if sometimes a very small one — throughout this period. At no time, however, was it sufficient to cover the overheads thrust upon it.

Possible evidence of increasing nervousness amongst the management can be deduced from the changes that took place in the run-up to the 1875 crisis. The first of these was the resignation of George Edward Forster from the board in April 1873. He became the company's solicitor instead, a position he had held previously under John Barrow, for whom he was one of the trustees and executors. The contract was initially for three years at £250 p.a., but was not renewed. Forster was obliged to sue the company for his remuneration, and this "disloyalty" was too much for the directors to stomach. David Davies, the contractor and now a Member of Parliament, came onto the board to replace Forster, who died in 1878.

Brown, one of the "sleeping" directors, resigned in July 1873 and was replaced by one Frederick L'Estrange Clark of Pembroke; he was followed by Poole in August, replaced by Charles Lord Denton from St Briavels. By a move that parallelled Forster's, Poole became company secretary, Joseph Butler resigning to make way. On Poole's shoulders therefore fell the responsibility of being appointed Receiver. The board then comprised John James Barrow as chairman, A.C. Sherriff, M.P., Deans, Davies, Clark and Denton, with the last three forming a finance committee. Only Davies and Clark of the six could truly claim a local background and, it might be suggested, an understanding of the line and its problems in other than purely financial terms. Most meetings took place in London, although the finance committee generally met at company offices in Carmarthen or, from time to time, at Pembroke Dock. These six directors remained until June 1875 when Deans, anticipating the forthcoming crisis, disposed of his shares and became ineligible. He was replaced by a Henry S. Ellis of Exeter. Davies resigned in July and Sherriff took no further active part in the company's affairs. Directors' remuneration was £150 p.a.

A word should also be said of the other employees of the company. James Weekes Szlumper continued as engineer during this period, and was responsible for "maintenance, examination, repair of permanent way, bridges, signals, stations, yards, superintending men, returns to the Board of Trade and the company secretary, examining land charges, etc." For this he was paid £150 p.a. plus £80 for performing similar duties on the Pembroke and Tenby Railway. Edward Hamer was the locomotive superintendent and traffic manager, at a salary of £300 p.a. Five others were employed in the general office at Aberystwyth, an accountant at £90 p.a., three clerks and a cleaner cum messenger.

The traffic department employed 30: stationmasters, clerks, porters, a crossing keeper, a wagon inspector, and four guards and a lampman at Aberystwyth. There were no station staff at either Aberystwyth or Pencader, as both were manned by the owning companies. All intervening stations then open with the exception of Llangybi but including Aberystwyth Harbour had station masters, a total of 12. Those at the more important stations were paid between £1 and £1 5s. per week. There were 20 in the locomotive department with a driver, fireman and cleaner allocated to each engine except, for some reason, "Aberystwyth". The remaining 8 worked in the repair shops at Aberystwyth. Also based at Aberystwyth were a carriage examiner and two carpenters, the permanent way inspector, two further carpenters employed on maintenance of structures, and a labourer. The remaining employees comprised eight permanent way gangs, each of four men, and one of five, together with two men quarrying stone, two sawyers, and a pointsman at Aberystwyth

Harbour. The overall total was thus 106.

A.C. Sherriff, when newly appointed a director, was asked to examine whether economies could be effected by combining staff with the Pembroke and Tenby Railway, his previous experience in railway traffic management making him the ideal candidate for this task. Some sort of joint working with the P. & T. had become a realistic possibility following J.J. Barrow's takeover of the M. & M.'s near neighbour and ally, a takeover which soon led to both companies being served by the same directors. Sherriff found that the numbers employed were certainly not excessive for independent companies, but that together they could manage with a common board of directors, one solicitor, one manager, and one secretary. Some savings could also be made by having repair activities concentrated at Pembroke Dock, with a "competent man or two" remaining at Aberystwyth.

Very little seems to have been done about Sherriff's report, presented in January 1873, although the recommendation that there should be just the one secretary was acted upon. Poole resigned his Pembroke and Tenby directorship and was appointed as secretary to that company in the following August, making the identical move on the Manchester and Milford at the same time. The secretary's office for both companies was established in Carmarthen in March 1874. Further developments had to await the formation of the M. & M. and P. & T. Joint Committee in 1879. Even in 1873, however, it was too late for any real fusion of the two companies' operations: the Great Western and Carmarthen and Cardigan Railways had already broken the interlopers' contact at Carmarthen.

CHAPTER 4

IN CHANCERY, 1875-1900

Poole's first task as Receiver for the Manchester and Milford Railway was to bring together the complex threads of the company's financial affairs, and establish just how disastrous the position really was. The directors — for at this stage the management of the railway remained ostensibly in their hands — were free to concentrate on ways of improving the operating position. Clearly, no amount of investigation into the extent of existing debts was going to prevent these accruing further as matters stood.

Their room for manoeuvre was small, so far as further economies in the operation of the line were concerned. There remained, though, the payments due to the Cambrian for the Llanidloes joint line and station. If not exactly a drain on the finances, since the bills were not being paid, they remained a source of increasing liability. And what better scapegoat for their present troubles? Had not the Mid Wales Railway browbeaten the Manchester and Milford into giving up its projected line from Strata Florida to the Llangurig branch in return for use of the Mid Wales' substitute over the same territory? Forget for the moment that the M. & M. would probably never have had the resources to complete the line: this the directors, in public at least, undoubtedly did. Forget that the Mid Wales was just as badly affected in its ability to raise funds in the difficult financial climate of the mid-1860's as the M. & M. Forget also that it was the Cambrian which was being made to suffer for the omissions of the Mid Wales: they were not one-and-the-same until 1888. The fact remained that the Mid Wales had failed in its undertaking yet still refused to relieve the Manchester and Milford of payments for something the M. & M. was thereby prevented from using.

The Mid Wales had in fact sought and obtained extensions of time in which to build its mountain line in both 1869 and 1872. The 1869 application was strenuously opposed by the M. & M., who sought to impose severe penalties on the Mid Wales should it again fail to do the job within the period specified. By 1876, when time was again expiring, it was quite apparent to the M.W.R.'s management that the proposed line had become a hopeless proposition, and an Abandonment Act was applied for. The Manchester and Milford, needless to say, opposed the Act, but was once again unsuccessful. Not only was no substitute connection between Strata Florida and Llangurig provided for, but the legislators were also not prepared to make any explicit arrangements to recompense the Manchester and

Milford. A clause which stated that "nothing in this Act contained shall be deemed to affect any alleged rights or liabilities of the M. & M. under an agreement between the M. & M. and Mid Wales of 28th October 1864" was deemed to be sufficient protection.

It was scant comfort to the Manchester and Milford, who believed it to be illusory, whatever the intentions of Parliament. Altogether, that august body can scarcely have drawn much satisfaction from its inept handling of matters pertaining to the M. & M., who felt obliged to seek the opinion of the Solicitor General. He was emphatic. "We are of the opinion that the M. & M. as a company has no legal remedy whatever against the Mid Wales company. The Act of 1876 clearly created no liability on the part of the Mid Wales . . . It simply remits the company to its rights under the agreement of 1864. The provisions of that agreement have however been strictly complied with. All that the Mid Wales thereby undertook to do was to apply for an Act . . . No doubt it was contemplated that the M.W.R., having obtained the Act, would make the line, but as the M.W.R. has managed to induce Parliament to release it from the obligation of building the line without imposing any liability to indemnify those who are injured by such abandonment, it is not in the power of any court of law to create such an obligation. Obviously, the case is an extremely hard one on the M. & M., but the only tribunal that can remedy it is Parliament. At law, the claim to redress is wholly unsupportable and unarguable".

That being the opinion of the Solicitor General, the company did the only thing it could: it initiated a Bill in the 1877 Session which would have required the M.W.R. to repay within one month any sums which the M. & M. had paid to the Cambrian in respect of the Llanidloes station and joint line. Alternatively, the Mid Wales could pay the Cambrian directly, leaving the M. & M. right out of it. All repayments due from the date the Mid Wales (Western Extensions Abandonment) Act of 1876 reached the Statute Book would have been covered. There was thus a punitive element in it, for the Mid Wales would end up paying two thirds of the Llanidloes station costs compared with the Cambrian's one third, when a more equitable solution might have been for the two user companies to divide the costs equally.

The House of Commons accepted the M. & M.'s view, and held that "it is owing to a certain extent to the fault of the Mid Wales that the Milford company cannot use the joint line and station". The Mid Wales brought a good measure of fiery eloquence to bear in rehearsing the well-worn arguments about the Manchester and Milford's difficulties, as exemplified by its inability to build more than four miles of line — between Penpontbren and Llangurig —

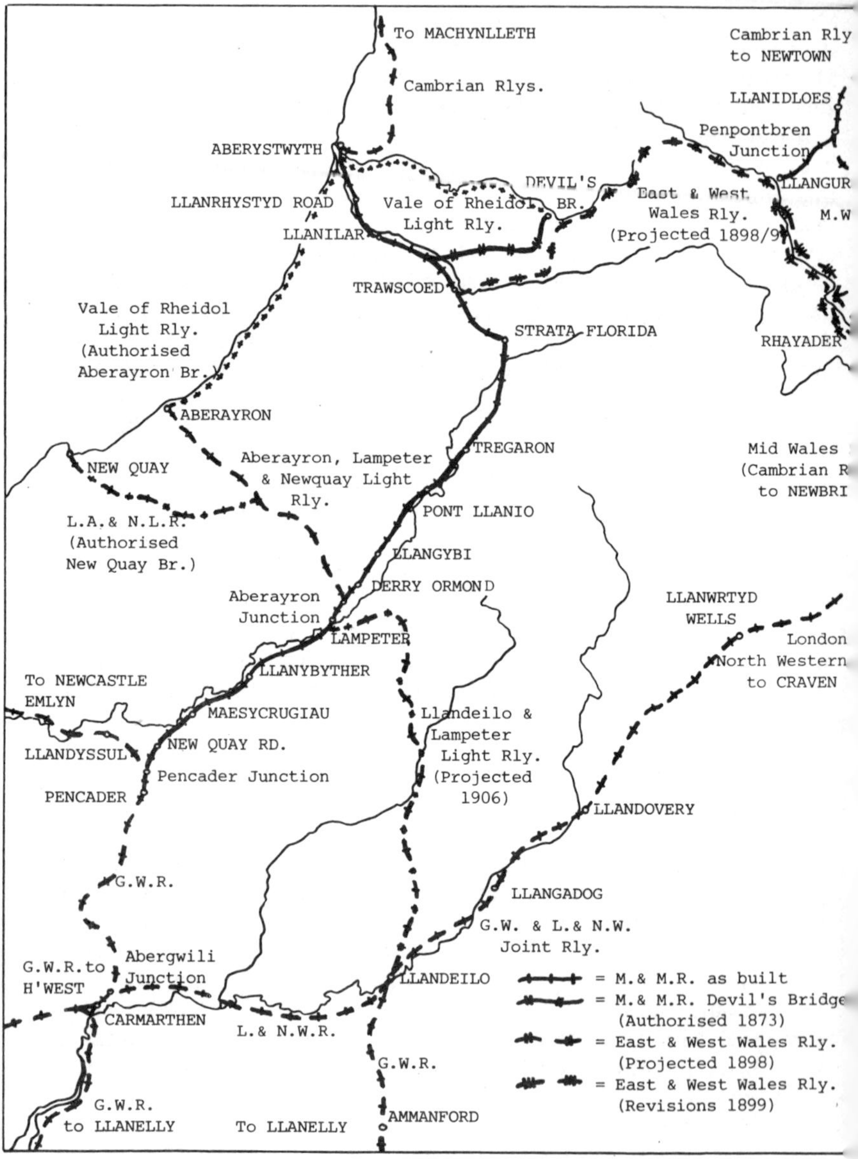

1873 - 1906. Later Proposals, Reasonable and Implausible.

while the Mid Wales built all its railway. It was also contended, with some truth, that the 1864 agreement was the M. & M.'s lifeline, rather than an imposition. The Mid Wales concluded that the Bill was "unreasonable, vexatious and vindictive, and altogether without precedent, and ought not to pass". In the last resort it didn't, being rejected by their Lordships. The Manchester and Milford's costs in the matter remained unpaid.

Meanwhile, developments on the railway were perforce limited, comprising only the most essential repairs and improvements in facilities. The board sought the construction of a goods shed at Llanybyther early in 1876, yet were still trying to justify it to the Court three years later. The expenditure was in fact sanctioned shortly after, together with that needed for refreshment rooms at Lampeter and station master's houses at Strata Florida and New Quay Road. Traders along the line played their part in developing the facilities: a wooden store at Llanybyther, a saw mill on railway land at Tregaron, a siding at the expense of the Rheidol Foundry at Aberystwyth; all were readily agreed to by the company.

As part of the search for economies, the engineer was asked to ensure that old sleepers were re-used as fencing or as fuel for the locomotives, and to see if land on the defunct Llangurig branch could not be let off for grazing! Maintenance of structures on this unused section of the M. & M. was still necessary, and was not made any easier by the frequent theft of bridge parapets for use as building materials: the engineer was further exhorted to find a shape for coping stones which would render them useless for other purposes. A horse was killed when it fell on the Llangurig branch, and led to considerations of fencing the route, but of course nothing immediate was done.

The M. & M. and M.W.R. were still being charged for a signalman employed at Penpontbren Junction, and not surprisingly tried to get the Cambrian to dispense with his services. The M. & M. also set about reducing the wages of its employees, and most had been cut by early in 1879. Standards were obviously being allowed to slip, and the company was beginning to attract unwanted attention from the Board of Trade. Quite apart from routine matters relating to continuous footboards and brakes, the Board was also questioning arrangements at the Aberystwyth Harbour and Ystrad Meurig quarry junctions.

Perhaps the most interesting possibility in the years following the appointment of a receiver was that of some form of joint operations with the Pembroke and Tenby Railway, of which John James Barrow was also the chairman. The reason for the Barrows' involvement in the affairs of the P. & T. became obvious enough once control of the M. & M. had been won. There was little prospect that the M. & M.

would, by its own endeavours, achieve its one-time objective of an outlet to Milford Haven. The Pembroke and Tenby represented just such an outlet. The fact that the Great Western stood, intransigent, between the two must have seemed more hopeful of change than the M. & M.'s crippled finances, which ruled out any thoughts of independent action.

By early 1879, J.J. Barrow was surrounded by mostly new faces on the two boards. His son, John Burton Barrow — already a P. & T. director — began a long connection with the Manchester and Milford in November 1876. H.S. Ellis resigned in mid-1878, numbers on both boards being restored with the appointment of W. Eagle-Bott and C. Stanley Williams, followed by William Wavell as replacement for Charles Lord Denton. In February 1879, J.J. Barrow stood down as chairman in favour of Eagle-Bott, whose main claim to prominence seems to be that he lived next door to Barrow in Westbourne Terrace, Hyde Park. In June, he, J.J. Barrow and Williams formed a committee "to investigate the general position of the companies in relation to receipts and expenditure, with a view to ascertaining how far arrangements can be organised to promote additional economy . . . to reduce expenses consistent with efficiency".

The committee soon decided to give six months' notice to a Mr Isaac Smedley, then the traffic manager of the Pembroke and Tenby, to Hamer, his opposite number on the M. & M., and to Szlumper, who was engineer to both companies. Eagle-Bott would write pointing out that the notice might not be acted upon, and was not a mark of displeasure. This was not altogether honest as it was already intended to reappoint Smedley as traffic manager for the two concerns, and to replace Szlumper who was considered unsatisfactory: it had recently emerged that the engineer had failed to report a defect which made the junction at Pencader unsafe for passengers, he had not kept a proper record of replacement sleepers used, and had allowed the condition of the two lines to deteriorate seriously. Szlumper's notice was therefore confirmed with the comment that there was a requirement for someone "more practically acquainted with mechanical minutiæ" to superintend the locomotive and carriage department.

The committee reported — on the basis of visits it made in the summer of 1879 — that both track maintenance and drainage were poor, and recommended that combined repair shops for the two companies be set up, possibly at Carmarthen where suitable land had been found subject to permission from the Carmarthen and Cardigan Railway. Single management for both lines was proposed, and the report concluded sulkily that "the directors have had the minimum voice in the management . . . instead of being consulted on all subjects".

Lionel R. Wood, previously of the North Eastern Railway, was appointed engineer to the two companies, succeeding Szlumper at the end of 1879. Smedley took on the traffic management of the M. & M. in addition to his existing duties on the P. & T., replacing Hamer. Hamer's misdemeanours soon came to light. For a start, he was held to have been unduly lavish with free passes and had allowed his brother to do paperwork, for which payment was later sought, and give orders to staff without authority. But most seriously, he had made arrangements with "Hamer's Mercantile Co. Ltd." for wharves at various of the company's stations, the arrangements conflicting with those already in force for other traders.

All might have been settled peaceably had not the Cambrian, with the "support" of Szlumper and Hamer, chosen that moment to intervene by petitioning the Court of Chancery for an official manager for the M. & M. At the time, the management of the company remained in the hands of the directors. The Court had done no more than appoint a receiver, Poole, and he was very much the directors' man. The Cambrian took particular exception to the proposed amalgamation of the M. & M. and P. & T. and to Poole's ambivalent role in relation to the directors. The Petition was initially dismissed, but succeeded on appeal. There was then some irresolution over whether the directors could again put forward a nomination for manager, their choice naturally being Smedley. Ultimately however, this course was rejected and in August 1880 a barrister, J. Cholmeley Russell, was appointed instead. This action effectively spelt the end of the M. & M. and P. & T. joint committee. Meetings continued to be held, but they were increasingly one-sided affairs involving only the Pembroke and Tenby. Bott, Barrow and Williams, meeting on New Years Eve 1881, concluded that "the committee could not be called joint after the appointment of an official manager for the Manchester and Milford". Its last recorded meeting was in April 1882.

Russell's appointment heralded another period of chronic turmoil on the M. & M. and he was soon in conflict with the directors over the extent of his powers. The first confrontation revolved around the new engineer and traffic manager. These appointments had been suspended while the Cambrian's petition was heard, but both Wood and Smedley were well-established by the time of Russell's arrival. Undeterred, Russell dismissed Wood in October 1880 and reappointed Szlumper.

The directors were incensed. Their patience was already exhausted as a result of the continued litigation in which the company had been embroiled. They could accept the legal requirement for a manager, but not the need to bring in someone unversed in the niceties of running an insolvent railway, particularly as Smedley was prepared to take on the responsibility without extra salary. They resolved "to lay the facts before the Court with a view to ascertaining how far the directors are superceded by the appointment of an official manager". In their view, Russell had "set up for himself . . . an extraordinary position of sole authority." Before the Court could pronounce, Eagle-Bott stood down as chairman, declining to retain an office which "Mr Russell assumed and claimed" whose "duties and responsibilities were undefined by the Court".

Smedley, who had been busy trying to reach agreement with the Cambrian over its claims, was also dismissed, so Russell was then well on the way to ridding himself of all the "directors' men". His own appointment as Receiver, replacing the secretary, Poole, was made in November 1880, and he took up the position from the following February. Russell claimed that his one concern was to run the line efficiently and economically. The directors took a different view, and their report for the half year to December 1880 was full of recriminations. They pointed out that the Receiver had from the outset gone against the directors' policy, and had insisted that all executive power rested with him, so that "of necessity" there would be disagreement on the management. The directors complained over the arbitrary way in which the engineer had been dismissed, and saw Szlumper's reinstatement, without consultation, as intolerable. Smedley's dismissal was attributed to his reluctance to agree to Russell's economy measures, which involved reductions in the number and speed of trains. The directors, with William Wavell temporarily in the chair, were unable to do more than voice their dissatisfaction. Smedley wrote to them on two occasions in 1881 to enlist their aid over his dismissal, but they had to own there was nothing they could do. Szlumper was conclusively re-installed and soon threatening a libel action against the directors.

While Russell was struggling to establish himself against the directors' opposition and to put the company's affairs on a sounder footing, critical negotiations had been under way with the Cambrian aimed at settling the liabilities over the Llanidloes joint undertaking once and for all. Smedley had reached an agreement with Lewis of the Cambrian in January 1881 by which the Cambrian was to get the Llangurig branch and the M. & M.'s share of the joint line and station. The Cambrian's outstanding claim to the end of 1880, around £8,500, was to be written off and the M. & M. was to be released from all past and future liability for the Llangurig line and the joint facilities on payment of £3,000, and once the working agreement was executed — or the Act authorising the transfer obtained as the case might be.

The approval of both boards of directors was secured within a fortnight. The next step was to embody the agreement in a wider scheme of arrangement covering the company's liabilities and submit this to the Chancery Court. The scheme's preamble indicated that the Manchester and Milford's capital structure had not changed significantly since 1875, with ordinary shares standing at £323,000, leaving £57,000 unissued. Almost all the preference stock — £175,000 in substitution for ordinary shares and £15,300 new 1865 stock — had been taken up. Loans stood at around £164,000, so the company could in theory still borrow £26,000. In practice, however, the rent charges represented a capital equivalent of nearly £25,000, and this had to be offset against the remaining powers to raise more money. So also had the excess of capital expenditure over receipts, ca. £50,000. At best, therefore, the company could not legally have found more than about another £8,000. Unpaid interest on loans had been mounting steadily since 1875, to around £100,000 at the time the scheme of arrangement was being put together. The same went for rent charges, with arrears of £11,000 and more "in the pipeline" pending conveyance of the land involved! Other new debts since the 1875 investigation included the costs of the 1876 and 1880 Devil's Bridge branch Acts, which had been met by J.J. Barrow.

The Barrows now agreed to advance the £3,000 which was to be paid to the Cambrian and to complete all outstanding land transactions in order to ease the scheme's acceptance. Four distinct new debenture stocks were proposed in the scheme to replace the existing rag-bag of liabilities. Debenture A — created to finance land purchase — was to carry interest at 5% and rank equally with rent charges as the first call on any surplus funds. Debenture B at 4% was intended to cover the Barrows' £3,000 payment to the Cambrian, arrears on rent charges, the costs of the various recent Acts and Bills, and a sum of £5,000 urgently needed to improve station and siding facilities and buy new rolling stock. Next in the pecking order was debenture C at 3%, to an amount equivalent to the existing 1860 and 1865 loans and arrears. Then came Debenture D with a miserable 2% interest, to be issued at 10s. in the £ to sundry other creditors. Last of all came the shareholders: scant prospect for them of any income from their investment!

The document concluded with provision for the discharge of the Receiver—the directors' hand at work!—and for the Chancery Court to make any changes it thought fit. Once again, though, the law rested its leaden hand upon the Manchester and Milford, and Vice Chancellor Hall declined either to tinker with the scheme or approve it. The directors were naturally disappointed. Not long after, however, they were taking the view that circumstances had altered so as to improve greatly the prospects of success on appeal to a higher court.

In whatever it was they had in mind, they were mistaken. In October the Cambrian, upset at the M. & M.'s failure to get its scheme accepted and at the prospect of interminable wrangling which this brought into view, rescinded the January 1881 agreement and began an action to recover the £8,500 owed. Shortly after, the M. & M.'s appeal was dismissed, so once again the only hope was to promote a Bill aimed at sorting out its present untenable position.

Desperation must have been the dominant emotion amongst the directors, so far-fetched was much of what was now proposed. The Bill not only repeated many aspects of the unsuccessful scheme of arrangement piecemeal, but also sought to go further, over the heads of the Cambrian's directors, and refer the 1881 agreement which they had so lately rescinded to the Cambrian's shareholders. If they too rejected it, the sum which the M. & M. should pay over was to be decided by an arbitrator. Next came provisions, similar to those defeated by the Mid Wales Railway in opposing the M. & M.'s 1877 Bill, which would enable anything paid to the Cambrian to be reclaimed from the Mid Wales. A further clause provided for the discharge of the Receiver and another set up a three year moratorium on law suits against the company other than in its capacity as a carrier.

Finally, the Bill sought to allow the Manchester and Milford to sell out to any company that was unwise enough to buy it, with no more authority than that of a majority of shareholders. This would have been regarded as rank provocation by the Cambrian, which was always neurotic in the extreme about the encroachment of "foreign" companies on its territory. The Cambrian itself was in no position to purchase the line, being once again on the verge of bankruptcy, and was therefore well to the fore in raising objections. It disliked, among other things, the proposal to refer its claim to an arbitrator, the failure to give its claim next priority after the rent charges, and the plan to discharge the Receiver, who had, after all, been installed at the Cambrian's behest.

The Great Western also opposed the M. & M. objecting to the clause which would ease a takeover; spuriously on the reckoning of the Cambrian, who considered that no one but the GWR would be interested in purchasing the line. The GWR, however, believed that its legitimate interests would become vulnerable to some hastily-conceived deal between the M. & M. and the Cambrian or the Mid Wales.

Szlumper too was among the objectors, as the stock which he had accepted at the request of J.J. Barrow in lieu of payment for services would now rank after the debenture expressly created to satisfy the claims of the Barrow family. Particularly irritating was the fact that some of these claims were for costs incurred in promoting "futile"

Bills in Parliament. Szlumper alleged that as Barrow was to all intents and purposes "the company", the effect of the Bill would be to sacrifice others' interests for Barrow's benefit, and not for the good of the company. It was claimed that Barrow then owned all but 5% of the shares and that he had from time to time represented the M. & M. as his own private property "and had always nominated the directors and provided them with the necessary qualifications". Faced also with the predictable opposition of the Mid Wales Railway, the Manchester and Milford's Bill stood little chance. The directors recorded their regret "that the Bill . . . by which they hoped to extricate the company from its difficulties, was thrown out by Parliament". As late as 1897, the company gave notice that it would try again, but thought better of it.

Returning to the operation of the railway during this particularly crisis-torn period, the timetables showed just three passenger trains each way for much of Poole's time as receiver. In July 1876 these were:

Up	*a.m.*	*p.m.*	*p.m.*	*Down*	*a.m.*	*p.m.*	*p.m.*
Aberystwyth	8.45	2.10	4.50	Pencader	7.00	3.10	7.45
Pencader	11.10	4.25	8.20	Aberystwyth	11.15	5.30	10.30

All trains also carried goods. An additional Down working was restored briefly from March 1879 for a period of three months. Departing from Pencader at 4.30 p.m., it was timed to reach Aberystwyth at 7. The other afternoon train was then retimed to 2 p.m. from Pencader, and ran on Tuesdays, Fridays and Saturdays only. The through connections via the GWR and Cambrian at this time involved a 6.30 a.m. departure from Manchester (Victoria) allowing Aberystwyth to be reached at 2.27 p.m., or as near to that as the Cambrian could manage, but hopefully in time for a Manchester and Milford connection at 2.40. Arrival times were then Pencader 4.45, Carmarthen at 6 o'clock, Carmarthen Junction 6.40, and New Milford 8.30 p.m.

In the reverse direction, there was a GWR train leaving New Milford at 10.30 a.m. arriving at Carmarthen Junction at 12.11 p.m. Then, however, it was necessary to wait until after 3 in the afternoon for a train to Carmarthen Town and Pencader, reached at 4.15 p.m. Small wonder that the traffic manager was instructed to see the Pembroke and Tenby, Great Western and Carmarthen and Cardigan about improving the situation. The M. & M. duly got its passengers to Aberystwyth at 7 in the evening, but it was then too late for connections for the North that day.

The June 1879 working timetable indicated the following schedules:

Miles		Goods+Pass (1.2.Parly)		Goods & Mineral		Goods+Pass (1.2.3.)		Goods+Pass (1.2.Parly)	
		arr.	dep.	arr.	dep.	arr.	dep.	arr.	dep.
—	Aberystwyth	—	7.45	—	8.30	—	2.35	—	4.45
1	Aber. Harbour	7.48	7.53	8.35	8.39	—	—	4.50	4.54
3	Llanrhystyd Rd.	7.58	8.00	8.48	8.53	2.42	2.43	5.00	5.06
6	Llanilar	8.08	8.12	9.05	9.13	2.49	2.50	5.15	5.30
9	Trawscoed	8.22	8.26	9.28	9.33	2.58	2.59	5.40	5.43
14	Strata Florida	8.56	9.00	10.15	10.25	3.23	3.25	6.23	6.33
19	Tregaron	9.10	9.12	10.40	10.55	3.34	3.35	6.45	6.55
21½	Pont Llanio	9.20	9.21	11.03	11.12	3.40	3.41	7.01	7.04
25¼	Llangybi	9.28	9.29	—	—	—	—	7.12	7.13
26½	Derry Ormond	9.32	9.34	11.27	11.32	3.50	3.52	7.16	7.18
28¾	Lampeter	9.41	9.46	11.42	12.07	3.57	4.00	7.24	7.35
34	Llanybyther	9.58	10.02	12.22	12.43	4.11	4.13	7.48	7.54
37¾	Maesycrugiau	10.13	10.14	12.52	1.00	4.19	4.20	8.04	8.09
39½	New Quay Road	10.20	10.24	1.13	1.20	4.25	4.27	8.16	8.20
41	Pencader Junc.	10.27	10.28	1.24	1.25	4.30	4.31	8.22	8.23
41½	Pencader	10.30	—	1.30	—	4.33	—	8.25	—

Times underlined indicated locations where up and down trains crossed. The 2.35 p.m. was clearly the premier train, with the very minimum of goods other than through traffic. This befitted its status as providing the sole tenuous justification for the line's "Manchester and Milford" title. In the Down direction, the train service had a curiously unbalanced appearance.

	Goods+Pass. (1.2.Parly)		Goods+Pass. (1.2.3.)		Goods & Mineral		Goods+Pass. (1.2.Parly)	
	arr.	dep.	arr.	dep.	arr.	dep.	arr.	dep.
Pencader	—	7.00	—	3.54	—	4.00	—	7.55
Pencader Junction	7.02	7.03	3.55	3.56	4.03	4.04	7.56	7.57
New Quay Road	7.11	7.20	4.00	4.01	4.08	4.14	8.01	8.02
Maesycrugiau	7.26	7.35	4.05	4.06	4.20	4.36	8.09	8.10
Llanybyther	7.48	8.05	4.13	4.15	4.46	5.00	8.18	8.24
Lampeter	8.20	8.40	4.24	4.26	5.15	5.44	8.34	8.42
Derry Ormond	8.47	8.50	4.29	4.30	5.50	5.55	8.48	8.50
Llangybi	8.54	8.55	4.34	4.35	—	—	8.52	8.55
Pont Llanio	9.10	9.30	4.40	4.41	6.15	6.20	9.05	9.07
Tregaron	9.40	9.50	4.47	4.48	6.35	6.45	9.14	9.15
Strata Florida	10.05	10.15	4.57	5.00	6.58	7.15	9.28	9.32
Trawscoed	10.35	10.40	5.19	5.20	7.40	7.50	9.54	9.55
Llanilar	10.48	10.52	5.26	5.27	8.00	8.10	10.03	10.05
Llanrhystyd Road	11.00	11.05	5.34	5.37	8.20	8.30	10.14	10.17
Aberystwyth Harbour	—	—	—	—	—	—	—	—
Aberystwyth	11.15	—	5.45	—	8.40	—	10.25	—

There was only one train in the morning, and this a miserable slow thing taking over four hours for little more than 40 miles. The 3.54 p.m. train was the one which provided such through connections as there were from south to north, and the "mixed" element would certainly have been kept to a minimum on this working. It was in fact the fastest over the line in either direction, having the benefit of Trawscoed bank in its favour: the northbound time between Strata Florida and Trawscoed was 19 minutes start to stop, compared with a best of 24 minutes towards Strata Florida. This benefit did not extend to goods trains, for which a gradient of this length and severity could be a distinct embarrassment. Goods trains were required to stop at the summit near Ystrad Meurig and pin down brakes. They were then forbidden to exceed 12 m.p.h. down the bank.

Times in the northbound direction were also helped by the absence of a booked call at Aberystwyth Harbour. Trains could stop there if required, but the harbour line was without run-round facilities, and could only be worked by Up trains. Llangybi was without facilities of any sort, and trains called on market and fair days only.

Smedley, when newly appointed general manager, was able to initiate some modest improvements in the train service, which were later to form the alleged background for his removal by Russell. From June 1880, two additional return workings were arranged, each running over just part of the route. The day's activity began at Pencader with the 6.45 a.m. mixed train, working only as far as Lampeter where it was due to arrive one hour later. This train returned at 8.05, arriving at Pencader at 8.50. At the other end of the line, there was a Mondays-only goods and empty carriage run to Tregaron, leaving Aberystwyth at 7.30 a.m. and arriving at 8.45. This became the "Special Market Train" in the reverse direction, leaving Tregaron at 9 o'clock and taking one hour and five minutes back to Aberystwyth.

The remaining trains all covered the full course of the railway, and were as follows:

		Mixed	*Goods*	*Mixed*	*Mixed*
Up		*a.m.*	*a.m.*	*p.m.*	*p.m.*
Aberystwyth	dep.	8.15	8.30	2.35	6.00
Pencader	arr.	10.35	2.30	4.33	8.45

		Pass-enger	*Mixed*	*Goods*	*Mixed*
Down		*a.m.*	*p.m.*	*p.m.*	*p.m.*
Pencader	dep.	10.05	3.54	4.00	7.55
Aberystwyth	arr.	12.30	5.45	8.40	10.15

The real benefit of the changes would have been felt by passengers wishing to travel towards Aberystwyth earlier in the day. They could now leave Pencader three hours later than under the previous timetable and still be in Aberystwyth for lunch. Goods traffic for stations to Lampeter was forwarded by the additional early morning train, allowing the first Down train over the whole line to operate at a much improved average speed. The Manchester and Milford continued to dignify the faster of its mixed trains with the title "through" goods and passenger. As the title suggests, only those wagons which were booked over the whole distance between Aberystwyth and Pencader were taken, and shunting at intermediate stations was thereby avoided.

One feature of the service, common to many railways with but a single line of rails yet of more than branch line length, was the number of occasions on which crossing of trains was called for. For example, the 8.15 from Aberystwyth crossed the Mondays-only cattle special at Strata Florida, and the morning passenger train from Pencader at Maesycrugiau. This was in turn met by the Up goods at Tregaron. The next Up train was intercepted by the 3.54 from Pencader at Llanybyther, and by the goods train which followed close behind at the next station, Maesycrugiau. The final Up train of the day, the 6 o'clock from Aberystwyth, crossed with that same goods working at Strata Florida, and with the last Down train at Llanybyther.

The difficulties of operating a timetable in these circumstances over a hilly forty mile line with indifferent locomotives and braking should not be underestimated: around two hours for the trip from Pencader to Aberystwyth was a fair performance. Unfortunately, the Manchester and Milford had early in its career acquired an unenviable reputation for time-keeping, a state of affairs which the new traffic manager, Smedley, quickly set about changing. Certainly, there was editorial comment in the Cambrian News in March 1880, remarking on the change under the title "Up and down the Coast, A Lesson in Punctuality". The first scene, a station on the M. & M., was set with a farmer requesting a ticket to Strata Florida . . .

Booking Clerk.	— The train has gone.
Farmer.	— What? Gone!
Clerk.	— Yes, a quarter of an hour ago.
Farmer.	— Why, it is only a quarter of an hour after time now. Do you mean to say it went at the right time.
Clerk.	— Yes, to the minute.
Farmer.	— Oh, to the minute. Well that's something fresh in these dull times.
Landowner. (to farmer)	— Ah Jones, we are in time I see.
(to Clerk)	— Ticket for Cardiff!
Clerk. (respectfully)	— The train has gone, sir.
Landowner. (amazed)	— Gone! When did it go?
Clerk.	— About twenty minutes ago.
Landowner.	— What, at the time advertised? I never heard of such a thing before.
Clerk.	— We have done it for a week now, and are always going to do it in future. Them's our orders. And there's a truck of lime for you sir.

Landowner. — Has that lime come already? I didn't expect it for a fortnight. How is it here so soon?

Clerk. — Goods are not to lie about the sidings until the passenger trains can take them on. There will be regular goods trains in future.

So it continued, in much the same vein. The second scene took place in a third class carriage.

1st passenger. — I missed the train yesterday. I was walking down only about one minute after time thinking I was rather too early if anything, when by George if the blessed engine didn't whistle and off the train went without me. I had to walk six miles, if you please. (Looks out of the window). We are spanking along at a rattling pace!

2nd passenger. — We are going and no mistake. What a draught there is.

3rd passenger. — Yes, the wind come through the holes where there ought to be either lamps or stoppers. It would cost very little to fill those lamp holes with blocks. (The train stops at a station). See, there are two men and a woman coming. They're running. (The station master gives the signal to start).

Guard. — We might as well wait a minute for them. We are in good time.

Stationmaster. — My orders are to go at the right time.

Guard. — All right. (Whistles. The train goes just as the men and woman reach the platform. They run at the carriages but are pushed back, and left behind).

The editorial concluded sagely, "I am told that the last train is going to come in at ten o'clock, that the first train in the morning is going to do the distance between Carmarthen and Aberystwyth in three hours instead of five, that goods are to be sent on promptly, that lamps are to be provided at night, and blocks to fill the holes in the day, that traffic is going to be pushed along, and that all together the M. & M. line is going to turn over a new leaf, and let us hope that is all that will be turned over."

Nor did the Manchester and Milford's new leaf escape comment in the correspondence columns. "Sir" wrote one habitual victim of the M. & M.'s way with a timetable, "I do not know if you ever travel by the M. & M. Railway. If you do, you must have found within the last fortnight a wonderful change with regard to its punctuality. I have travelled on it for six years and never missed a train, but I missed one last week, and I was only ten minutes late . . . I write to say that I am heartily glad of it, for I too well remember the wretched weary hours I have sat waiting "after time" at those miserable wooden huts called stations. I travelled with a gentleman from London last week who said it was the first time he had been on this railway, but that he had been told many a time that it was the worst railway in England(!) I coincided with him, but at the same time I said that I thought there was an improvement lately; and before we got as far as Pencader he confessed that it was not so bad after all. It does a fellow good to see the way that station masters, porters and guards are tripping about at the stations. I hope it may continue. If it does, I am sure it will be for the company's good. I know for a fact that gentlemen who have been travelling from the north order their carriages to meet them at Aberystwyth instead of having them waiting an unknown time at M. & M. stations. I say again that I am deeply grateful for the change . . . I shall now travel with pleasure and much more frequently." We can but speculate on how long the Manchester and Milford's efforts at good timekeeping lasted.

Surprisingly, Russell's appointment and Smedley's dismissal did not lead to a reduction in either the speed or the number of trains. Perhaps when he came to a closer look at what was involved, Russell found that the prospective savings from any further economies would have been offset by a fall in the traffic receipts. There were changes to both departure and journey times, but they were only of a minor nature. One short-lived experiment in the Autumn of 1881 was the extension of the Mondays-only cattle special to run as far as Lampeter. From October 1884, the morning passenger train from Pencader ran mixed, but by mid-1886, there had actually been some improvements in booked times in this direction. Compared with the situation in 1880, the morning train was allowed 2 hours 15 minutes, a ten minute improvement, the afternoon train which provided the line's south-to-north connections, 1 hr. 47 min., five minutes less than previously, and the evening train 2 hrs. 15 min., also better by five minutes.

For a short period from late in 1886, the Mondays-only empty carriage stock and goods working from Aberystwyth was altered, and appeared in the public timetables as a passenger service. On the first Monday of the month, it again ran as far as Lampeter, connecting with the early morning Pencader-Lampeter-Pencader turn. An additional trip over the entire line thus became possible on these days, leaving Aberystwyth at 6.45 a.m. and reaching Pencader at 8.50. In the Down direction, departure was also at 6.45 a.m., but the journey included a 35 minute wait at Lampeter, and overall took one hour longer. Perhaps the service was not well-patronised, or perhaps the need to open up booking offices at an early hour at the Aberystwyth end of the line caused staffing problems out of proportion to the benefits: it was not long previously that the company had been under some pressure on the question of working hours. In any event, the experiment did not last long on this occasion, although it was repeated in the period 1890-4, running through to Lampeter every Monday.

By the end of 1888, therefore, the service was as follows:

Up	*1st Mon. in month*	*Other Mondays*	*a.m.*	*a.m.*	*Goods a.m.*	*p.m.*	*p.m.*
Aberystwyth	6.30	7.00	—	8.10	8.20	2.30	6.15
Tregaron	—	8.40	—	—	—	—	—
Lampeter	8.07	—	8.10	—	—	—	—
Pencader	—	—	8.50	10.39	2.05	4.40	9.00

The Mondays-only train was for empty carriage stock and through goods only.

Down	*a.m.*	*1st Mon. in month*	*Other Mondays*	*a.m.*	*p.m.*	*Goods p.m.*	*p.m.*
Pencader	6.45	—	—	10.10	4.01	4.07	8.05
Lampeter	7.45	8.20	—	—	—	—	—
Tregaron	—	—	8.50	—	—	—	—
Aberystwyth	—	9.50	9.50	12.20	5.48	8.57	10.20

By August 1880 the staff on whom the day-to-day running of the line depended had increased to a total of 120 excluding both manager and engineer. There were then six in the general office at Aberystwyth. Each of the eleven stations on the line, that is excluding Aberystwyth and Pencader, and Llangybi which remained unmanned, employed a "chief clerk" as stationmaster, and there was a similar position at Aberystwyth Harbour. Assistant clerks were found at Llanybyther, Lampeter (2), Tregaron and Trawscoed, and porters at New Quay Road, Llanybyther, Lampeter (2), Tregaron and Strata Florida. Finally within the traffic department total were an inspector, four guards and a lampman, all based at Aberystwyth, a cleaner at Lampeter, and a gatekeeper for the level crossing between Maesycrugiau and Llanybyther.

The locomotive department employed 16: four drivers, firemen and cleaners, a foreman, fitter, apprentice and a coalman. This may have seemed none too many to keep the M. & M.'s locomotives running, but there was certainly no shortage on the carriage and wagon repair side: a total of 17 including eight carpenters, the remainder being smiths, sawyers and the like, with just one inspector. Finally, there were ten permanent way gangs of four apiece with an inspector at Aberystwyth, and four painters, three carpenters, a labourer and a carter to look after structures along the railway.

Russell's task was no easy one, and was not made any simpler by the continued hostility of the directors. His reports, intended for the ears of his masters in the Court of Chancery, tended to show matters in the most favourable light, but nonetheless allow us to follow the struggle to keep the line operating. Russell's first concern after appointment as Manager was for the state of the permanent way, which personal inspection had shown to be in a seriously deficient condition. In his first six months, it had been necessary to replace rotten sleepers in the equivalent of 1½ miles of track, and much else besides, the figures being quoted by the official manager "to give some idea of the state into which the line had been allowed to fall". Further repairs became imperative following a serious flood just before Christmas 1880 which carried away about 100 yards of the trackbed and interrupted through running for a number of days. Russell was able to report that Szlumper had quickly made arrangements to carry on the traffic, being able to do so "owing to his being resident at Aberystwyth", thus vindicating Russell's earlier insistence on having locally-based management.

An early change of policy was to purchase the two engines, No. 4 "Aberystwyth" and "No. 5", which had previously been on hire. The price agreed was £2,100 plus interest, and it was reckoned that the engines would be fully paid for in about two years at a cost little greater than the previous hire charges. There would then be an end to the indignity of running a railway with engines clearly marked as someone else's property! Nonetheless, repairs to the motive power continued to be a heavy drain, with "Lady Elizabeth" and "No. 5" both requiring their fireboxes renewed, "Carmarthen" needing new cylinders, and "General Wood", cylinders, tyres and firebox. "Aberystwyth" succeeded in breaking a crank axle, so it is not surprising that Russell was soon advocating the need for new engines.

Despite the substantial renewals, permanent way was also a cause for concern. The trouble was that no stocks of rail had been built up against the day, fast approaching, when large scale replacement would be needed. Hitherto, worn out rails had been replaced by part-worn ones bought secondhand. This stock was now all but exhausted, and its use had compounded the difficulties. With so much nearly worn-out track, progressive renewal over an extended period of years matched to the M. & M.'s ability to find the money would scarcely be possible.

Russell's reports showed that during 1881 and 1882, not far short of £8,000 had been paid into court for distribution to rent charge holders. Around £500 had been used to complete a land purchase, a similar sum incurred for legal costs on the abortive scheme of arrangement, and £2,200 spent on purchase of the two engines. His comparison of 1879 and 1880, effectively the last years of management by the directors, with 1881 and 1882 as representative of his own efforts, certainly indicated an upwards trend for income, although to what extent this was due to Russell is questionable. Traffic receipts were the major factor, rising from £16,000 to £18,000. Expenditure

Pencader Junction, with M.&M.R. diverting to the right. July 1904 (L.&G.R.P.)

New Quay Road station in Manchester and Milford Railway days (National Library).

Pencader station, looking south towards Carmarthen. One of the M.&M.R. Sharp Stewart engines can be seen beyond the down platform. Undated, but probably taken in the 1890's (Kidderminster Art Gallery and Museum)

M.&M.R. no.5 on up train made up of Great Western carriages, drawing into Tregaron in July 1904 (L.&G.R.P.)

The up platform at Strata Florida, July 1904 (L.&G.R.P.)

Former site of Penpontbren Junction, with M.&M.R. earthworks and bridge on the left, Cambrian Railways towards Llanidloes on the right. 1904 (L.&G.R.P.)

Lampeter station looking south, 23 July 1904 (L.&G.R.P.)

M.&M.R. no.5 leaving Pencader in July 1904 with bogie-third no.10 or 11, composite no.12 or 13, and four-wheeled brake van no.6 or 18. (G. M. Perkins)

"Cader Idris" as GWR no.1306 at Newcastle Emlyn with GWR carriages (G. M. Perkins per C. C. Green)

Former L&NWR Crewe Goods no.3111, purchased in 1891 and shown here standing at the Llanybyther down platform. Driver Joseph Salmon on buffer beam, fireman David Baker and P.W. inspector Owen on footplate.

No.5 with an early carriage and goods brake van at Tregaron (Glyn Griffiths per C. C. Green)

GWR Dean Goods no.2351 running as M.&M.R. no.9, on up train at Llangybi. The leading and third carriage in the train are ex-Mersey Railway (L.&G.R.P.)

Carmarthen train at Aberystwyth, in charge of an unidentified Dean goods. All the carriages are in the lake livery of the 1910-22 period (National Library of Wales)

had been reduced over the period, but the major improvement was in fact achieved in the second of the two "directors" years. Russell was nonetheless able to point to surpluses on revenue of £1,100 and £2,700 in 1879 and 1880, compared with "his" £3,300 and £3,700 in 1881 and 1882.

It was not to be expected that the results would satisfy the directors, now reduced to four — J.J. and J.B. Barrow, C. Stanley Williams and William Wavell — with the death of Clark and the resignation of Bott. First they complained that a better result had been obtained by cutting back on maintenance, so refuting Russell's statements regarding the poor condition of the line he had taken over. Then the following year, they complained that expenditure had increased sharply, implying that costs were out of control.

It proved possible to postpone major outlay on the track by reusing iron rails from the disused Llangurig branch, and 1½ miles were so dealt with in 1882. However, the reprieve was a short one. A beginning was made in 1884, when more than £2,000 was spent on 400 tons of double-headed steel rails weighing 70 lbs. to the yard. These were laid between Maesycrugiau and Llanybyther, and proved sufficient for 3½ miles. Russell reckoned that this activity would have to be repeated for several years, commenting that "as five sixths of the rails on the line have been down since the railway was opened . . . the outlay is unavoidable". As a result, he thought it unlikely that revenue surpluses would be large enough during this period to make any further inroads in the rent charge arrears. In other words, they would be lucky to meet these charges as they accrued.

The directors, who had otherwise remained strangely mute at this time, were duly scandalised. When Russell sought and obtained permission from the Chancery Court to buy the next batch of rails, the directors commissioned an "independent" view of the necessity for this continuing outlay. Independent, it certainly was not, for their choice of whom to employ to make the inspection was both predictable and provocative: Smedley, the former traffic manager, and Wood, the former engineer, both of whom had Russell to thank for the short duration of their careers with the M. & M. Smedley and Wood's first report in mid-June 1885 complained that the time they had been allowed for the inspection was insufficient to confirm or refute Russell's standpoint, although what they did see was sufficient to convince them of the need for some further investment. Yet they wrote "we feel that there need be no difficulty in impugning his statement as to the absorption of the revenue during the next eight or nine years. When we come to compare his actual working for the last four years as against that of the directors for 1880, it is clear that he is not developing the line as he claims credit for, and the expenditure in the running department has so largely increased as to make it palpable that the concern is not receiving proper and practical attention".

The following week, Smedley and Wood walked the whole line under Szlumper's eagle eye, and were able to report that about eight miles had been relaid, while old rails now in stock would be sufficient for a further two miles, leaving 31½ to be attended to. They accepted the need for the 400 tons of rails Russell wented to buy, plus another 400 tons, after which they thought the permanent way could be maintained for several years without major expenditure. Smedley concluded that even if the whole of the remaining distance was to be relaid, £2,000 p.a. for five years would suffice at current prices. Since £2,000 appears to have bought the equivalent of 3½ miles of track, his calculation must have taken into account additional funds realised from sale of old rails.

Fortunately for Russell, traffic continued to grow modestly, permitting one or two other useful items of expenditure to be met from revenue: a crane for the timber traffic at Llanrhystyd Road, a new goods shed at Llanybyther, repairs to the quarry line at Ystrad Meurig, even an increase in his own salary. Other items, the M. & M. could well have done without. The Cambrian raised its charges for the use of Aberystwyth station, and the company found it necessary to reduce third class fares from July 1885. Also, at a particularly awkward time early in 1887, when one engine was having new tyres fitted in the workshops, another broke a crank axle. With only three engines fit for service, it was necessary to hire another until one of the two under repair could be rostered again, and this brought a £100 bill.

But worst of all, in October 1886 there was a disastrous flood which washed away embankment and the railway in two places alongside the River Ystwyth and again near Lampeter. The stores at Aberystwyth were also flooded to a depth of over four feet. The company's employees worked hard to restore through communication, and this was achieved in about a week. The Manchester and Milford's line was of course especially prone to flooding, since it followed the Ystwyth and Teifi for much of its length. The problem was most severe around Llanilar, and it was a washout here which contributed to the ultimate closure of the line in the British Railways era. The old wooden bridge which carried the railway over the River Rheidol into Aberystwyth had also become unsafe, so the company was obliged either to rebuild or replace it. Russell considered that a replacement of iron girders carried on stone piers would be the best course, and it is this bridge, opened in January 1888, which served until the line's closure. There was one beneficial side-effect of the flood. It also prompted the County Council to build a new stone road bridge over the Rheidol, for which nearly 4,500 tons of stone were moved by rail from the Ystrad Meurig quarries.

After seven years of managing the railway, and despite all tribulations, Russell felt able to view the situation with some satisfaction. With what justification it is difficult to discern. There had been some recent improvement in the operating position, with surpluses of £2,700, £3,600 and £4,400 for the years 1885-7, but unpaid debenture interest continued to mount at a depressing rate. The rent charges were, however, being met, and a beginning had been made in reducing the backlog. By the end of 1887, Russell could also point to considerable progress with the major work of track renewal. 17½ miles had been replaced, mostly at the southern end, but including 3½ miles with bull-headed rail on the Trawscoed incline. 1888 marked the high point of the M. & M.'s profitability, with a surplus of £5,750 on revenue account. Never again was this figure to be approached, with the result that the company floundered from year to year, its equipment becoming more and more decrepit, and its backlog of debt forever mounting.

By 1889, Russell was advocating expenditure on a wide range of items. £6,000 was the figure mentioned for new engines and carriages, plus rebuilding of three old carriages. The timber bridge carrying the line over the Teifi by the Bog of Tregaron, just south of Strata Florida station, needed replacement. It was proposed to substitute an iron girder bridge on stone abutments similar to but smaller than that at Aberystwyth. Nearly £700 was expended on fencing the Llangurig branch, an obligation from which the M. & M. could not extract itself even though the branch was derelict. Szlumper reported that new boilers were necessary for four of the locomotives, and these were ordered. The year also saw the Regulation of Railways Act reach the Statute Book. As a result, the Board of Trade insisted that the Manchester and Milford interlock points and signals, install the block system, and equip all passenger trains with automatic brakes.

Russell saw the answer to the apparently insuperable problem of finding the necessary funds as a new scheme of arrangement. His estimate of what was required amounted to £22,000, including the items already mentioned together with completion of track renewal, new station houses, goods sheds and more siding accommodation. A scheme comprising £55,000 rent-charge stock carrying 4% interest, £20,000 "A" stock also at 4%, £165,000 3% "B" debenture and £150,000 2% "C" debenture could, he felt, provide for the settlement of all debts, including that to the Cambrian, and leave sufficient for the investment he was proposing. Barrow was unenthusiastic. He had after all been through the whole unsavoury process of seeking court approval for such a scheme once before. Barrow's view was that rail replacement need only cost £500 p.a. and that selling off old rails together with money in the bank would be enough for a new engine plus sundry other works. The Board of Trade's requirements could, he thought, be financed by the Board itself. Rather surprisingly, Barrow regarded repayment of the Cambrian's debt, quoted at £24,000, as of greater importance than, for example, the failure to meet interest on loans. The sums owing to him were put at £70,000 although this was in fact only part of the true amount.

Szlumper's warning on the need for new boilers had unfortunately come too late. In August 1890, that on "Carmarthen" exploded at Maesycrugiau, miraculously hurting no one, although the engine was damaged beyond repair. Colonel Rich of the Board of Trade held an inquiry into the accident and, no doubt greatly to Szlumper's relief, reported that the explosion occurred through a defect which could not be detected, and which arose from a method of construction long since abandoned. The four new boilers from Sharp Stewart cost £2,600: three were supplied and one was retained by the makers to be fitted to the new locomotive ordered to replace "Carmarthen".

Russell noted "an unfortunate concurrence of mishaps which deprived the company of two of its locomotives — "Carmarthen" obviously, and another unspecified — when a third — "General Wood" — was in to be fitted with a new boiler". His main concern was the need to hire alternative motive power, comprising two engines from the GWR at £4 a day supplemented, according to one source, by a light engine purchased from the LNWR and familiarly known as the "coffee pot". This was probably a reference to the LNWR "Crewe" type locomotive purchased early the next year. Amazingly, the first the board heard of the explosion was when the Secretary read about it in a newspaper: so much for the directors being in touch with the company's affairs.

Expenditure in 1890 reach new heights, almost £20,000. Two new composite carriages were purchased, costing £880, and three third class vehicles were either rebuilt, according to Russell, or replaced according to Szlumper, for £275 apiece. The locomotive repair shops at Aberystwyth, entirely of timber and now rotten and unsafe, were replaced by a larger structure of galvanised iron, and to complete the picture, it also proved necessary to line the tunnel at New Quay Road at a cost of nearly £700. Not surprisingly, track relaying had to be suspended for the time being.

The next two years were fortunately rather quieter, the major events being the arrival of one new and one second-hand engine. The Board of Trade had, however, issued an order in respect of a wide range of safety items, without actually making any provisions for finding the money required, and this order had be complied with somehow. Two years only were allowed for installation of the block system, and two and a half for interlocking and fitting of continuous brakes. A Board of Trade certificate was issued in August 1892 for £9,289, being the sum which the BoT considered appropriate for the work. The certificate did not of itself create the funds. It merely allowed the M. & M. to create new loans which would rank after the rent charges but before the existing debenture; loans which would not otherwise be permitted as matters stood. Difficulty might still be expected in finding anyone willing to lend, since the company was scarcely a safe investment. Advertisements offering £9,000 of debenture placed on three occasions in The Times in October and December 1893 failed to elicit more than one enquiry. This single would-be investor asked for a copy of the accounts, and was then heard of no more!

In view of these difficulties, an extension of time was sought from the Board of Trade, who permitted completion of the work to be deferred to November 1894. Russell had estimated the cost of the block telegraph, continuous brakes, interlocking — to include Pencader Junction — and contingencies at £9,500. However, it soon became clear that this wasn't going to be enough. Seven of the fifteen passenger carriages were found to be unfit for the application of vacuum brake, so the only way in which the regulations could be complied with was by purchasing new stock. The stock which could and had been vacuum fitted was enough for only two trains each way daily. The estimated cost of six new carriages and a brake van, less the allowance originally made for continuous brakes on the carriages which these would replace, was £2,500. An engine with vacuum brake would also be needed, price £2,200. Finally, Russell had seriously underestimated the cost of the electric train staff system between Pencader and Lampeter and the block telegraph installed from there to Aberystwyth.

A further Board of Trade certificate therefore became imperative. An extra £5,411 was granted in November 1893, making a total which could be borrowed of £14,700. The stock was, however, taken up only slowly. By the end of 1893, no more than £2,000 had been subscribed or promised. By 1894, the figure was £6,000, all of it coming from Barrow. The company's long-suffering benefactor subscribed another £3,000 in 1895 and ca. £2,000 in 1897/8. A further £450 of this debenture was issued in 1900, the remainder never seeing the light of day.

Considering the difficulties in raising the money for the work, Russell was able to make good progress with the requirements set by the Board of Trade. A contract was let in June 1894 to the well-known firm of Saxby and Farmer for the erection of cabins, signals and all necessary locking and interlocking, for almost £4,800. This included equipment at all M. & M. stations, excluding therefore Pencader and Aberystwyth, but including Ystrad Meurig quarry, Aberystwyth Harbour, and crossing gates close to the station at Tregaron. An inspection of the new installations was made in January 1896 by Colonel Yorke, the Government's inspector, Russell, Szlumper, W. A.

Young, the traffic manager, and T. E. Owen of the permanent way department, together with a representative of Saxby and Farmer. All was not in order at first, and some changes had to be made, mainly to improve the signalmen's view of proceedings and to afford better protection for passenger lines by substituting "safety sidings" for the "scotch blocks" which had ill-advisedly been installed. A new inspection was undertaken in September 1898.

The last five years of the nineteenth century appear to have witnessed something of a metamorphosis. The M. & M. began to lose its overtly ramshackle character. Modern signalling equipment had been installed. Russell had had his way with the purchase of replacement rolling stock: a new engine was delivered in 1896, preceded in 1895 by five eight-wheeled carriages, all but the first such vehicles on the railway. One remaining anachronism, however, was the continued practice of running mixed trains, with the public timetables of the period indicating:

		Mixed	*Wed.Fri.Sat.*		*Mixed*
	1.2.3.	*1.2.Parly.*	*only 1.2.3.*	*1.2.3.*	*1.2.3.*
Up	*a.m.*	*a.m.*	*a.m.*	*p.m.*	*p.m.*
Aberystwyth	—	8.25	10.30	2.55	5.05
Lampeter	7.55	—	—	—	—
Pencader	8.30	10.30	12.25	5.00	7.30

	Mixed	*Mon.Thur.*	*Mixed*		
	1.2.3.	*only 1.2.3.*	*1.2.Parly*	*1.2.3.*	*1.2.3.*
Down	*a.m.*	*a.m.*	*a.m.*	*p.m.*	*p.m.*
Pencader	6.50	7.45	8.42	2.30	6.05
Lampeter	7.35	—	—	—	—
Aberystwyth	—	9.55	12.07	4.20	8.30

All but the last train of the day arriving at Pencader, plus the Mondays and Thursday only in the opposite direction, had reasonable connections over the former Carmarthen and Cardigan line, generally taking about an hour between Carmarthen and Pencader. Altogether, there was nothing very brilliant in the running, but nor was it entirely disreputable for a line such as the Manchester and Milford's.

The lot of waiting as well as travelling passengers was also eased to some degree. Llanybyther station, originally of wood, had burnt down and was replaced by an improved structure of brick and stone. A new waiting room was built at Lampeter, to be followed by renewal of the rest of the station including, just before the turn of the century, much of the goods facilities. After Lampeter, the next station in line for upgrading was Tregaron, whose timber structure had become rotten with age and beyond repair.

Perhaps all these superficial signs of new prosperity prompted the Cambrian to reassert its claims, feeling no doubt that rather too much of the M. & M.'s revenue was being siphoned off to pay for new facilities and rather too little to satisfying the creditors. The Cambrian continued to submit accounts every six months for expenses in connection with the Llanidloes joint line and station, and in mid-1895 again sued for payment. The Manchester and Milford had, of course, no defence other than to resort to Parliament, a course which was proposed for the 1897 Session, but not proceeded with. By 1899, the sum owing to the Cambrian came to more than £26,000, and a further writ was issued covering charges for the period 1895-1900. The only purpose which these legal actions seem to have served was to get the Cambrian's status as creditor officially recognised and proven: that concern could hardly expect to see its ill-deserved money.

The Cambrian was, however, able to extract some compensation from its other point of contact with the M. & M. at Aberystwyth. The agreement which had been in force here since the beginning of 1883 was for the M. & M. to pay one third of passenger expenses, its proportion of goods expenses, together with charges for rent and maintenance related to the original cost of the station. By 1899, the M. & M.'s bill for the costs of passenger handling had more than doubled, quite out of proportion to the growth in traffic.

Before turning to a new century and the negotiations which led to leasing by, and ultimately amalgamation with, the Great Western, mention must be made of two railways projected into the Manchester and Milford's territory. The first could be expected on balance to have little impact on the M. & M.'s traffic. This scheme came to fruition, albeit only in part. The second might have benefitted the M. & M., but came to nought.

It will come as no surprise that the first of the two proposed lines was none other than the Vale of Rheidol Light Railway. What should perhaps come as a surprise is that this line was built at all, and at such a late date. No one could claim that, since the M. & M.'s abortive attempts on Devil's Bridge, either the traffic or the money-raising potential of the district had greatly increased. True, tourism was now gaining in importance, and in this regard a line up the Rheidol valley had much to offer. New mines were also opening, although they could do little more than replace the lead workings further inland which were then in decline.

Perhaps the greatest spur was the passing of the Light Railways Act of 1896, which wakened promotors to new and cheaper ways of building railways. An Act for a line to Devil's Bridge was obtained in 1897 following a survey by Szlumper, now Sir James. The Act authorised construction over the 12 miles from Aberystwyth to a gauge of 1 ft. 11⅝ ins., all on capital of £68,000. It is no part of this story to recount the history of the Vale of Rheidol. Suffice it to say that the line opened to passenger traffic in December 1902, and that Szlumper and Russell were both members of the Vale of Rheidol's board, although Russell had resigned by the beginning of 1899; also that the ambitions of the V. of R. were as grand as its resources were limited.

Funds for the construction of the M. & M.'s new neighbour were slow in appearing. Nevertheless, the V. of R. sought an order early in 1898 from the Light Railway Commissioners for an extension along the coast to Aberayron. The M. & M.'s directors saw reason to object: Aberayron they regarded as "their" territory. They need not have concerned themselves. Nothing was ever done about the extension despite an offer by Cardiganshire County Council to advance £18,000 towards its cost. A scheme was soon afoot to build a standard gauge light railway to Aberayron, but from Lampeter — a much more attractive prospect for the Manchester and Milford.

The other scheme to emerge just before the turn of the century was for the "East and West Wales Railway". One part of the line proposed corresponded in effect with that planned by the Mid Wales Railway in 1865, on which the M. & M. had pinned its hopes, and in which it had been frustrated. From a junction at Trawscoed, with running powers from there to Aberystwyth, the E. & W. Wales would have crossed to the north of the Ystwyth at Pen-y-Bont, just over a mile upstream, following the river to Pontrhydygroes. The familiar route via Devil's Bridge and a tunnel between Blaen Myherin and Pant Mawr would then have been adopted. From Pant Mawr, the line was projected alongside the Wye to Llangurig and Rhayader, running parallel with the existing Mid Wales route for the last three miles. The E. & W. Wales was, however, to continue beyond Rhayader, crossing the Mid Wales and executing a complete "U" turn to head first east, then north, and finally east again. The Central Wales railway was to be bridged at Cross Gates, not far from Pen-y-bont station and north from Llandrindod Wells, the end of the proposed line coming at New Radnor, with an end-on connection with the GWR.

One would be forgiven for wondering just where the line would finish, so far-fetched was this scheme. The M. & M.'s directors must have been unsure, for they were obliged to retire to Sir James Szlumper's office in order to view the plans. However, they took it seriously enough, "liking the idea of being linked with the Midlands". Russell was persuaded to withdraw his objections, based on disruption at Trawscoed station and the siphoning off of M. & M. traffic for points east of Cardiff. The minor modifications to the scheme proposed by the M. & M. were readily accepted by the promotors.

The East and West Wales Railway Bill was thrown out by the Commons on financial grounds. Nothing daunted, a revised Bill was prepared for the 1899 Session, this time with the M. & M. in opposition following failure to agree terms. The line between Llangurig and Rhayader was altered in the 1899 scheme to follow the east bank of the Wye, and to leave its course upstream of Rhayader. Powers for a separate station at Aberystwyth were sought, together with running powers once more between Aberystwyth and Trawscoed. There were also to be running powers over the Knighton and Eardisley line into New Radnor station. This time, the scheme was abandoned before being considered by Parliament. The Manchester and Milford could enjoy the dominance of its beautiful but impoverished territory for a few more years.

CHAPTER 5

AMALGAMATION IN PROSPECT, 1900-1911

By the end of the century it had become abundantly clear that the only solution to the M. & M.'s ever-mounting difficulties lay in selling out to one of the railway's bigger neighbours. Even Russell viewed expenditure on the line in terms of increasing its value to a prospective purchaser. A meeting was held between the directors and their Great Western counterparts in mid-1896, at which the Great Western was asked if it would buy the line for £40,000 in GWR 5% debenture stock and £210,000 in cash. Not at that price was the reply. Early the following year, J. J. Barrow wrote to the Great Western's general manager suggesting a lease or working agreement for a percentage of the receipts. The Great Western was prepared to negotiate, but from a start-point of a fixed annual rental no greater than £2,500. This was not at all the scale of things Barrow had in mind, and the matter was dropped for the time being.

The next approach was made by Russell early in 1903, but before the Great Western could reconsider the question, John James Barrow died. His importance in the evolution of the Manchester and Milford Railway cannot be understated, despite the constraints imposed upon his direction by the existence of a manager appointed by the Chancery Court. J. J. Barrow had been involved with the M. & M. since 1863-4, and the major responsibility had rested on his shoulders since his father's death in 1871. The continuity of the Barrow family was not now lost, however. As previously noted, John Burton Barrow succeeded as chairman in August 1903. William Wavell returned to the board from the same date, and Charles Deans Barrow, J.B.'s stepbrother, made up the number a year later. For the final years of the company's existence, the directors were thus the following:

John Burton Barrow	Aspley Guise, Bedfordshire.
Leonard Norman Barrow	Normanton Hall, Southwell, Notts.
Charles Deans Barrow	Holmewood, Tunbridge Wells.
A. Griffiths Boscawen, M.P.	Harwarten, Tunbridge Wells.
William Wavell	Sussex Gardens, Hyde Park, London.
Col. C. Stanley Williams	Ivy House, Edenbridge, Kent.

Addresses have been quoted to show just how remote the directors were from the operations they sought to control: the original concept of a "Landholders' Line" seems to have gone by default. John Burton Barrow continued the initiative begun by his father, although as so often when the Great Western was involved, the negotiations were a long uphill struggle. Russell's original proposal had been for a rental based on an increasing percentage of gross earnings, but with a guaranteed minimum. The idea behind the lower percentages in the early years was to give the purchaser something in hand with which to improve station accommodation, but the GWR claimed it would take £60,000, equivalent to £2,400 p.a., to bring the line up to its standard. Russell could only report that the whole matter was still very undefined.

The Manchester and Milford next sought to show how the Great Western could easily make economies if it took over the line's operation. The GWR was, however, more concerned with the M. & M.'s position in relation to the Cambrian Railways. This could be stated quite simply. The Cambrian was a judgment creditor and therefore had the right to have a manager and receiver appointed by the Chancery Court; but it had no prospect of seeing its claims satisfied. The payments due to the Cambrian could not come from the working expenses until the M. & M. began "working" to Llanidloes station, which of course it would never do. The Cambrian's claims therefore ranked as ordinary debt and after the rent charges, interest on the loans created under the Board of Trade Certificates, and interest now amounting to no less than £275,000 on the original loans. What mattered, therefore, was to own these prior securities so as to be entitled to the surplus net revenue. As things stood, the Barrows could claim almost all the excess once the rent charges had been paid, as they held the debenture. Ownership of the share capital was of little value, since it afforded no financial benefit and only nominal control while the line remained in Chancery.

Here, of course, was the crux of the affair. For the GWR to achieve any worthwhile control, it had both to buy out the Barrow interest, either absolutely or in the form of a lease or working agreement, and to propitiate the Cambrian. Negotiations had already stumbled at the first of these hurdles without any real consideration having been given to the second, so the M. & M was not in a position to pursue the course which would have suited it very well; namely, to play off the one company against the other as rival suitors. The Cambrian's involvement was more of a damper than a spur to the Great Western's interest.

The Manchester and Milford was, quite reasonably, awake to the possibilities of a deal with the Cambrian as an alternative should the Great Western falter. Relations with the Cambrian had never been cordial, however, and that company's own weak financial standing was also a drawback. There was bickering over the charges levied for facilities at Aberystwyth, and the running sore over payments for Llanidloes. The new century began with plans being made for a separate station at Aberystwyth, although in the event, these were shelved. In 1902, a Bill was mooted with the objective of releasing the

M. & M. from commitments at the Llanidloes end, but this too was deferred. Complaints were made to the Cambrian over the removal of M. & M. rails remaining at Penpontbren Junction, and over increased charges for the Llanidloes line, for which accounts contined to be submitted: yet another action was instigated late that year with the intention, it must be imagined, of having the status of the M. & M.'s debts to the Cambrian confirmed and clarified. Yet no more than a few months afterwards, the two concerns were talking seriously about a lease of the line.

In August 1903, an offer was received for a 99 year lease, under which the M. & M. was to get 4% of the combined net receipts of the two companies subject to an annual minimum of £4,000. The M. & M. was however to pay interest on all capital expenditure on the line and its rolling stock. The debt for the Llanidloes line was to remain and accumulate, but the Cambrian would not claim payment while the agreement lasted. The Great Western soon got wind of the Cambrian's proposal. In fact, it was reported direct to them by Mrs Barrow, J.J. Barrow's widow, who stated that she had had a "handsome offer" of £4,000 a year from the Cambrian. In October 1903, the two general managers met to talk over the matter. The Great Western confirmed that it was not anxious to take over the line, but what would be the Cambrian's view? The Cambrian said it would see it as an unfriendly move, and the meeting concluded amicably enough with the GWR agreeing to withdraw completely in favour of the Cambrian if that company would develop the line and give the Great Western proper access. The Cambrian's general manager later reported that he had offered a comprehensive agreement which would allow the GWR its present facilities following a Cambrian takeover or, if a dispute arose, full running powers.

By the beginning of 1904 therefore, events seemed to be favouring the smaller of the M. & M.'s two neighbours. Negotiations with the Great Western had reached deadlock, and the Great Western had all but deferred to the Cambrian, who had an offer on the table which could well form the basis for an agreement. That company's confidence was, however, misplaced. The Great Western asked Russell not to consider the question of its purchase of the line as altogether closed and Russell, in reporting this to J.B. Barrow, recommended that if the Cambrian could not be prevailed upon to offer at least £5,000 p.a., its offer should be declined.

Meanwhile, it was necessary for the M. & M. to try by some means or another to rid itself of its obligations at Llanidloes. By 1904, more than £55,000 was owing in respect of investment that the M. & M. had never been able to use, and of operating costs which benefitted the company not one penny. A further application was therefore made to Parliament. This time the more informal approach of a petition to the House of Lords was adopted, and paid off. Henceforth, the company was only to pay interest on its original one third share of the cost of Llanidloes station. Their Lordships could not, of course, absolve the Manchester and Milford from past liability. The company accordingly wrote to the Cambrian to the effect that its proposals would only be considered if modified to cancel all the existing debts for Llanidloes.

This the Cambrian was now ready to do. A Bill was steered through Parliament in the 1904 Session by which the M. & M.'s liability could be removed. Thereupon the M. & M., with what can only be seen as amazing effrontery, turned down the Cambrian's terms. Then in May 1905, a brief note in the M. & M.'s minutes recorded that the Great Western had approached the company with a view to working the line. This time agreement was quickly arrived at, and within days all was signed and sealed.

The agreement, to commence on July 1st 1905, gave the GWR responsibility for maintaining the line, operating the train service, and fixing tolls for through traffic. The M. & M. was still to determine traffic rates for local business and pay the directors, secretary, auditors and receiver, and any compensation for employees who, for reasons such as old age, were considered unsuitable for employment by the GWR. From the gross receipts, the M. & M. was to get 19%. This was to be used, first, to pay the rent for Pencader station, then the Cambrian's charges at Aberystwyth, management costs, rent charges and interest on loans. Minimum payments were to be on a sliding scale: £3,100 p.a. in 1906-8, £4,100 p.a. in 1909-13, and £5,100 in subsequent years. Should the sums available come to more than the minimum — an unlikely occurence — the M. & M. would not see an immediate benefit as the GWR was then to be reimbursed for engine costs and sundry other outgoings. The agreement also covered construction of a separate station at Aberystwyth on which the M. & M. was to pay running costs up to the level of charges for use of the Cambrian station. Traffic from the M. & M. was to be routed over the GWR wherever possible and the GWR was to loan the sum needed to pay off the balance on two recently-acquired ex-LNWR engines, and to purchase the M. & M.'s stores, locomotives and rolling stock at a valuation.

The Cambrian's reaction when the news leaked out is best left to the imagination. It too had a draft contract prepared bearing the same date as the Great Western's agreement and almost identical in content. The Cambrian's terms actually appeared to be better, with the M. & M.'s share of gross receipts set at 25% and with higher guaranteed minima. The only other major difference concerned Aberystwyth station: the Cambrian scheme, needless to say, made no mention of the need for independent facilities.

The intended running powers agreement arranged between the GWR and the M. & M. was known in outline at least to the Cambrian's management on June 7th 1905. A week later, the press had got hold of the story. The Aberystwyth Observer reported that another rumour was in circulation to the effect that the Great Western was trying to buy the line. A second local paper noted that Grierson, who had succeeded Russell as Official Manager and Receiver in July 1904, denied rumours. "Both companies were working together to deal with tourist traffic", he said.

The Manchester and Milford applied to the Chancery Court at the end of June for sanction of its arrangement with the Great Western. The Court, however, opted to wait until the Cambrian had a chance to make its comments known, which it did in no uncertain terms. From London, the Cambrian's representative was soon able to write that "we were successful beyond our expectations and have put a spoke in the M. & M. wheel. As the Great Western was to start working on the 1st (July), the M. & M. asked us not to delay matters, but I have told them that after the way they have treated us, we will do nothing we can help to assist them". On July 4th, movements of Great Western engines and staff on the M. & M. were reported back to Oswestry. Particular excitement was caused by one engine, stabled overnight at Aberystwyth, which had been labelled "M&M". On the 6th, the Cambrian's counter-proposal was sent to the Manchester and Milford, and letters were also dispatched to seek affidavits from well-known railway experts to establish that the offer was better than the Great Western's. By the end of July, the first battle had been won by the Cambrian. The Manchester and Milford withdrew its request for sanction of the Great Western takeover, and agreed that the Cambrian would be consulted in any future moves. The Cambrian News was unimpressed. The newspaper's belief was that for its namesake to be in charge of all local railways would be the death of the district.

Thus rebuffed in the Court of Chancery, the Great Western was obliged to reconsider its tactics. The Court felt it had no jurisdiction to do anything that would appear in the nature of removing the Receiver or of interfering with his powers, and believed that the solution lay in applying to Parliament for confirmation of the agreement. In the event, the nature of the agreement was changed to a lease for a period of 999 years, and in this form it was approved by the Manchester and Milford board in December 1905 and by a special meeting of proprietors in January 1906. All that remained was to incorporate the new agreement in a Bill, and by one means or another overcome or buy off opposition to its progress through Parliament.

Matthew Vaughan Davies, a local M.P., was amongst the first called to give evidence when the Bill came before Parliament. He claimed that there was local support for a Great Western takeover, and suggested that the Cambrian's inability to pay a dividend indicated that it had difficulty working its present system. The Lord Bishop of St David's supported Davies' evidence, pointing out that what was needed was faster trains, better stock and improved permanent way. Mr Evan Davies, a cattle dealer from Llangybi, claimed he had problems getting wagons for his cattle from the Cambrian onto the M. & M., and Thomas Benjamin Grierson, the new Official Manager and Receiver, explained how his attempts to canvass extra traffic met with opposition from the Cambrian, whereas the Great Western permitted all sorts of through trains and had lent rolling stock to the M. & M. Because of the Cambrian's attitude, the company really needed an independent station at Aberystwyth, but of course couldn't afford it. The Mayor and Town Clerk of Aberystwyth noted how conditions had improved over the last year or so since the start of closer working relations with the Great Western; a view supported by other local people. Perhaps the most telling comment, though, was that of William Felix Poole, the M. & M.'s secretary, who was asked why the Cambrian's 1905 offer was refused. His reply was that the M. & M. preferred the secure 19% proffered by the GWR to the riskier 25% in the Cambrian's proposal. The Cambrian's weaker financial standing told against it.

Opposition from the LNWR and Midland was soon bartered away behind the scenes. This left the Cambrian, who agreed to £11,000 in full settlement of the existing, £63,000, debt and future liability in respect of the Llanidloes line and station. The Cambrian had the option to take over the derelict Llangurig branch without payment, but subject to all the attendant commitments. The Great Western agreed not to seek an independent station at Aberystwyth for as long as the Cambrian co-operated over the accommodation of traffic in the existing structure, and to continue its existing through carriage workings over the Cambrian.

The agreement regarding Aberystwyth station concerned only passenger traffic. The Great Western was therefore free to develop the goods side as it saw fit, either by extending the M. & M. facilities or by building a new goods station. Land was available to the southwest of the existing platforms, and this had in fact been earmarked many years before by the M. & M. The reasons for the long-standing difficulties over Aberystwyth are hard to understand as the station itself had always been envisaged for the use of two companies. Yet despite some changes made soon after opening and more extensive rebuilding in 1893, it does not seem to have worked well until much later, when the Cambrian had itself become part of the GWR and the station was again remodelled.

The Cambrian no doubt felt it had now secured its position as well as could reasonably be expected, although it remained less than happy about the removal of the Receiver. Opposition was withdrawn, and the amended Bill passed into law in May. The lease was to begin on July 1st 1906. The newspapers were quick off the mark in giving the arrangements their blessing. The day after the Cambrian withdrew its opposition, one reporter wrote "The GWR has come to stay. There is now no fear of a Cambrian Railways' monopoly as there was some years ago when the Cambrian made a bid for the line. We expect great things from the Great Western, and also want some of their splendid motor buses to connect Aberayron and Newquay with the railway". This last at least he got. The Cambrian News saved its main comment until the Great Western had actually taken up the reins, when it was noted that there was little visible sign of change other than the introduction of the summer timetable and comings and goings among middle-ranking Great Western staff. It was intended to keep much of the M. & M. stock in use "with GWR imprinted on", and to employ as many as possible of the M. & M.'s workforce. However, eight employees were retiring and Mrs Barrow was providing for these.

The plight of the eight for whom work could not be found was not a happy one, and the Cambrian News talked of men being thrown "helpless into the world". The blow was eased by the generosity of Mrs Barrow, who paid most of those involved a year's salary, ranging from £200 for the traffic manager after 23 years with the railway to £41 12s. to a screwer with 31 years' service. The others so provided for were all aged 67 or over. The saddest case was that of driver Benbow who, after serving the Manchester and Milford for the whole of its independent career, wrote to say that he would be entirely destitute unless Mrs Barrow could help him.

Some of the other employees were only taken on by the Great Western for a limited period and without responsibility for retirement provisions. These were all men aged between 58 and 68 and included five who had been with the railway since it opened, and a further five who had more than 35 years each to their credit. Others were obliged to accept employment in different functions from those to which they were used, notably three firemen who were found to be colour-blind! Many of the younger men were expected to move away from Aberystwyth, where a much smaller establishment would be maintained in future.

In following the progress of relations between the M. & M. and its two larger neighbours, other developments which took place during the early years of the new century have been passed over. The death of J.J. Barrow and the retirement of the Receiver, J.C. Russell, have however received passing mention. While the next generation of Barrows took over nominal responsibility, the power behind the

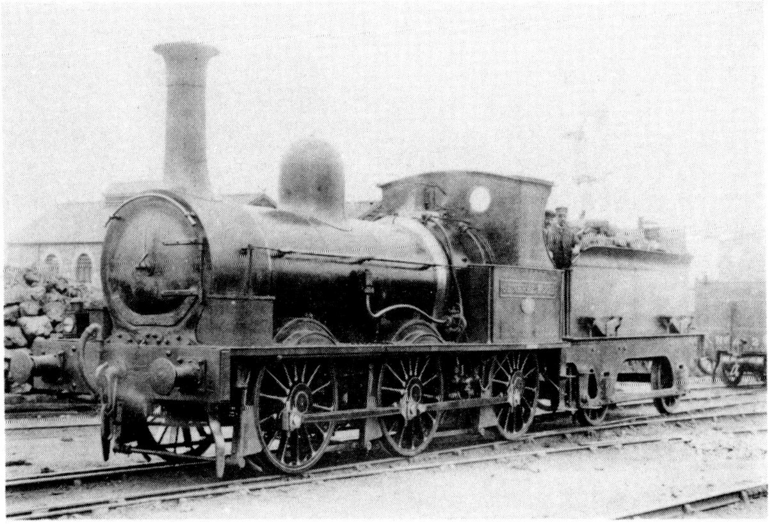

"General Wood" as running with new boiler and cab. (F. Hannan per C. C. Green)

No. 1 (General Wood) before reboilering, and bearing no evidence of nameplates (Glyn Griffiths per C. C. Green)

M.&M.R. no. 6 "Cader Idris" (Mrs Humphreys per C. C. Green)

The new no. 2., "Plynlimmon"

M.&M.R. no.4, "Aberystwyth", sometimes known as "The Old Boat". Driver James Benbow, fireman David Davies on footplate by the leading splasher, and wheeltapper Evan Lewis (L.&G.R.P.)

Manchester and Milford Railway no.4 "Aberystwyth" as built by Manning Wardle, showing the original green livery (Real Photos)

Ex-L.&N.W.R. standard "coal" engine, purchased by the M.&M.R. to replace "General Wood", and seen here running as GWR no. 1338 (Real Photos)

Driver Edward Benbow and colleagues pose with Lady Elizabeth (Glyn Griffiths per C. C. Green)

Tri-composite carriage no. 13; livery dark tan with cream upper panels and gold lettering shaded left and below in red (Weh-Lyn Collection, per C. C. Green)

M.&M.R. no.2 "Carmarthen", after its boiler exploded at Maesycrugiau in August 1890 (L.&G.R.P.)

Washout near Llanilar in October 1886. The permanent way inspector, T. E. Owen stands second from the left. David Baker, fireman of the ballast train in the distance, and later to have such a narrow escape when "Carmarthen" exploded, stands astride the track, fifth from the camera (L.&G.R.P.)

Up train approaching Derry Ormond station in June 1962 (M. Hale)

The warehouse on the Quay at Aberystwyth in Sept. 1962, note buffer stop still in situ to left of picture (C. C. Green)

throne remained the widow of the late John James Barrow. One of her first acts was to investigate the nature of her inheritance. The report which she commissioned, completed in mid-1904, was far from uniformly critical, and served to show how much the general state of affairs had improved in recent years.

The permanent way, it was stated, was in fair order and only required attention to the ballasting in one or two places. However, the workforce on maintenance was considered excessive, partly because some of the men were too old to do an effective day's work, and partly because one gang doubled up on such jobs as cattle loading. Not all the signalling was working correctly and some of the stations were dilapidated. The cost of repairs and renewals in the locomotive department, although too high, was thought to be incapable of reduction while the company was forced to operate as it did. A major complaint was that annual train mileage was excessive in relation to the traffic, having risen by 20% in the last ten years. Since wages could not be reduced or traffic significantly increased, this was about the only area where an improvement in the net profit could be sought. The arrangements by which the Cambrian was supposed to be responsible for carriage cleaning at Aberystwyth were also sharply criticised. It transpired that two M. & M. employees had to be engaged full time on such work, otherwise it would not get done.

Traffic on the line being as light as it was, the report suggested that the offices of goods manager and superintendent of the line should be merged, and that experiments taking place elsewhere with steam and electric railmotors should be watched closely: this type of equipment might be just the thing for the Manchester and Milford Railway. Final recommendations were that the Post Office should be encouraged to part with substantially more than the £8 per mile per annum it was then paying for the carriage of mails, substituting a figure closer to the £50 per mile or more that the Cambrian was said to be receiving; and that steps should be taken to end the outlay on the defunct Llangurig branch.

It is difficult to justify the charge of excessive train mileage, at least by reference to the published passenger timetables. That for mid-1903 showed only three trains daily for passengers departing from Aberystwyth, with an additional Saturdays-only working beginning at Lampeter at 7.50 and arriving at Pencader at 8.30 a.m. All but one of these trains was indicated in the timetable as mixed. In the other direction, there were four trains on which passengers could travel, the first departing from Pencader at 7 a.m. and due to arrive at Aberystwyth at 9.28. With this exception, journey times were around two hours, so most of the goods traffic would have been worked forward by goods rather than by mixed train. It was in this area, perhaps, that reductions in train mileage could be obtained. The connections offered by the Manchester and Milford Railway in the closing years of its independent career were, from the North:

GWR	Manchester (Exch.)	dep. 7.45 a.m.	10.45 a.m.	—
,,	Oswestry	arr. 10.12 ,,	1.55 p.m.	—
Cambrian	Oswestry	dep. 10.57 ,,	2.42 ,,	—
LNWR	Manchester	dep. 8.35 ,,	11.50 ,,	11.55 p.m.
,,	Whitchurch	arr. 9.57 ,,	1.44 p.m.	2.13 a.m.
Cambrian	Whitchurch	dep. 10.05 ,,	1.50 ,,	2.25 ,,
,,	Oswestry	,, 10.57 ,,	2.42 ,,	3.25 ,,
,,	Aberystwyth	arr. 2.25 p.m.	5.30 ,,	6.20 ,,
M & M	Aberystwyth	dep. 3.00 ,,	6.15 ,,	8.45 ,,
,,	Pencader	arr. 5.00 ,,	8.30 ,,	10.40 ,,
GWR	Carmarthen	,, 6.15 ,,	—	11.45 ,,
,,	Carmarthen	dep. 6.48 ,,	—	1.20 p.m.
,,	New Milford	arr. 8.25 ,,	—	3.10 ,,

In the northbound direction, the published connections were distinctly less helpful:

GWR	New Milford	dep. —	10.40 a.m.	1.00 p.m.
,,	Carmarthen	arr. —	12.45 p.m.	4.28 ,,
,,	Carmarthen	dep. —	1.40 ,,	5.10 ,,
,,	Pencader	arr. —	2.25 ,,	6.00 ,,
M & M	Pencader	dep. 10.55 a.m.	2.35 ,,	6.15 ,,
,,	Aberystwyth	arr. 12.55 p.m.	4.29 ,,	8.23 ,,
Cambrian	Aberystwyth	dep. 1.10 ,,	5.40 ,,	—
,,	Oswestry	arr. 4.05 ,,	9.05 ,,	—
,,	Whitchurch	,, —	10.25 ,,	—
LNWR	Whitchurch	dep. —	10.39 ,,	—
,,	Liverpool	arr. —	12.40 a.m.	—
,,	Manchester	,, —	1.10 ,,	—
Cambrian	Oswestry	arr. 4.05 p.m.	—	—
GWR	Oswestry	dep. 6.07 ,,	—	—
,,	Manchester (Exch.)	arr. 8.37 ,,	—	—

There was a connection for the Manchester and Milford's 10.55 a.m. train from Carmarthen, but not from anywhere further west. The utility of this particular connection was further undermined by the long wait for the Great Western train at Oswestry. However, in all this discussion of through traffic between Milford and the North, it must be remembered that there were rather less complicated ways of making the journey, notably from Carmarthen over the LNWR to Llandeilo and thence over the Central Wales line to Shrewsbury. The Great Western could hardly be expected to fight very hard for the limited amount of business seeking to use any of the various north-to-southwest routes on offer.

Where the Great Western did show an interest was in the development of tourist traffic. Express trains, hauled by GWR engines and with through carriages giving passengers from Paddington, Newport (Mon.), Cardiff and of course Carmarthen, the facility of a journey to Aberystwyth without changing, stopped only at Lampeter, Tregaron and Strata Florida on the Manchester and Milford line. Other express trains between Carmarthen and Aberystwyth were run three days a week in the season, with an additional stop to those named above at Pencader. In this case, motive power was generally provided by the M. & M. with passenger stock coming from both railways. These "limited stop" trains were first introduced in July 1902. Excursion traffic, particularly from South Wales, had now reached sizeable proportions. A contemporary commentator has described how, on the occasion of his visit, two heavy excursion trains, each consisting of eight or nine GWR bogie carriages and each hauled by one of the ex-LNWR goods engines, left Aberystwyth one evening for Llanelly. Their progress up Trawscoed bank is best left to the imagination.

Despite much clamour from the University and local authorities, the regular train service still terminated at Pencader. As indicated in the timetables, the company continued to rely on the Great Western to provide connections to and from Carmarthen. The new Manager and Receiver, Grierson, recognised the desirability of exercising running powers to Carmarthen, but as usual the question of costs and payments was the stumbling block.

Grierson was himself able to contribute to a modest reduction in management costs by additionally taking over the functions of engineer and locomotive superintendent. These had been restored to James Szlumper once Russell had established his control in 1880, although Szlumper had recently, in June 1902, stepped down as locomotive superintendent in favour of his son Charles. Nepotism seems to have been rampant on the Manchester and Milford, as by the time the Great Western took over, one R.F.H. Grierson was employed as assistant engineer and Humphrey Barrow was gaining railway experience as assistant locomotive superintendent.

Another aspect of Mrs Barrow's report which Grierson embraced with enthusiasm was the suggestion of employing railmotors for the light local passenger traffic on the line. Nothing, however, came of this, any more than of another of his proposals, to exploit the Tregaron Bog on a commercial scale for peat fuel. Grierson found reason to differ from the conclusions of the report regarding the permanent way, and with his predecessor as engineer, Szlumper, who had been responsible for it. The new Manager and Receiver noted that the track was once more in a deplorable state, with thousands of sleepers rotten, and some of the timber bridges so bad that the rails were assisting the timbers in supporting the trains "which is against the Board of Trade's requirements"! There were also no plans of the line, so how Szlumper had managed all those years is a matter for speculation. On the running side, Grierson found that the company was desperately short of goods and cattle vans, and bemoaned the fact that every time there was a cattle fair, he was obliged to borrow stock from the Cambrian or Great Western, who thereby siphoned off much of the profit from the extra traffic. Extensions of the electric train staff were put in hand to replace the block telegraph system in use at the Aberystwyth end of the line. This was despite a collision at Maesycrugiau, caused by improper use of the train staff by M. & M. employees, in which a workman was injured.

These operational matters aside, the manager's other main concern was with two new railways projected into M. & M. territory. One, the Lampeter, Aberayron and Newquay Light Railway, the M. & M. was generally in favour of, as it could be expected to bring traffic onto the line. The other, to be known as the Llandeilo and Lampeter Light Railway, the company was strongly opposed to for just the opposite reason.

The L.A. & N. Light Railway was born of the failure of the Vale of Rheidol company to attain its objective of a connection to Aberayron, a small coastal town built around harbour and small shipbuilding yards. A proposal to build a line between Lampeter and Aberayron was first floated in 1903. By early-1904, co-operation with the M. & M. was in principle assured, although when the proposal came before the Light Railway Commissioners for consideration, the M. & M. was annoyed to find that powers were being sought to enter into working agreements with railways generally, and not just itself. The terms offered by the Manchester and Milford were to work the line at cost plus 25% of the profits, and an attempt by the L. & A. to get a minimum guaranteed profit provision was stoutly, and wisely, resisted. A branch to Newquay, on the coast south of Aberayron, was mooted in mid-1904. This would have diverged from the Aberayron line roughly midway along its length, and serves to show the persistent and incurable optimism of railway promoters in this part of the country. Despite the Light Railway configuration and relatively modest engineering works required, the cost envisaged for the Lampeter-Aberayron line alone was no negligible sum. Fund-raising was also proceeding far from smoothly, a loan from the County Council causing particular difficulties. Nonetheless, it was in respect of the Lampeter, Aberayron and Newquay Railway that a Light Railway Order was sought and granted in 1906.

It was reported to the Manchester and Milford board in October 1908 that a contract had been signed for the line's construction. The railway was finally opened in April 1911 and, with the M. & M.'s own amalgamation then all but a reality, it was worked from the outset by the Great Western. The existing station facilities at Lampeter proved adequate for traffic from the branch. The junction, after some initial

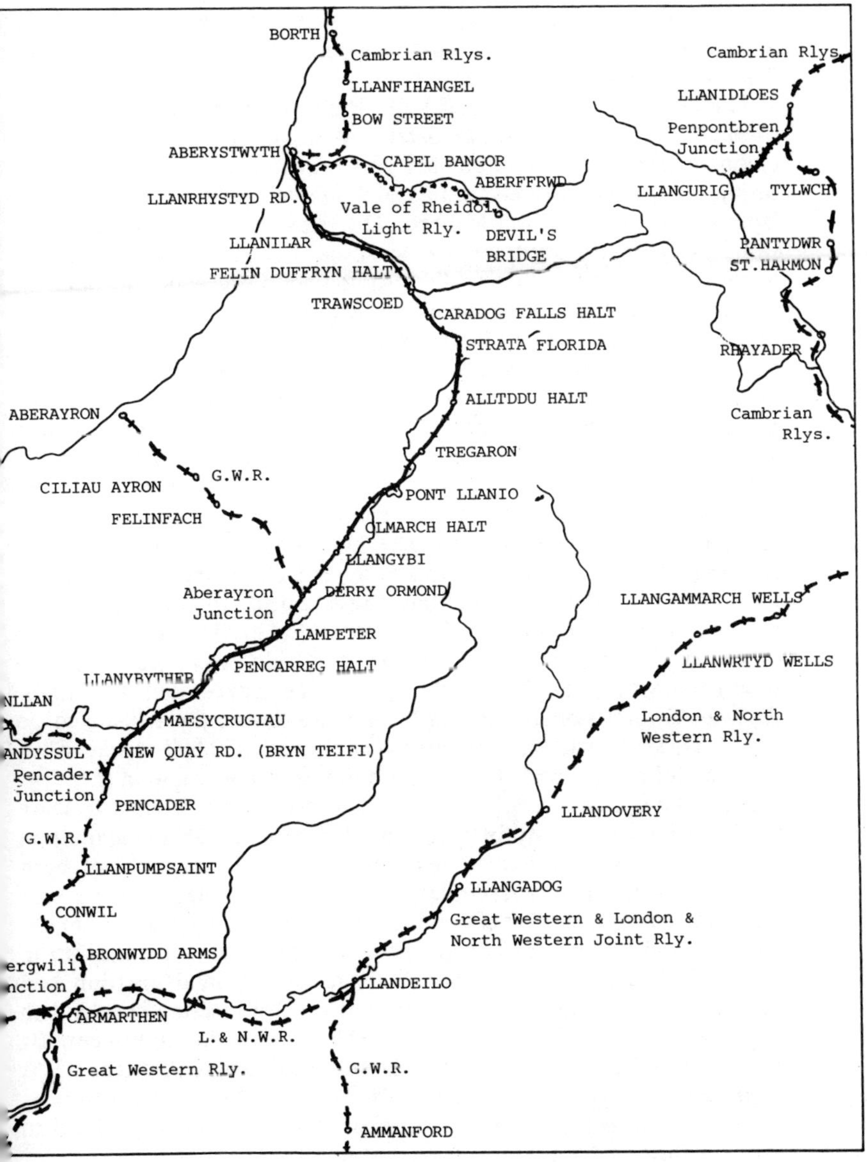

1. The Final Configuration of Railways in Cardiganshire.

indecision, was laid in about 1½ miles north of Lampeter, and there were ultimately seven intermediate stops before reaching Aberayron. The line to Newquay was never built.

The Llandeilo and Lampeter Light Railway was at one time thought of in connection with the Lampeter and Aberayron as two parts of a chain of light railways stretching to Cardigan Bay. However, it was promoted quite separately and as such met with sustained opposition from the Manchester and Milford. The route proposed was much the same as that envisaged for the Swansea and Aberystwyth Junction Railway some forty years earlier. At the southern end, independent passenger facilities were planned, but with a connection onto the main line immediately outside Llandeilo station. Deviations from the earlier plans were mainly with a view to minimising earthworks, at the expense of sharper curves: maximum speeds between 15 and 25 m.p.h. were intended. In order to reach Lampeter, the route would have swung west two miles before Llanfair Clydogau, a meeting-point then being arranged a good half mile out on the Pencader side of the Manchester and Milford station. There was not, however, to be a junction with the existing railway. Instead, an independent line crossing the M. & M.'s to make an end-on connection with the Lampeter and Aberayron Railway was planned. In this way, at the cost of a new bridge over the Teifi, substantial earthworks, disruption in the town, and a second Lampeter station, there could be no problems with joint facilities! Despite the opposition, the Light Railway Commissioners were in favour of allowing the scheme to go ahead. However, with an estimated cost of over £150,000, it was much too fanciful to be a real threat, and nothing further came of it.

After the uproar over the Great Western's initial attempts to lease the Manchester and Milford Railway, the progress to amalgamation was as uncontroversial as it was inevitable. Relations had not been altogether smooth since 1906, largely as a result of haggling over the treatment of almost £57,000 which the GWR had spent on maintenance, and which it reckoned was necessary to bring the line up to standard. However, by October 1910, terms for amalgamation had been agreed. In January 1911, a special general meeting was held to approve the draft of a Bill which would sanction the agreement. By June, the Bill had been successfully steered through Parliament. At their last meeting, with J.B. and L.N. Barrow, Wavell and Williams present, the directors were able to report that the company ceased to exist on July 1st 1911.

The Manchester and Milford (Vesting) Act itself contained little that was unexpected. The preamble pointed out that when the Great Western leased the line, unpaid debenture interest amounted to £306,000 and debts on "temporary" loans, £94,000. Thus far under the lease, the GWR always had to subsidise the minimum payments to the M. & M. Even when the minimum rose to £5,100 p.a. in 1913, this would still leave only £2,700 after paying the rent charges and interest on the priority debentures, which were those issued under the Board of Trade certificates for the purchase of new rolling stock. Yet interest payable on the other loans was more than £8,000 p.a., so the debt could only increase. In this situation, the only sensible thing to do was to rationalise matters by complete amalgamation, whereby all accrued debt would be expunged in the winding up of the company.

Under the terms of the agreement, ordinary and preference shareholders got nothing, as might be expected. The Act empowered the Great Western to issue new 2½% stock to be exchanged at the rate of £92 GWR stock for every £100 of the former M. & M. ordinary debenture. This was not as generous as it seemed, as almost all the M. & M.'s debenture carried 5% interest. Even so, it was at least money in the pocket rather than sunk in the M. & M.! The priority debenture, which was worth something because of its higher placing in the "pecking order" for surplus funds, was replaced by more GWR 2½% stock, issued in the ratio of two GWR units to one M. & M. so that the yield was exactly equivalent. The Great Western also took over the continuing liability in respect of the rent charges for land. Other than this, its only concern was to escape from any possible claims arising from the Manchester and Milford's fifty year struggle against insolvency. The company was left to untangle its position and wind itself up as best it might. One problem was spared the M. & M.: the Great Western had the task of disposing of the derelict Llangurig branch, the Cambrian having declined to take up its earlier option.

CHAPTER 6

LOCOMOTIVES AND ROLLING STOCK, 1866-1906

The first engine known to have been employed on the Manchester and Milford Railway in any capacity was a contractors' locomotive of a well-known standard type produced by Manning Wardle, works number 172. It was built in 1865 and delivered, new, to David Davies at Lampeter. This engine was apparently named "Teifi" for the duration of its time on the line. Manning Wardle's diagram for their Class K, to which "Teifi" conforms in most respects, shows a 0-6-0 saddle tank locomotive with 11ins. by 17ins. cylinders and with all that manufacturer's usual hallmarks, most notably the bent iron cab. Other major dimensions were: wheelbase, 5ft. 5in. + 4ft. 10in., wheels 3ft. 1⅜in. in diameter, total heating surface 345 sq. ft., and tank capacity 420 gallons. Cylinder diameter has also been quoted elsewhere as 12in.

Before turning to the earliest locomotives used in revenue-earning service, reference must be made to another engine, reputedly named "Montgomery", of whose existence little is known. Edward Benbow, for many years the driver of "Lady Elizabeth", recalled for the Welsh Gazette in July 1906 that he had been in charge of the transportation of this engine to the Manchester and Milford at the time of the line's construction. The route taken was from Caersws to Aberystwyth over the Cambrian, and thence to Llanybyther on a trolley pulled by 50 horses. Benbow himself recalled this as the first engine on the line, a statement which the manner of delivery would tend to confirm. It is thus entirely plausible that "Montgomery" was another contractors' engine, actually preceding "Teifi" on construction duties.

No such obscurity surrounds the first three engines to work the Manchester and Milford's train service. These were No. 1, a six-coupled goods engine of standard Sharp Stewart design, maker's No. 1596 from May 1865, and Nos. 2 and 3, passenger engines of the 2-4-0 wheel arrangement, also to a standard Sharp Stewart design, works numbers 1713 and 1756, of June and July 1866.

It will be seen from the dates that only the one engine was available to work the service when the line was first opened to Lampeter, for which purpose it was, of course, sufficient. The two passenger locomotives were delivered in time for the opening throughout to Aberystwyth. All three had been ordered by the contractors, Davies and Beeston, but were later sold to the M. & M.

As early as January 1865, the question of names for engines was the subject of correspondence. John Barrow "didn't care whether the (first) engine was called Lady Elizabeth or General Wood". Who Lady Elizabeth was is not clear. General Wood we meet once in the context of an incomplete land purchase, so we may presume he was a local landowner. In the event, it was his name which graced the goods engine, No. 1. No. 2 was named "Carmarthen" and No. 3 became "Lady Elizabeth". Dimensions were as follows:

	"General Wood"	*"Carmarthen" and "Lady Elizabeth"*
Coupled wheels	4ft. 6ins.	5ft. 6ins.
Leading wheels	—	3ft. 6ins.
Wheelbase	6ft 9ins + 8ft. 0ins.	6ft. 6ins + 7ft. 9ins.
Cylinders	16ins. by 24ins.	16ins. by 20ins.
Boiler: barrel (outside)	10ft. 4ins. by 3ft. 11½ins.	10ft. 0ins. by 3ft. 10ins.
tubes (2ins. dia.)	156	157
tube heating surface	870.0 sq. ft.	843.4 sq. ft.
firebox " "	81.5 " "	71.4 " "
total " "	951.5 " "	914.8 " "
grate area	14.0 " "	11.6 " "
pressure	120 lbs/sq. in.	120 lbs/sq. in.
Engine weight	26t. 0cwt.	24t. 18cwt.
— distributed	9t. 8c. + 10t. + 6t. 12c.	8t. 3c. + 9t. 9c. + 7t. 6c.
Tender: water	1,200 gallons	1,200 gallons
coal	3 tons	3 tons
wheels (4)	3ft. 6ins. dia.	3ft. 6ins. dia.
Tender weight — in working order	17t. 18cwt.	17t. 18cwt.

With their light weight, modest size and low working pressure, these engines could hardly be called powerful, even in relation to the needs of the Manchester and Milford, although they compared well enough with the standards of their time. In any event, there was much to be said for keeping to unadventurous, well-proven designs for a railway which could expect to have only very basic engineering facilities. Also, being "off the shelf", they could be purchased at a competitive price and at short notice. Similar engines were to be found on other relatively minor railways in the United Kingdom, notably the Pembroke and Tenby. "Pembroke" of the P. & T. came from the same batch as the M. & M.'s "Carmarthen", and carried the immediately preceding works number.

These first three locomotives appear to have served the company well and uneventfully, at least until trouble of a spectacular nature arose in 1890. There could have been but few problems in the intervening years, as the records make no mention of "General

Wood", "Carmarthen" and "Lady Elizabeth" except to note the repairs and maintenance, all of a more of less routine nature, which were carried out. It may be mentioned in passing that up to 1872, the company's returns showed only two locomotives as being owned by the M. & M. The correspondence on the subject between the secretary, Butler, and Hamer, then traffic superintendent, leaves some doubt as to whether even these worthy gentlemen were quite sure that the total should be three! Then in November 1890, Butler's successor as secretary was obliged to note that, in going through the papers, he could find no record of "Carmarthen" ever having been paid for!

The need for additional motive power was soon felt, a need which its financial position prevented the company from satisfying. The initiative was therefore taken by John Barrow who went out and purchased a further locomotive from Manning Wardle, seemingly without seeking the advice of anyone better qualified than he to assess the company's requirements. The engine in question carried Manning Wardle's works No. 238, and was another 0-6-0 saddle tank locomotive, not dissimilar to the contractors' engine "Teifi". As such, it was hopelessly undersized for the duties it was expected to perform. By early November 1867, the engine — M. & M. No. 4 "Lampeter" as it had become — was reported to be doing full work and running the 1.20 p.m. mixed train from Aberystwyth. Four days later, a further report to Barrow remarked that the engine was by no means a favourite, but that on its first day it had run 200 miles "which was hard as the engine was just out of shops and the bearings all new". On the Saturday "Lampeter" had been an hour late at the station of that name with the 6.10 train, "but on Saturdays, the 6.10 is a heavy train anyway". On this occasion, it had been loaded with five trucks of lead ore, each weighing about 12 tons in all, as well as passenger coaches and van. It seemed to the inspector almost as though a deliberate attempt had been made to cause the engine to fail. "If he (the inspector) had been there, the engine would not have been allowed to start with that load". The diagram, maker's class M in this case, indicates a locomotive with 3ft. 0in. diameter wheels, cylinders 13in. by 18in., and wheelbase 5ft. 10in. + 5ft. 8in. This permitted a rather larger boiler than was the case with "Teifi", giving 542 sq. ft. of heating surface, and supporting a tank of 550 gallons capacity. Nonetheless, with such generally diminutive proportions, it is perhaps a wonder that "Lampeter" arrived only one hour late.

"Lampeter's" timekeeping on trains brought immediate complaints from passengers, one at least seeking financial compensation. If it was bad enough to warrant particular notice alongside the general standards quickly established by the M. & M., it must indeed have been bad. Within a week, the engine was relegated to ballasting duties on the Carmarthen and Cardigan Railway, over which the M. & M.

was then laying a third rail in order to run standard gauge trains through to Carmarthen. This work, for which a light Manning Wardle saddle tank was much better suited, could not however continue indefinitely. It was in fact finished in February 1868. Well before this date, Barrow was searching for ways of disposing of "Lampeter", one suggestion being an exchange with the Cambrian for one of that company's bigger engines. The suggestion was ruled out through fears of being "done" (sic) by the Cambrian, and proved superfluous when Manning Wardle said they would take "Lampeter" back in part-payment for another engine.

In January 1868, Barrow received a cheque for £1,300 for "Lampeter", and Manning Wardle an order for a 16-inch goods engine "of the same power as Sharp's" for £2,500. The new engine also took the number 4 on the Manchester and Milford, but was named "Aberystwyth". The Manning Wardle works number was 255, and it arrived on the line on July 1st that year. "Aberystwyth" was a six-coupled goods tender engine with dimensions very similar to those of Sharp Stewart's "General Wood". Driving wheel diameter, wheel-base and cylinders were precisely the same. The boiler was slightly bigger, the barrel being 10ft. 6in. long and 4ft. 0in. in diameter, with 171 2in. diameter tubes giving a tube heating surface of 925.5 sq. ft. Firebox heating surface was 90.5 sq. ft., for a total of 1,015 sq. ft., usefully greater than that for "General Wood". The firebox was concealed within a raised casing, 4ft. 11½in. long, and this was joined to the barrel lagging by a quarter circle of polished brass, an attractive feature also shared by the other three engines at work on the line. Other brass work abounded, including a dome of exceptional height, an imposing safety valve casing, and beading round the splashers.

The photograph showing this engine in early condition, possibly as new, reveals that brakes were fitted to the tender only. Again, this was common enough for the period. The engine alone weighed about 25 tons, a little less than "General Wood", and in small degree attributable to retention of the familiar bent iron spectacle plate instead of the more comprehensive cab which seems to have been original equipment on the Sharp Stewart engines. The same photograph shows quite clearly that the engine was not painted black which, with orange lining and retention of much of the polished brasswork, was the livery in later years. "Aberystwyth" in company, presumably, with the other motive power was originally given a green livery. Unfortunately, the precise shade and details of the rather elaborate lining, together with the date at which the changeover to black took place, are unrecorded.

Decoration in the early years of the black livery was also quite elaborate. In addition to orange infilling of the main panels, sand-boxes were lined orange, and the running plate similarly pencil-edged.

Boiler bands carried a single narrow orange line, and there was one band on the firebox, close to the cab. Buffer beams were red with a white rim to the iron plate, leaving an edging of black timber, and carried the engine's number shaded right and below in black. Buffer beam ends were lined white with an orange panel.

No indication of ownership appears to have been affixed to "Aberystwyth" at the factory, although there were large manufacturers' plates on the cab sidesheets and on the tender frames above the middle axlebox. Even in later years, M. & M. ownership was denoted by no more than a small rectangular plate on the valance above the centre driving wheels, a form of identification found on most of the other engines, including at least the first of the ex-LNWR machines.

"Aberystwyth" seems to have had a somewhat blighted existence on the Manchester and Milford Railway. Within two months of entering service it had developed cracked spokes, which Manning Wardle promptly agreed to put right. The M. & M., who seemed to rate everyone else's business ethics about as highly as its own, sought an undertaking that the wheels would be replaced before the engine was paid for. In November 1868, we find Manning Wardle writing to complain that Barrow had stopped payment on a bond for £1,000, when all that was required was to hold the bond until he was satisfied that repairs had been carried out properly. The makers also pointed out that they had not shirked their responsibilities in regard to "Aberystwyth", and moreover that they had gone out of their way to help over "Lampeter", which had been purchased without their advice as to its suitability. Manning Wardle subsequently agreed to accept £800 immediately, and a further £200 when the wheels and axle had been replaced. For the while, relations were restored.

In the meantime, "Aberystwyth" had succeeded in fracturing a cylinder cover. Hamer wrote gloomily to Barrow, who was of course the owner of the locomotive as well as chairman of the company, "We are going to have constant trouble and expense with this engine". In response to a request for stronger covers, Manning Wardle pointed out that they were weaker than the cylinders by design, so that in the event of a build-up of water in the cylinders, the covers would fail first and in that way avoid more expensive damage.

Despite the experience with "Lampeter", tank engines seemed to have exercised a fascination for the management. In May 1869, Manning Wardle was asked to submit a design for a goods tank engine capable of hauling twenty loaded wagons, each carrying 8 tons, up a 1 in 60 gradient at 10 m.p.h. The tracing which was prepared showed a six-coupled saddle tank engine generally similar to, but rather larger than, the more familiar types produced by this firm, and already met with in "Teifi" and "Lampeter".

The specification for the engine mentioned inside frames, inside cylinders 17in. by 24in., a 15ft. 6in. wheelbase and 4ft. 0in. diameter wheels with 2¼in. thick treads. There was to be one long-stroke pump worked from the crosshead, and one Giffard's injector feeding water from the saddle tank of 800 gallons capacity. Buffer beams were to be oak, with "Brown's" buffers. Also mentioned were wrought iron rail-guards at both ends, a boiler 10ft. 9in. long by 4ft. 1in. outside diameter constructed of ½in. plates with longitudinal seams double-rivetted, two safety valves and dome, a coke box on the footplating behind the firebox shell, sandboxes in front of the leading wheels and a "powerful break to be worked from the footplate and act on one side of all the wheels". There was to be a steam jet in the firebox, a weather screen of iron with glass spectacles in brass frames and with the top bent back partly over the driver's footplate, water gauges, gauge cocks, clack boxes, whistle and steam pressure gauge. The specification also called for a boiler with total heating surface of 1,180 sq. ft., tested for operation at 150 lbs./sq. in., lagged with pine and covered with sheet iron. Finally, painting was to be with two coats, followed by a rub down, and then application of a top coat, lining out and varnishing.

For some reason, an engine to this design was not proceeded with. Instead, Barrow financed the purchase of a further engine from Sharp Stewart, makers No. 2036. This was a goods engine, similar to "General Wood". It was completed at the Atlas Works, Manchester, in May 1870, and delivered in June, at which time Hamer sought guidance on what the directors wanted it called. The directors quickly decided against naming the engine, so it became plain "No. 5". Sharp Stewart were paid that same month, but Manning Wardle were less lucky. They submitted a claim for £60 owing and unpaid in October 1870, and complained that they had not been dealt fairly with. "Despite getting estimates from us, you have bought another engine from another firm since then". Unfortunately for the M. & M., "Aberystwyth" had to be put on shed not many months later and parts sought from Manning Wardle. The makers thereupon refused to send them unless their account was settled first.

There does seem to be some evidence to support the Manchester and Milford's prejudice that "Aberystwyth" was a troublesome engine. Up to the end of September 1875, "No. 5" had cost some £500 to repair, about £9 per month. Over the rather longer period that "Aberystwyth" had then been in service, the figure was nearly £1,000, or £11 per month. Taking the three year period from 1877 to 1879, a further comparison of the two engines owned by Barrow showed repairs and maintenance of £800 for the Manning Wardle engine, and £550 for the rather newer Sharp Stewart equivalent. If "Aberystwyth" did have a weakness, it seems to have lain in the area of wheels and motion. As well as the early troubles, the engine broke its crank axle in 1881, and a further replacement was needed in 1886.

These five locomotives were sufficient for the company's needs for many years. The timetable was generally operated with four engines, with one either as a spare or under repair; and there were only four locomotive crews at this period. The enginemen's lot must have been a hard and at certain times an eventful one, not least when careering down Trawscoed bank. Edward Benbow, who claimed to have driven the first train between Lampeter and Pencader and only retired when the GWR leased the line and withdrew his regular engine "Lady Elizabeth", had some lucky escapes in the course of a long career on the M. & M. "Lady Elizabeth" came off the rails near Aberystwyth on one occasion, overturning down an embankment and ending up in a ditch. Apparently there was little damage to either crew or engine. On another night, Benbow felt a dreadful lurch near Llanybyther, the buffers locked behind, and he looked back to see part of the line hanging in mid-air. Similar trouble could occur where the railway crossed Tregaron Bog. Another driver, Richard Jones, recalled that the line once gave way here under a ballast train, and alleged that it then took a fortnight to fill the hole properly.

Richard Jones made a rival claim to the distinction of driving the first train, as well as the last before the Great Western took over, on both occasions in company with Edward Edwards as guard. Both men came to the M. & M. from the contractors, Davies and Beeston. Jones worked contractors' locomotives during construction of the line, and Edwards had been foreman of a gang of excavators: it has been said that many of the best jobs on the railway were secured by David Davies for his "boys" from Llandinam.

Very early in the company's career, in fulfilment of Stephenson's famous dictum regarding the likely outcome of a collision between a locomotive and a cow, just such an animal "jumped" over the fence at Pont Llanio, and was killed by a passing goods train. Two passengers who jumped out of a moving train between Llanybyther and Maesycrugiau were luckier in this respect, such being the dilatoriness of M. & M. trains, but were prosecuted at Llandyssul Petty Sessions for their transgression. Another passenger, one Jane Williams, who jumped from a moving train at Strata Florida was less fortunate, and broke a leg. She had the temerity to claim compensation from the company. On a much more serious note, a porter was killed by a train whilst on duty at Llanybyther station in December 1878.

Much the most noteworthy accident, however, once more involved an engine — No. 2, "Carmarthen" — and its crew, in August 1890. Over the years, repairs had been carried out on all the engines' boilers as they became necessary. Nonetheless, by 1890 the oldest had been in use for almost 25 years, and were getting beyond repair. Szlumper had counselled the need for replacements, and four were in fact on order from Sharp Stewart for the four engines of their manufacture. But before they could be fitted, that on "Carmarthen" exploded while the engine was working a mineral train at Maesycrugiau. Half a ton of boiler casing was blown into the River Teifi, 400 yards away, and the chimney finished up in the fifth wagon from the engine. The driver, Richard Jones, lost no more than his cap and the fireman, one David Baker, was similarly fortunate.

Pending an inquiry into the affair, the other engines were ordered to operate with reduced pressure, which must have made them well-nigh useless. Three of the four new boilers were fitted with all possible speed, and the Manchester and Milford entered into what might be termed the second phase of its locomotive history. "Carmarthen" itself was scrapped without further ado. Despite this experience, insurance against another explosion was not deemed to be a worth-while precaution until 1901.

"General Wood" had been equipped with its new boiler by year-end. According to the acknowledged authority on absorbed GWR locomotives, the replacement had a barrel 10ft. 2¾in. long in two rings of 4ft. 1in. and 4ft. 2in. diameter, allowing room for 134 2in. tubes and 38 of 1¾in. diameter, and a tube heating surface of 919.25 sq. ft. The raised firebox casing was 5ft. by 4ft., the firebox itself 4ft. 4in. by 3ft. 4in., giving 88.25 sq. ft. of heating surface, and a grate area of just over 14 sq. ft. Pressure was now 150 lbs./sq. in. "Lady Elizabeth" and "No. 5" received their replacement boilers in 1891. That on "Lady Elizabeth" was reported as having a barrel 9ft. 8in. long by 4ft. 4in. outside diameter with 168 2in. tubes. Corresponding figures for "No. 5" were 10ft. 4in. by 4ft. 2in. and 172 tubes. By 1906, pressure was 140 lbs./sq. in., although it was presumably set initially at the higher level noted for "General Wood".

Once the decision was taken not to try and repair "Carmarthen", the Manchester and Milford was left with a boiler on order for which there was no immediate use, and a deficiency in the motive power department. It was therefore only natural to retain the fourth boiler at Sharp Stewart's and incorporate it in a new engine. This was delivered in 1891, and took the number 2 once carried by "Carmarthen". It was, however, named "Plynlimmon" after the mountain which lies between Aberystwyth and Llanidloes, under whose shadow M. & M. trains might almost have run had the line been built beyond Pant Mawr. "Plynlimmon", Sharp Stewart's No. 3710, was a 2-4-2 tank engine of much more modern appearance, and was soon doing useful work on the railway. Main dimensions were as follow:

Coupled wheel dia.	5ft. 6ins.	Boiler barrel.	9ft. 7ins. by 4ft. 2ins. & 4ft. 1in.
Carrying wheel dia.	3ft. 6ins.	Firebox casing.	4ft. 9ins. by 3ft. 8ins.
Wheelbase.	6ft. 6ins. + 7ft. 6ins. + 6ft. 6ins. = 20ft. 6ins.	Firebox.	4ft. 1in. by 3ft. 1in. by 5ft. 2½in. high
		Tubes.	168, 2ins. dia.
Weight.	11t. + 12t. 10c. + 10t. + 9t. 16c. = 43t. 6c.	Tube heating.	866.3 sq. ft.
		Firebox heating.	82.3 sq. ft.
Tank capacity	1,000 gallons	Total heating.	948.6 sq. ft.
Cylinders.	17ins. by 22ins. str.	Grate area.	12.9 sq. ft.
Tractive effort.	12,138 lbs.	Pressure	140 lb./sq. in.

The above are shown on the Great Western diagram. Minor variations appear elsewhere, notably in the list of engines used by the GWR as the basis for a valuation of Manchester and Milford rolling stock. This list appears as an appendix, and may well be the source for the oft-quoted 5ft. 0in. driving wheel diameter. This figure is clearly wrong, as can be seen from photographs of "Plynlimmon". Ownership, incidentally, was still indicated by the customary vestigial plate on the valance, although symmetry here dictated a position mid-way along the coupled wheelbase. "Plynlimmon" distinguished itself, or its crew, early in its M. & M. career by running away, unattended, from Pencader towards New Quay Road. It then ran back down the gradient towards the junction, whereupon it was hit by the 8.30 a.m. up goods which was travelling at greater speed in the same direction. There were no injuries, but the impact was sufficient to damage track and a Great Western wagon in the goods train.

The cost of new engine and boilers was very much more than the company's finances could sustain at one time, so it was necessary, at least for accounting purposes, to defer part of the outlay. Russell reported that the boilers had been all but fully charged out by the end of 1892. "Plynlimmon", however, was being entered in the accounts at £500 p.a. With an initial cost for the engine of £2,000, this burden would not terminate until 1895.

The accident to "Carmarthen" had revealed just how vulnerable the company was with such limited motive power in reserve. Pending the arrival of "Plynlimmon" in mid-1891, there were at best only the four engines available which were needed to operate the timetable. The real situation was worse. Day-to-day maintenance and repair could rarely be postponed, and there was the task of boiler replacement to be seen to. The train service could only be kept going with the aid of hired locomotives, an expensive expedient. The M. & M. therefore set about securing a further locomotive with some urgency; this and the need for minimum cost dictating the solution of a second-hand machine.

In January 1891, a 2-4-0 tender engine of the "Crewe" or "Allan" type, with 15¼in. by 20in. outside inclined cylinders, was acquired from the London and North Western Railway for the sum of £705. This engine, with its part-outside frames and 3ft. 6in. leading wheels supported by outside journals and underhung springs, both looked and was ancient. It had originally been built at Crewe, works number 352, at the end of 1855, taking No. 80 on the LNWR's North Eastern Division. After successive renumberings to 480 and 1933, it became No. 3111 in October 1889. Driving wheels were 5ft. 0in. in diameter, with axle loadings 9t. 14cwt, and 6t. 4cwt. A further 6t. 12cwt. on the leading wheels made a total for the engine of 22½ tons, so there should have been no complaints from the M. & M.'s permanent way department on this score. The tender was similarly modest, weighing 13t. 11cwt. and being carried on four 3ft. 6in. wheels. Capacities were for 2 tons of coal and 1,100 gallons of water.

It is not certain that this engine ever carried a number on the Manchester and Milford. If it did, it cannot be detected on the only known photograph, and was not painted on the front buffer beam after the manner of the company's other motive power. "No. 2" has been quoted, but this would have caused confusion on the arrival of the new No. 2, "Plynlimmon". Of course, the engine may well have been intended as no more than a stop-gap while "Plynlimmon" was awaited. Whatever the expectation, Russell was soon able to report that the ex-LNWR machine was doing useful work, and it was not until June 1899 that the directors decided to sell it. No offers were received at the asking price of £200, and a sale was finally concluded in April 1900 at £150.

The next addition to the company's motive power came in 1896. It proved possible to include an allowance for a new engine as part of the sum which could be raised on the strength of the Board of Trade certificates. Provided someone could be found to lend the money, the cost would not have to be carried in the operating result, as had been the case for "Plynlimmon". The new engine was an enlarged version of "Plynlimmon", from the same makers, and cost just under £2,000. Dimensions for No. 6 "Cader Idris" — Sharp Stewart's No. 4128 — were shown on the later GWR diagram as follows:

Coupled wheel dia.	5ft. 2ins.	Boiler barrel.	9ft. 7ins. by 4ft. 4ins. & 4ft. 3ins.
Carrying wheel dia.	3ft. 6ins.	Firebox casing.	5ft. 6ins. by 3ft. 8ins.
Wheelbase.	6ft. 6ins. + 8ft 3ins. + 6ft. 6ins. = 21ft. 3ins.	Firebox.	4ft. 10ins. by 3ft. 1in. by 5ft. 2½ins. high
		Tubes.	179, 2in. dia.
Weight.	8t. 14c. + 15t. + 15t. + 8t. 14c. = 47t. 8c.	Tube heating.	923 sq. ft.
		Firebox heating.	91.5 sq. ft.
Tank capacity	1,290 gallons	Total heating.	1,014,5 sq. ft.
Cylinders.	17ins. by 22ins. str.	Grate area	15.25 sq. ft.
Tractive effort.	12,921 lbs.	Pressure	140 lb./sq. in.

Once again, there are minor inconsistencies with dimensions given in the descriptive list of engines dating from 1906. Wheels, for example, were quoted in the list as 5ft. 0in. diameter, although the difference is less glaring here than in the case of "Plynlimmon". Sharp Stewart by this time favoured flush casings for boilers, so the absence of the familiar circular-section beading between barrel and firebox was the easiest way to distinguish the two tank engines from a distance. Closer to, it would have been noticed that "Cader Idris" lacked all indication of ownership, although ill-proportioned combined oval "M & M R" and number plates were later attached to the bunker sides, displacing the maker's plates to a position high up on the cab panels.

It might be thought that with seven engines available once "Cader Idris" entered service, the Manchester and Milford was very much better endowed with motive power than it had been previously. Such, however, was not altogether the case. For one thing, seasonal and excursion traffic over the line was beginning to make itself felt, and to pose operating problems for which a reserve of locomotive power was desireable. As an example, one Thomas Price, a local farmer, began to organise a series of highly successful excursions at about this time. There was also heavy traffic in 1896 when the Prince of Wales, later King Edward VII, and Princess Alexandra visited Aberystwyth for the Prince's installation as Chancellor of the University; and later, early in the present century, when Buffalo Bill's Wild West Show "came to town".

Such traffic was not the only reason. The older of the Manchester and Milford's engines were becoming worn out, and could not long be relied on to haul heavier trains of bogie carriages up and down the company's steeply graded route. No. 4 "Aberystwyth" was perhaps in the worst condition, having borne its share of the traffic without other than strictly essential renewals since 1868. Manning Wardle had already claimed that it was in dire need of a good overhaul in 1878. By the early 1890's, the case for rebuilding had become pressing, but the engine could not be spared in the period following the debacle with "Carmarthen". Russell then sought to get rid of "Aberystwyth" and to replace it with a new machine. In the end though, it was decided to return the locomotive to Manning Wardle for rebuilding, and this was done in 1897.

Much delay was occasioned by the engineering strike that year, and by the fact that "Aberystwyth" proved to be in rather worse condition than feared. The engine had been expected back in time for the summer traffic of 1898, but the work — including vacuum brake fitments — was not completed until later in the year, when its cost had risen to almost £1,700. As rebuilt, "Aberystwyth" was graced with a flush-topped boiler 4ft. 5in. in diameter and pressed to 160 lbs./sq.

in., and a cab of spartan and far from pleasing appearance. Cylinder diameter was enlarged to 17ins., and weight went up to 30 tons, making the rebuilt "Aberystwyth" the most powerful of the Manchester and Milford's locomotives.

The company must have been well-satisfied with the second-hand engine bought from the London and North Western Railway, as the opportunity was taken to purchase another from the same source. M. & M. No. 7 was one of the LNWR's standard "Coal" engines, built in 1889 as Crewe works number 3093. On the LNWR, it had initially been No. 1095, but carried No. 3561 at the time of disposal. Wheels were 4ft. 3in. in diameter, cylinders 17in. by 24in., and weight 29½ tons. It cost the M. & M. £1,650, and arrived in Wales in March 1902. This was followed by a similar machine of rather more ancient vintage, intended as a direct replacement for "General Wood". Russell reported the necessity for such a purchase in November 1903, when "General Wood" was stated to be almost beyond repair. He again pressed the matter in February 1904, following yet another breakdown. Even then, a decision was delayed while negotiations continued with the Cambrian and GWR over a working arrangement. However, when these negotiations showed no prospect of an early conclusion, it was decided to proceed with the purchase. LNWR No. 3088 had originally emerged from Crewe in 1880 with works No. 2388 and traffic No. 2387, and cost the M. & M. the same sum as before: £1,650. At first sight, therefore, the engine appears to have been less of a bargain, although it may well have had a recent major overhaul to compensate for its greater age. Certainly, the new M. & M. No. 1 survived for a number of years on the GWR in marked contrast to its stablemate No. 7. Dimensions from the GWR diagram are quoted below: once again there are minor differences from the 1906 list shown in the appendix.

Coupled wheel dia.	4ft. 4ins.	Boiler barrel.	9ft. 10ins. by 4ft. 2ins. & 4ft. 0in.
Wheelbase.	7ft. 3ins. + 8ft. 3ins. = 15ft. 6ins.	Firebox casing.	5ft. 5ins. by 4ft. 0½ins.
Weight.	10t. 6c. + 10t. 8c. + 10t. 6c. = 31 tons.	Firebox.	4ft. 9ins. by 3ft. 5½ins. by 5ft. 7ins. high
		Tubes.	194, 1⅞ins.
Cylinders	17ins. by 24ins.	Tube heating.	960.2 sq. ft.
Pressure	150 lb./sq. in.	Firebox heating	94.6 sq. ft.
Grate area	17.1 sq. ft.	Total heating	1,054.8 sq. ft.

"General Wood" 's ultimate fate is not recorded, although a recommendation was made by the official manager to sell the engine plus two tenders for £120 late in 1904. Disposal could well have been before the end of the year as the returns show no increase in the tally of locomotives at the close of 1904. By the same token, we can only guess at which tenders were involved, since the returns show both that from "Carmarthen" and that from the old LNWR 2-4-0 as still in existence.

Tourist traffic reached new levels in 1905, when the GWR introduced an improved train service over the M. & M. to Aberystwyth. Largely with this in view, three "Dean Goods" 0-6-0 tender engines were loaned to the company from the end of June that year. These were GWR Nos. 2301, 2351 and 2532, and thus included the first engine of the class, from which the alternative "2301" designation derived. On the Manchester and Milford, they became respectively Nos. 8, 9 and 10, indicated by Great Western style number plates on the cab sides. In other respects too, the engines looked little different in M. & M. guise: they appear to have retained their standard GWR green livery.

Nos. 8 (2301) and 9 (2351) were initially shedded at Carmarthen Junction, while No. 10 (2532) was based at Aberystwyth. After the Great Western leased the M. & M. in 1906, the company's motive power and rolling stock was absorbed, and the three GWR engines reverted to their earlier numbers. No. 2301 remained at Carmarthen until October 1907 when it left Wales. However, it returned in May 1910 for a further three years — but not necessarily to work regularly over the former M. & M. line as there were other possibilities for engines based at Carmarthen Junction. No. 2351 returned to Swindon for five months from June 1906, but was also then seen again at Carmarthen, with brief interludes at Pencader and Aberystwyth, before it too left West Wales in the autumn of 1911. No. 2532 remained longest in the area and was shedded at Carmarthen Junction and Aberystwyth for much of the eight years until the outbreak of war.

The Great Western was not altogether generous in its assessment of the Manchester and Milford's locomotives, altough the M. & M. was not perhaps the sort of concern one would choose to buy such equipment from out of choice. The two ex-LNWR engines, Nos. 1 and 7, attracted respectively valuations of £750 and £600 which, in the case of the former, represented depreciation of rather over 50% in the space of two years. Perhaps the GWR noted that, whatever had happened since, it was originally built in 1880. "Plynlimmon" and "Cader Idris", being the two most modern engines on the line, were similarly valued at £750 and £700, "Cader Idris" surprisingly attracting the lower figure of the two. The remaining engines were little better than scrap, the Sharp Stewart pair "Lady Elizabeth" and "No. 5" meriting £250 apiece and "Aberystwyth", by dint of its more recent rebuilding, £350. All told therefore, the valuation amounted to £3,650, about the price of a substantial modern machine of the sort that Churchward was beginning to turn out for the GWR.

Nor did the Great Western do very much with its new acquisitions other than, where feasible, allow them to wear themselves out gently in service. The tank engines at least might have merited a longer life with their new owners, being outlived by many years by GWR designs of much greater vintage. As a generalisation, it is probably true to say that the GWR rarely looked on absorbed engines in a favourable light when these were of a size whose work could equally well be done by standard designs. It tended to be the very small machines, tailor made for some particular duty for which more modern engines were unsuitable on weight or clearance grounds, which survived the longest.

The Manchester and Milford engines were all allocated numbers in the 13xx series generally reserved for locomotives from the absorbed railways. The passenger engines "Plynlimmon", "Lady Elizabeth" and "Cader Idris" were grouped together as Nos. 1304, 1305 and 1306, and the goods engines likewise as No. 1338 (M. & M. No. 1), 1339 (No. 4), 1340 (No. 5) and 1341 (No. 7); this despite the fact that elsewhere "Plynlimmon" and "Cader Idris" were referred to as goods tank engines by the GWR.

The Manning Wardle engine, No. 1339, was cut up at Neath in December 1906, having covered little more than 1,000 miles in the preceding six months. It is unlikely, therefore, that this engine ever carried the GWR number allotted to it. One of the former LNWR engines, No. 1341, suffered a similar fate at Swindon in November of 1906, having by then managed 4,000 miles in Great Western service. Nos. 1305 and 1340 were sold to E. Cornforth of Trentham in August 1906, so it is unlikely that these two old Sharp Stewart engines ran from the date that the GWR took over. This then left the two tank engines — neither of which was modified noticably by the GWR apart from the fitting of a brass safety valve bonnet to "Cader Idris" — and the other ex-LNWR machine. This soon sported a very small Great Western pattern tender, no doubt greatly to the confusion of the less knowledgeable amongst contemporary observers. The tender in question held no more than 2,000 gallons, and weighed when full 27t. 7cwt. "Cader Idris" appears to have retained its name for some time with its new owners; but not so "Plynlimmon".

"Plynlimmon", now allocated No. 1304, was whisked away from Aberystwyth for a major overhaul at Swindon for three months in the spring of 1907. It then returned to Neath, where it stayed until once more recalled to Swindon for further repairs in March-June 1909. Mileage with the GWR was then 16,000. After another six months based at Neath, No. 1304 returned closer to old haunts at Carmarthen Junction and Pencader, from which point it seems to have spent some of its time working services over the former Carmarthen and Cardigan line to Haverfordwest. A long spell at Swindon works followed between June and November 1912, after which it returned to

Carmarthen and Pencader once more. It was finally withdrawn to Swindon on May 8th 1916 and condemned in July or August of that year. Mileage over the previous ten years was then reckoned at 128,000.

"Cader Idris", No. 1306, was immediately sent to Neath for overhaul, and this may account for the retention of its name, on the assumption that Neath practice was more tolerant of such oddities. Outshopped in October 1906, it too was then rostered successively at Carmarthen and Pencader, clocking up 92,000 miles before major overhaul at Swindon between April and August 1910. It afterwards returned to its previous sheds, and seems then to have been paired with No. 1304. When one was at Carmarthen Junction, the other was at Pencader, and vice versa. With 206,000 GWR miles to its credit, No. 1306 was again recalled for repairs, spread over almost nine months between June 1915 and February 1916. It then saw the war out on familiar territory, making its final journey to Neath on February 10th 1919, and being condemned in April. The distance covered in Great Western ownership was not far short of 300,000 miles; by no means discreditable.

No. 1338 was the shortest-lived of the three. All of its service life until the end of 1912 was spent based at Aberystwyth, with major repairs at Swindon in February-June 1908 and again in 1911 and 1912. This engine likewise then gravitated to Carmarthen. It was withdrawn on August 17th 1915 and condemned at Swindon in December, at which time the distance covered with the GWR was calculated at 118,000 miles.

A resumé of the locomotives which ran on the Manchester and Milford Railway is given below.

Name	*M&M No.*	*GWR No.*	*Maker*	*Acquired*	*Disposed*	*Remarks*
"Montgomery"	—	—	Unknown	1865?	1867?	Existence unconfirmed.
"Teifi"	—	—	M.W.	1865	1867?	Contractors' engine.
"General Wood"	1	—	S.S.	1865	1904	First traffic loco.
"Carmarthen"	2	—	S.S.	1866	1890	Boiler exploded.
"Lady Elizabeth"	3	(1305)	S.S.	1866	1906	Sold at once by GWR.
"Lampeter"	4	—	M.W.	1867	1868	Part exchanged.
"Aberystwyth"	4	(1339)	M.W.	1868	1906	Cut up at Neath.
(Proposed design)	—	—	M.W.	(1869)	—	Never proceeded with.
(Unnamed)	5	(1340)	S.S.	1870	1906	Sold at once by GWR.
("Crewe" 2-4-0)	2?	—	LNWR	1891	1900	Built 1855. Sold £150.
"Plynlimmon"	2	1304	S.S.	1891	1916	Condemned at Swindon.
"Cader Idris"	6	1306	S.S.	1896	1919	Condemned at Neath.
("Coal" 0-6-0)	7	(1341)	LNWR	1902	1906	Built 1889.
("Coal" 0-6-0)	1	1338	LNWR	1904	1915	Replaced General Wood.
("Dean Goods")	8	2301	GWR	1905	1906	On loan from GWR.
("Dean Goods")	9	2351	GWR	1905	1906	On loan from GWR.
("Dean Goods")	10	2532	GWR	1905	1906	On loan from GWR.

A total of 15 four-wheeled carriages sufficed for the needs of the passenger service in the years immediately after opening. The finances were such as to permit the purchase of no more than six outright, the remainder being on "deferred payment", broadly equivalent to the hire purchase concept of our times. Payments terminated and the carriages in question came into full ownership late in 1872. Neither the builders nor the running numbers can be stated with certainty. However, there is some weak evidence to suggest that the owned stock came from Ashbury and the hired vehicles from the Midland Wagon Co., and rather stronger grounds for suggesting the following scheme of numbering:

	Owned	*Deferred Payment*
Third class	nos. 1-3	nos. 9-14
Composite, first & second	nos. 4, 5	nos. 7, 8
Brake vans	no. 6	no. 15

The next additions were a horse box and a carriage truck in the second half of 1871, and these became respectively Nos. 16 and 17.

Later, it was found that there was need for a further brake van. One was accordingly purchased, being delivered at Aberystwyth in August 1875, and numbered 18. These eighteen vehicles proved adequate until Russell's early years as official manager and receiver, by which time the company had of necessity already embarked on a policy of "make-do and mend" which was to last until the GWR takeover. Amongst the first vehicles to be extensively renewed under this policy were two composite carriages in the spring of 1883. These two composites were described by Russell as "large" to distinguish them from the others, thus indicating that there were in fact differences in design as well as in origin amongst the early vehicles.

A new composite carriage was acquired in 1883 from the Metropolitan Railway Carriage and Wagon Company, having been built at the Saltley, Birmingham works of J. Wright and Co. at a cost of £498. This carriage was of particular interest in being one of the very few applications in Britain of the Cleminson flexible wheelbase principle. The idea behind Cleminson's design was to obtain better riding characteristics together with increased passenger accommodation without the complication of bogies. The design made use of three pairs of wheels. The centre pair was allowed limited sideways movement, and was connected by radius bars to the subframes carrying the outer wheels, which could pivot slightly. In this way, the outer wheels could turn into curves and the middle wheels take up a relatively correct displacement from the longitudinal centre line of the chassis, the whole giving in theory a jerk-free ride. Also, by eliminating the flange-grinding effects of a rigid wheelbase on sharp curves, it was possible to incorporate a much longer wheelbase than might otherwise be acceptable, and construct a correspondingly larger vehicle.

The Manchester and Milford carriage incorporated no less than seven rather cramped compartments; five for third class and one second and one first. The wooden chassis was 37ft. 11in. by 7ft. 10in. over headstocks, with spiral springs for buffing and drawgear. It is not certain that the M. & M. number, 8, was that originally carried, as there should still have been one of the original carriages bearing that number. It was the expressed intention, however, that the new vehicle would replace one old carriage and a brake van no longer required as such, so that the former No. 8 could have been renumbered onto a duplicate list. In the event, none of the existing stock was disposed of as a result of the acquisition of the Cleminson carriage, or indeed for several years subsequently. The decision was taken instead to rebuild and renew the second pair of composite carriages, and this was put in hand in 1884, together with work on a number of the other passenger vehicles. No. 8 was allocated GWR No. 7897 in 1906, renumbered at Neath in April 1907, but condemned in August of the following year.

By the end of 1888, Russell was reporting the need for new passenger carriages, and an order for two composites was given to Ashbury's in 1889. Nos. 19 and 20 were delivered in 1890. Each contained two second and two first class compartments, and was carried on four wheels. They were renumbered by the Great Western at Tenby, No. 19 becoming No. 7895 in March 1907 and No. 20, No. 7896 in April, but both were condemned the following month. With the arrival of the two new composites, two of the old were converted and downrated to thirds.

The Manchester and Milford received something of a shock to the system with the Board of Trade's directive that all passenger trains should have continuous brakes. A review of the existing vehicles showed that seven from a total of sixteen purely passenger carriages, that is excluding from consideration the three brake vans, horse box and carriage truck, were quite unsuitable for equipment with automatic vacuum brake. These seven were too old and too weak and decrepit. Something had to be done urgently.

A start was made with an order in 1892 for a third class, luggage and brake carriage from Ashbury's at a cost of £800. Strangely, its arrival in the following year was mentioned by neither Russell nor the directors. The carriage was carried on eight wheels and had three third class compartments plus a substantial area for guard and luggage within a body variously noted as 37ft. 7in. or 37ft. 10in. long. Width over guard's lookouts was 8ft. 11in. and total wheelbase was quoted as 27ft. 8in. or 27ft. 10in. There were glazed double doors to the luggage area which was further illuminated by a pair of rooflights. This vehicle may possiblly have been built with a rigid or semi-rigid wheelbase, although by 1911 if not sooner, it was mounted on the earliest pattern of Dean four-point suspension bogies with wheels at 6ft. 4in. centres and scroll irons and suspension mountings outside the bogie wheelbase. Like many of the contemporary Great Western carriages to which this type of bogie was originally fitted, the M. & M.'s first eight-wheeler survived for a good number of years.

As M. & M. No. 15, it was a direct replacement for the brake van formerly carrying that number. This was scrapped, together with one of the remaining two original composites. By the end of 1893 therefore, the company's passenger stock totalled twenty vehicles, as follows:

Type	*Description*	*Running numbers*	*Built*	*Rebuilt*
Composite	Original 4-wheeled	?	1865-7	1883-4
(Total = 4)	Cleminson tri-compo.	8	1883	—
	Ashbury 4-wheeled	19, 20	1890	—
Third class	Original 4-wheeled	1-3	1865-7	various
(Total = 11)	,, ,, ,,	9-14	,,	,,
	Original, ex-compo.	?,?	,,	1890
Brake third	Ashbury 8-wheeled	15	1892/3	—
Brake van	Original 4-wheeled	6	1865	?
	Early 4-wheeled	18	1875	?
Non-passenger	Horsebox	16	1871	?
	Carriage truck	17	1871	?

The Manchester and Milford was successful in winning an extension of time in which to meet the Board of Trade's requirements, so the next new passenger stock did not arrive until 1895. By this date, the means of raising capital had been created under the Board of Trade's certificates, and the money once more provided by the Barrow family. At the beginning of the year, the Court of Chancery had authorised £3,600 for immediate outlay on carriages from the sum sanctioned by the BoT, and followed this in June with permission to spend a further £1,800 from revenue.

Five vehicles were involved, all with low arc roofs and steel frames. The full thirds were built by the Metropolitan Railway Carriage and Wagon Co., and the others either by that concern or more probably by Ashbury, at a total cost of almost £6,200 — rather more than originally envisaged. Main features were as follows:

		10	11	12	13	14
M. & M. number		10	11	12	13	14
Type		Third	Third	Compo.	Compo.	Bk. Compo.
No. of compartments		8	8	1st: 2 2nd: - 3rd: 5	1st: 2 2nd: - 3rd: 5	1st: ? 2nd: ? 3rd: ?
Dimensions:	body length	41ft 11ins.	41ft. 11ins.	40ft. 11ins.	40ft. 11ins.	43ft. 2ins.
	body width	8ft.	8ft.	8ft.	8ft.	8ft.
	wheelbase	35ft. 6ins.	35ft. 6ins.	33ft. 9ins.	33ft. 9ins.	35ft. 9ins.
Cost		£1,231	£1,231	£1,496	£1,496	£740

As seems to be all too commonly the case with Manchester and Milford locomotives and rolling stock, a number of variant dimensions are quoted and a number of details remain obscure. A wheelbase of 35ft. 8in. is given for Nos. 10 and 11 in the list of stock taken over in 1906, together with length of 42ft. 3in. and width of 8ft. 2in. The Great Western diagrams for Nos. 12 and 13 also show overall wheelbase of 33ft. 6in. All five had the 8ft. 6in. pattern Dean bogie which was then in current use on the Great Western, although No. 13 may once have had the 6ft. 4in. type, and a question mark must stand over No. 14. The borrowing of the unique and unmistakable GWR suspension system was a curious feature of the later phase of M. & M. passenger rolling stock. Just what sort of vehicle No. 14 was in original condition it is difficult to say. The low cost was particularly noteworthy, and may point — as for No. 15 — to initial construction as a rigid eight-wheeler. Once again, though, there is photographic evidence from a later date for Dean bogies. In this case, the change — if change there was — may have come late in 1904 when the M. & M. rebuilt the carriage with one first and one second class saloon with lavatory in between, retaining guard's and luggage facilities. As such, it is easy to imagine that it proved very useful, particularly for the summer holiday season's traffic.

All five carriages survived absorption by the GWR, as would be expected for such relatively modern stock, although the two full thirds continued in traffic for a surprisingly short time thereafter. Both were condemned in April 1910. Their extremely narrow compartments, no more than 5ft. 1⅜in. between partitions, and poor standard of upholstery were probably much to blame. Mr T.R. Perkins, recounting a railway tour made to Wales in 1900 for one of the railway periodicals, recalled particularly that these carriages were without cushions for the seat backs, in marked contrast to the older non-bogie stock which had them.

The arrival of these new carriages permitted the immediate withdrawal of the seven which were unsuitable for the fitment of automatic vacuum brake. The last of the original composite carriages and six of the thirds, including the two earlier converted from composites, were gone by the end of 1895. Also withdrawn was one of the brake vans, although this appears to have escaped scrapping as it crept quietly back into the stock returns in 1903.

It was additionally planned to buy a new horsebox alongside the other new stock, although whether this was done or not is not recorded. The vehicle the Great Western inherited in 1906 was wooden-framed, and included a groom's compartment. There was just one single-block brake, plus through vacuum pipe. The Great Western allocated it No. 841 in place of the previous M. & M. number, 1. If the horsebox was not in fact a new one in 1895 but the old No. 16

renovated, the renumbering probably took place at this time in common with renumbering of some of the older carriages.

No further changes of significance occurred in the Manchester and Milford's passenger stock list up until the time when the Great Western took over. The carriage truck was scrapped in 1899, and one of the remaining five four-wheeled thirds went in 1905. Also in that year, when second class had few years left to it in general application on British railways, the two eight-wheeled first and third class composites were — according to the stock returns — redesignated to tri-composites. The two first class compartments were then flanked by the two seconds, with two third class compartments at one end and one at the other.

Bogie design was not the only thing that the Manchester and Milford aped from the GWR. The carriage colour scheme was very similar as well, with the two base colours being chocolate and cream. A drawing of the Metropolitan R.C. & W. thirds shows an inter-twined "MMR" monogram, again almost identical in form to that employed on contemporary Great Western carriages. Whether this found general application or not is open to question, but no other obvious indication of ownership was to be seen. The same drawing also indicates that class designation was spelt out in simple sans serif characters, as distinct from the GWR's rather heavily stylised letter-face. Similar-sized sans serif numerals without prefix, located centrally in the waist panels between the end compartment and that adjacent at each end, indicated the carriage number.

Before reviewing the fate of M. & M. passenger stock under its new owners, reference must be made to a transaction which gave a quite different appearance to some of the company's trains in the years immediately before the Great Western leased the line. When Russell retired from the post of Manager and Receiver and was replaced by T.B. Grierson, this gentleman in the manner of so many new brooms set about making an impression. Within three months, he was recommending the purchase of new stock, and before another three months could elapse, he had snapped up twelve second-hand carriages from the Mersey Railway, which had just gone over to electric traction. One of the younger generation of Barrows accompanied a carriage inspector to Lancashire to view the stock in question, on which a total price of £540 was agreed. Unfortunately for Grierson, all this was happening concurrently with negotiations with the GWR for a lease of the line, and that company definitely didn't want its side of the deal loaded with a job-lot of ex-Mersey carriages. Grierson was therefore ordered to sell them again, and this he managed to do late in 1906, incurring a loss of £180 on the transaction. Their stay on the M. & M. was thus of short duration, and they do not even appear to have been repainted. Three of the twelve ultimately passed to the

Brecon and Merthyr Railway.

The carriages handed over to the Great Western in 1906 are listed below:

	*Third Class Brake Third**		*1st/2nd Compo. Tri-Compo.**		*Brake Vans*	
	M & M	*GWR*	*M & M*	*GWR*	*M & M*	*GWR*
4-wheeled	2-5	3976-9	19, 20	7895-6	6, 18	1421-2
6-wheeled			8*	7897		
8-wheeled	10, 11	3980-1	12,* 13*	7898-9		
	15*	3982	14	7900		

No. 14, as already noted, included a guard's and luggage compartment. Whether, subsequent to the 1904 rebuilding, this was a first/second or a first/third brake composite is not clear. In the company's returns, it was always shown as first/third, but Grierson described it as first/second, as did the 1906 listing. Assuming that it was regarded as a family saloon operationally, the lower class accommodation for the servants may well have been unbranded.

All the four and six-wheeled stock, including the horsebox, were valued by the GWR at £15 each, a total of £150. The eight-wheeled thirds attracted £120 apiece; the tri-composites, £160; the brake third £115, and the saloon brake composite £155. The total for the bogie vehicles was therefore £830, and for all passenger stock £980.

The early demise of the three composites Nos. 7895-7 has already been mentioned. None of the other non-bogie carriages fared any better. No. 4 (3978) was already grounded and in use as a greenhouse in 1906. The other thirds were renumbered at Neath or Tenby in January 1907, but were then condemned in July that year (No. 5/3979), and in the following May (No. 3/3977) and June 1908 (No. 2/3976). The dimensions for these carriages recorded at the time of the Great Western's lease, and shown in an appendix, indicate some intriguing minor variations. These point to differences in the original construction, rebuilding on a substantial scale, or else quite simply inaccurate measurement. All were, however, recorded as having five compartments. It appears that they may well have been open internally above the seat backs, with lighting provided by no more than two rape oil lamps, strategically located to penetrate the gloom to a similarly inadequate extent in each compartment. The records are also noteworthy in showing these carriages as being built in 1890 by Ashbury's. It is difficult to see how this can be so, since only the two four-wheeled composites were reported as purchased in 1890. It is much more likely that 1890 in this case refers to rebuilding, with which the Ashbury Company may well have had a hand in the supply of fittings, etc. The two vans were likewise soon gone, No. 18 being condemned in March 1907, and preceding its nominally elder cousin No. 6 by ten months.

In marked contrast to the rapid massacre of the old and sub-standard amongst the Manchester and Milford's stock at the hands of the Great Western, four of the bogie carriages, the two tricomposites, the saloon and the brake third, had a surprisingly long career with their new owners. One, albeit so extensively rebuilt as to be no longer recognisably M. & M., survives today preserved on the Dart Valley Railway.

The two tri-composites, Nos. 7898 and 7899 were not long with their new owners before being modified. With the coming abolition of second class, there was little call for additional vehicles offering this type of accommodation, particularly in such cramped style. Consequently, both had two end compartments gutted to form a single guard's and luggage area, and the remaining second class compartment demoted. In this form, they were allocated GWR diagrams E90 and E91 respectively. The only difference that can be detected lay in the way in which conversion was carried out, and its effect on the external panelling: whatever might have been the earlier position, there was definitely now no difference in the bogies, the Dean 8ft. 6in. type being common to both. No. 7898 had guard's doors where the inner of the two compartments had once been, and an extra door carved right at the end at each side to give double doors for luggage purposes. "Carved" is probably a good word with which to describe the conversion, as there were no apparent changes to either windows or panels. No. 7899 had the guard's doors where the outermost compartment was formerly located, and double doors cut where the inner of the two had been. On this conversion, the new doors were diagonally opposed, and the mouldings were altered to correspond.

Both were subsequently branded for use on the Culm Valley line in Devon. A photograph shows one of the two there in company with the former Watlington and Princes Risborough Railway engine, GWR No. 1384. This dates arrival of the ex-M. & M. carriages in the Culm Valley at 1911 at the latest. There they stayed for a good many years: with certainty beyond 1927 when both were demoted to third class and brake carriages, and allocated diagram D97. No. 7899 was demoted first, becoming No. 606 in February, and No. 7898 followed in June, when it was renumbered to 657. Even in this form, they had some years remaining. No. 606 was condemned in June 1936, and No. 657 at the end of 1938. The brake third, No. 3982 also gravitated to the Culm Valley at an early date, and appears in a photograph and in the GWR diagram D50 with the short-wheelbase Dean bogies. Guard's lookouts were removed in April 1927, and the carriage was condemned three years later.

The saloon, No. 7900, was withdrawn as early as February 1908 when, instead of being scrapped, it was used to form the basis of a new vehicle. As such, it reappeared in August 1910 as the Taunton

Division engineering department's inspection saloon No. 6479 on Swindon's lot No. 1170 and diagram Q1. Later renumbered to 80977, it is this carriage which still survives, although how much is original M. & M. is debatable. It seems likely that the chassis was retained almost in its entirety, but not the body. Without knowing how it appeared in early life, it is tempting to see the lines of the former saloon in the Great Western's departmental carriage. The records, however, show an increase in body length from 43ft. 2in. to 43ft. 6in., which would correspond to the expected difference between the typical GWR turnunder and the flat or near-flat ends of M. & M. carriage bodies.

Throughout its life, the Manchester and Milford Railway operated with just over 100 goods vehicles. MacDermott records a total of 117, and whilst this was the maximum ever operated at one time, and thus correct for the years 1893-5 and from 1899 to 1905, by the time the Great Western took over in 1906, the total was reduced by scrapping to precisely 100. These comprised 7 ballast wagons, 17 low-sided mineral wagons, at one time used mainly for lead traffic, 46 for goods, coal and locomotive coal, 14 covered vans, 10 cattle trucks, 4 timber wagons, and 2 brake vans.

Details of all these vehicles, so far as they were recorded, are given in the appendix. The Great Western Railway probably scrapped the great majority at the first possible opportunity and some, indicated by an "S" in the table, almost certainly never carried the new numbers which were allotted to them. All but one of the open vehicles appear still to have been dumb-buffered and, as a result of the unavoidable financial stringency, many would have seen the very minimum of maintenance over the years. The substantial expense needed to rebuild them to current standards could therefore scarcely be justified. The Manchester and Milford was, however, in possession of a number of relatively new cattle and goods vans built by the Metropolitan Carriage and Wagon Co., and these would no doubt have seen some more years useful service with the Great Western.

The repair statistics which survive for the years 1876-7, although containing errors and not therefore to be relied on in detail, do throw some light on the probable ways in which goods vehicles were numbered in the early years. A part of the company's goods stock was also operated on a hire purchase basis until 1872, when it became fully-owned. With fair certainty, numbers in the range 1-81 were allocated to owned vehicles, and numbers between 101 and 138 to the hired wagons, as follows:

Type	*Nos.*	*Total*
Ballast and low sided mineral (lead traffic)	5-31	27
Goods wagons (19), coal wagons (25) and vans (5)	32-80	49
Brake van	81	1
Total owned = 77		
Coal wagons	101-120	20
Cattle trucks	121-132	12
Timber trucks	133-136	4
Brake van	137	1
Total hired = 37		
Total fleet = 114		

Nos. 1-4 were probably intended for mineral or goods wagons which for some reason never reached or stayed with the M. & M. The five vans were probably numbered at random between 32 and 80 as they came into service. However, by 1876/7 they were beginning to be re-allocated onto numbers between 70 and 80, these later becoming the sole preserve of the van stock. When the company acquired a third goods brake van, which it first did in 1870 at a cost of £72, this became No. 138, even though it was owned and might thus more logically have been No. 82. The company was able to operate with just two goods brake vans between 1871 and 1874, and again in 1895-8 and immediately before the Great Western took over. At some stage, No. 137 was the one taken out of service and not replaced, as this number was carried by a high-sided wagon for goods or coal in 1906: some open wagons were displaced in 1893 and 1898/9 in order that additions to the van fleet could be numbered consecutively with those already in service.

The first such additions were five covered vans in 1893. At least two of the original five had already been rebuilt for meat traffic, so the need for new general purpose vehicles must have been pressing. The Manchester and Milford was itself listed as builder, so it is possible that salvageable parts from three recently scrapped open wagons found their way into the vans. The assertion that the M. & M. built its own stock must be treated with caution, although it was probably correct in this case. Almost all goods vehicles were so described in the GWR records, whereas we know that such of the original stock as did not come from the contractors was bought in. It is clear, though, that the company developed a substantial renovation and repair capability, so that there would often have been little left in the wagons inherited in 1906 from the nominally-equivalent wagons in the 1870's. For example, from October 1880, when the rebuilding of four cattle trucks was completed, to the end of 1884, no less than 38 open wagons were reconstructed at Aberystwyth together with a brake van, meat van and three covered vans. The workshops also handled around 180 repairs — major and trivial — in the course of a typical year. So there is some justification in considering the M. & M. as builder.

The next additions were made early in 1899 when four further goods vans, Nos. 67-70, four more cattle wagons, Nos. 121-4, and a brake van, No. 81, were purchased from the Metropolitan Co. The expenditure, £346 on the vans, £388 on the cattle trucks, and £146 on the brake van, was met from revenue. Six open wagons and two old cattle trucks were taken out of stock at the same time. The Great Western clearly didn't regard the M. & M.'s goods vehicles as much of an asset when it was obliged to value them in 1906. Even the relatively new brake van attracted only a purely nominal £5 — the same as an older van of Ashbury origin which had been demoted to breakdown use. All goods and cattle vans, new and old, were valued at £10 ea., and everything else at £5, for a total of £620.

CHAPTER 7

AFON TEIFI TO AFON YSTWYTH — A TRIP DOWN THE LINE

A traveller of 75 years ago could well have made his first acquaintance with the Manchester and Milford Railway on alighting from a Great Western train at Pencader. Here, he would have found a two-platformed station of a size more closely related to its status as a junction than to the modest requirements of the village. Road, railway and River Tyweli, a tributary of the Teifi, shared the narrow confines of the valley at Pencader. Looking north, a glimpse might have been caught of the river to the left as the eye followed the single line of rails disappearing into the leafy distance. Turning towards the south, back down the line to Carmarthen, the shunting of wagons into the goods shed or in the yard may have disturbed the tranquil scene; or perhaps one of the company's engines have attracted attention as it was turned, coaled and watered in the two road locomotive depot.

Intending M. & M. passengers had to avail themselves of a small waiting room on the down platform: the main station building was located on the "Carmarthen" side, to which there was access via a massive covered footbridge. Also on the down platform was a large signal box housing a 35 lever frame. In later years, 14 of these levers were redundant; a surplus partly attributable to changes in the track layout which took place between the wars. Two "middle" sidings and a catch point were taken out at that time, and the loop extended in their place.

Once given the signal to start, the M. & M.'s train would have eased gently out towards Pencader Junction, located half a mile beyond the station and by the Great Western's 260¾ mile post. A small signal box at the junction marked the start of the Manchester and Milford Railway proper. Soon after, the former C. & C. line to Newcastle Emlyn bridged the Tyweli and then appeared to drop quickly away to the left; for the M. & M. had by now begun its sharp climb out of the valley. For 1½ miles, gradients of between 1 in 59 and 1 in 83 were encountered, before the train clattered over the points for the New Quay Road station loop and its two sidings, past a ten-lever signal cabin on the Up side, and into the single platform, also on the Up side. The stop was formerly named Cross Inn (Llanfihangel) and in later years, logically but not very helpfully, became Bryn Teifi. The first confrontation with a "proper" M. & M. station would be unlikely to impress. New Quay Road boasted one of the company's primitive and miserable wood and corrugated iron shacks, although it no doubt served well enough for the few passengers who used it.

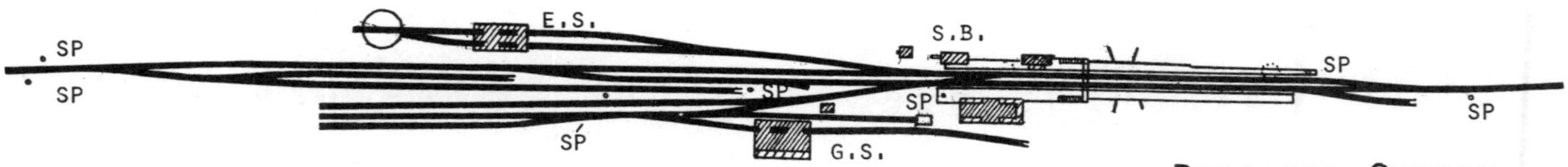

PENCADER STATION

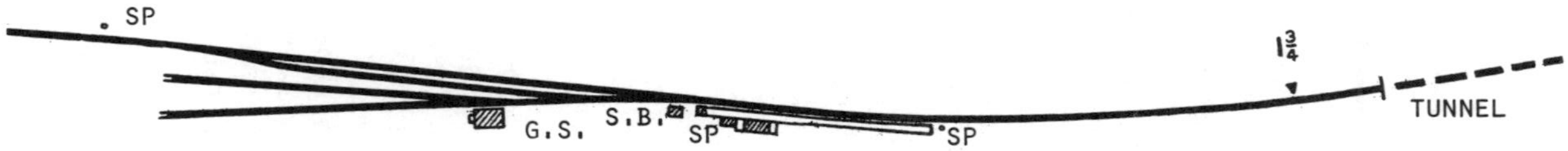

NEW QUAY ROAD STATION
(CROSS INN)

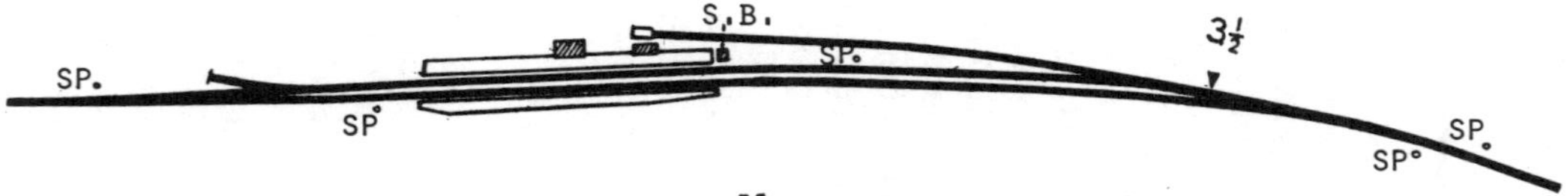

MAES-Y-CRUGIAU STATION

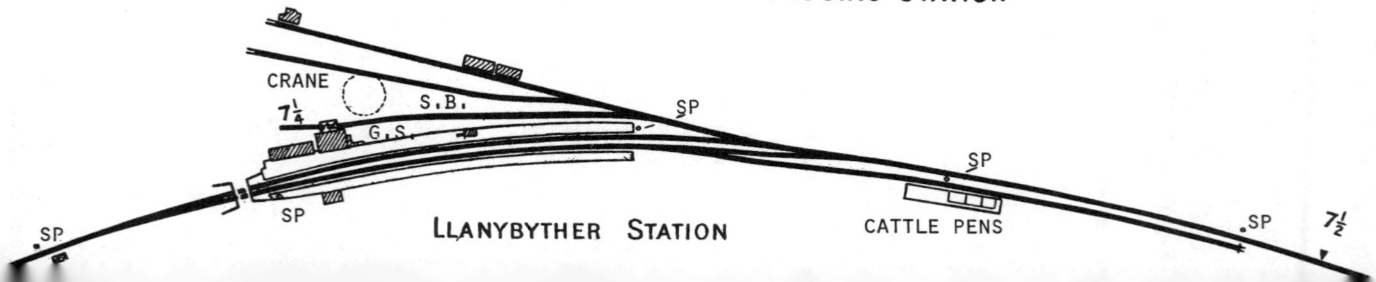

LLANYBYTHER STATION

North of the station, the line plunged into a 100 yard long tunnel under the "Cross Inn" and the road to New Quay. It had once been the intention to make a deviation instead of building the tunnel, but the alternative would have needed three road bridges, so it was doubtless not considered worthwhile. Cross Inn tunnel, a damp and troublesome place, marked the southern summit of the line. Once negotiated, the M. & M.'s train would have rattled off downhill, accelerating at an alarming rate on gradients as steep as 1 in 47 into the valley of the Teifi. Our passenger would have caught his first sight of the river on the left, meandering languidly through pastures, sparkling or sullen according to the whim of the weather, before he felt the train slow by the three mile post. Here, the Maesycrugiau fixed distant signal was reached, and the gradient turned once more against Aberystwyth trains.

Maesycrugiau station boasted two platforms, but needed no more than a single siding on the Down side to cater for its modest freight needs: there was also a short escape siding to stop wagons left in the loop during shunting from running back towards New Quay Road. Signalling, here as elsewhere on the Manchester and Milford, was straightforward, with fixed distant, home and starter for each direction, plus an outer starter beyond the loop for Down trains and, in GWR days, a ground signal guarding the siding. Control of loop and siding points and loop point locks accounted for ten levers from the twelve lever frame in the signal box. In later years, difficulties in sighting the Up home through an overbridge and round the curve just north of the station led to outer starter and Up home being combined on one post. Such combinations were to be found elsewhere on the line in M. & M. days, notably at the tunnel end of New Quay Road station, where Down starter and Up home were likewise so arranged. Maesycrugiau itself comprised barely more than a cluster of houses, so the station warranted no better than the usual squat M. & M. structure on the Down platform, later augmented by a pair of the Great Western's standard pagoda huts.

Onwards towards Aberystwyth, the line followed the Teifi in a north-easterly direction, never in the course of many miles straying further than was dictated by the river's tortuous course, winding through a broad valley below the western slopes of the Cambrian Mountains. Gradients were now undulating, although mostly adverse in order to follow the natural rise of the valley floor. Short stretches at 1 in 75 or 1 in 80 were to be found, but these were barely enough to tax even the old Sharp Stewart tender engines at the leisurely speeds called for with the M. & M.'s modestly-loaded passenger trains. Certainly, the travelling public would have had plenty of time to note the passing scene: a level crossing with its keeper's house 5¼ miles out from the junction, a substantial bridge half a mile later over a road and one of the many streams flowing down from the hills to swell the Teifi, then the Teifi itself close by on the left, washing the footings of the railway embankment, the Llanybyther fixed distant near the seven mile post, and so under a road bridge and into Llanybyther station.

Llanybyther vied with Tregaron for the status of the second-most important community, after Lampeter, served by the railway. The village was chiefly notable for its flannel works and a large agricultural implement factory near the line which specialised in the building of water wheels, a form of power much used in the area. Lastly, and by no means least from the traffic viewpoint, there were monthly cattle fairs which transformed the station yard into a hubbub of activity. By the time of our visit early in the present century, Llanybyther boasted a brick-built station building; the only one on the railway apart from Lampeter. It retained nonetheless the modest dimensions of the more prosaic structures to be found elsewhere, and was dwarfed by the solidly-constructed stone goods shed which stood alongside, and backed onto the Down platform. Three sidings fanned out on the Down or Aberystwyth side to make a sizeable yard. The yard's connection to the loop was worked from a twelve-lever frame in the signal box, which also controlled a single lay-back siding on the Up side, starting just short of the Up platform and equipped with cattle pens. All remaining levers were then needed for the loop points and the basic combination of home and starter signals for each direction, plus an outer starter for Aberystwyth-bound trains. A fifteen-lever frame was substituted in later years to cater for the added needs of shunting arms. The signal box was to be found on the Down platform from the time of Saxby and Farmer's installation, although not, it seems, before then. An early photograph of the station shows the Down platform to be devoid of such a structure, without indicating where else it might be. The same picture also reveals a signal post of quite enormous height carrying the old two-arm station signal. This was later replaced by one of more normal albeit still tall stature carrying just the Up starter.

Passengers would have had a few minutes leisure before the train restarted in which to take in the surroundings: the neat row of houses behind the goods yard, the Black Lion Hotel on a slight eminence beyond the station, on a corner where the denizens of Llanybyther doubtless congregated. Such signs of civilisation would soon have been left behind, however, as open country was regained, and as the Teifi once more wound towards and alongside the railway before receding to the west. An unending backdrop of hills unfolded on the landward side; hills which were sometimes close at hand, rolling, cultivated, sometimes further removed, giving occasional glimpses up the valleys and through the trees to the mountains beyond.

Eight miles out from the junction, a half mile bank at 1 in 81 was

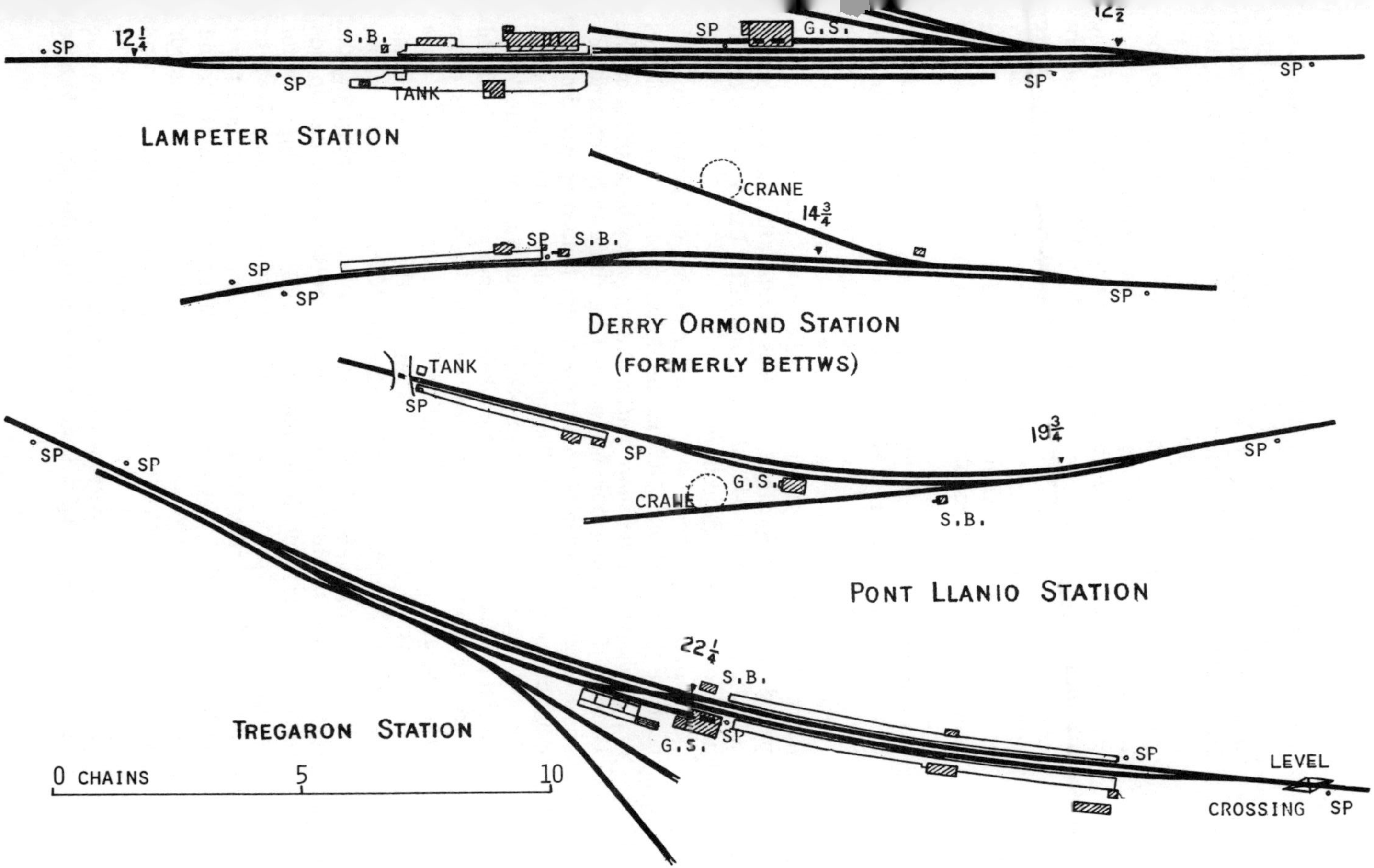
LAMPETER STATION
SP
12 1/4
S.B.
SP
TANK
SP
G.S.
SP
12 1/2
SP
DERRY ORMOND STATION
(FORMERLY BETTWS)
CRANE
14 3/4
SP
S.B.
SP
SP
SP
PONT LLANIO STATION
TANK
SP
SP
G.S.
19 3/4
SP
S.B.
TREGARON STATION
SP
SP
22 1/4
S.B.
G.S.
SP
SP
LEVEL
CROSSING
SP
0 CHAINS
5
10

encountered, so the train would have been proceeding quite slowly as it passed the point on the Up side where Pencarreg Halt was later built. Opposite lay Pencarreg Lake, cut off from the Teifi by a knoll of higher ground. On towards Lampeter, river, railway and road followed each other closely: now, as then, the railway's course can be seen at no great distance for much of the way along the road from Llanybyther to Lampeter. Nearing Lampeter, the line swung north on an embankment, dominating the flat acres verging the Teifi and offering a glimpse over the grey slate roofs of houses huddled at the southern extremity of the town. Rattling in quick succession across three bridges, including a girder structure above the Lampeter-Llandovery road and a 78ft. 6in. span over the Teifi, the train would have slowed near the fixed distant, just short of the twelve mile post, and drawn to a halt at the station.

Lampeter, or Llanbedr Pont Steffan, was very much the traffic hub of the Manchester and Milford system. From as early as the 12th century, Pont Steffan had been a crossing point for the River Teifi. In the 13th century, the town was established as a borough, yet it sheltered a population of little more than 1,700 in our period; serving to illustrate just how limited the railway's traffic potential really was. In M. & M. days and after, Lampeter was chiefly noted for its theological college.

The station layout was not dissimilar to that at Llanybyther, with separate Up and Down platforms straddling the loop, main buildings and goods yard on the Down side, and a single lay-back siding on the Up side. The station building was a long single-story construction, whose squatness was emphasised by a canopy formed by extending the slate roof over the platform. The original ten-lever signal box stood at the southern end of the Down platform, but was superceded by a standard Great Western structure, brought into use in May 1916 and sited just beyond the Up platform towards Aberystwyth. This cabin also supplanted Aberayron Junction Box in course of time. In more recent years, all but two of the 23 levers in the new Lampeter frame were in use. Five levers controlled the signals for Aberystwyth trains, respectively home, starter, outer starter and two arms indicating the route selected at Aberayron Junction. Station signals on the Up side comprised outer home, home and starter, plus two shunting arms for the siding, the Up distant on the station approach being fixed, as customary. Five further levers worked the loop points and locks and the Up siding, whilst a sixth provided the release for the north ground frame. This in turn gave access to the array of five sidings in the goods yard. The remaining five levers in use were power worked to control Aberayron Junction and the stop and distant signals protecting its approach from both Aberystwyth and Aberayron. At the time of our tour, however, signalling at Lampeter was more rudimentary, with no more than the usual quota of distant, home and starter in each direction, plus an outer starter for Aberystwyth trains, sited on the Up side of the line.

Lampeter preserved a more rural aspect than Llanybyther by virtue of the station's location on the extreme eastern edge of the town. Our traveller might well have taken advantage of the protracted stop to stretch his legs in the station yard, and here he could not fail to note all the usual activity of a small country town; in the goods yard to his right, at the saw mill in the other direction, or along Station Terrace, whose line of houses led towards Lampeter itself. Perhaps there would also have been a horse bus for Aberayron, soon to be replaced by one of the Great Western's familiar motor buses. Yet hills and woodland were never far from view. On the other side of the line, the countryside all but encroached onto the Up platform, where there was to be found a modest stone waiting room, a couple of oil lamps, and a massive water tower for the needs of the locomotives.

North from Lampeter, the line climbed noticeably, at 1 in 67, 71 and 89, as far as the 13 mile post. The subsequent site of Aberayron Junction was passed just over half a mile later: until after the date of the company's lease to the GWR there was, of course, nothing to be seen here. The way led on into boggy land alongside the Afon Dulas, a stream which wound down past Lampeter to join the Teifi south of the station. The Teifi itself now lay over a mile distant to the south-east, hidden from view by an intervening ridge of high land.

Derry Ormond station was reached just short of the 14¾ mile post. If Lampeter represented the best that the M. & M. could offer, Derry Ormond was surely amongst the worst. A miserable little corrugated-iron hut stood on a wind and rainswept platform on the Down side, seemingly miles from any human habitation. The name itself derived from a nearby park and the residence of the local squire, one Inglis-Jones; the former name, Bettws, from a church. There appear to have been but few inhabitants, so it is perhaps unfair to be unduly critical of what was, after all, little more than a halt. Halt or not, Derry Ormond boasted a signal cabin, also on the platform, to control the usual minimum of signals and the southern end of the loop. The remote, Aberystwyth, end plus a single siding were worked from a ground frame.

From Derry Ormond, it was precisely a mile and a quarter on moderate rising gradients to Llangybi. Llangybi was regarded as an unmanned station rather than a halt, and not all trains stopped there. Its chief use was for market and excursion traffic, and it was completely without goods facilities, comprising nothing more than a 300ft. long platform located on the Up side between two overbridges. So if station it truly were, it must have vied for the honour of being the most basic in the Kingdom. One of the overbridges carried the road between Llangybi, a cluster of houses a few hundred yards distant, and Llanfair Clydogau, a village which straddled the Teifi a good mile's stride in the opposite direction.

Seventeen miles out from the junction, the railway began to ascend quite steeply once more, past the later site of Olmarch Halt — in recent years a 70ft. long wood-framed platform and open-fronted shelter on the Up side — and up between areas of high land before an equally sharp descent back into the valley of the Teifi. The remains of a Roman fort could be detected here, guarding the Roman causeway, Sarn Helen, which now turned away towards Aberystwyth. The river wound yet again close at hand near the 19¼ mile post, although this time on the southern side of the railway. Shortly after, through a road bridge, stood Pont Llanio station.

Pont Llanio was another typical M. & M. structure, set on a single platform on the river side of the line. Opposite, the land rose in a rocky slope into which a water tower was set. The loop was located beyond the Aberystwyth end of the platform, a single siding trailing back towards the station on the land left by a gentle bend in the river. A small signal cabin with eight levers, sited where the siding joined the loop, sufficed. Pont Llanio was one of the places which had fallen foul of the Government's inspector a few years earlier, because the curve in the line badly impaired the signalman's visibility. As a result, the signal box was removed from its original position by the platform-end. As a further aid to visibility, the Up starter and Down home were carried on a single post on the platform side of the road bridge, with the Down arm visible above the bridge. The station boasted a small stone goods shed, but the milk factory which later dominated Pont Llanio, and the siding which served the factory, were not yet built. The "pont" of Pont Llanio carried the road from the station by three arches over the Teifi, past the Derry Arms pub and a few scattered dwellings, and off to Llandewi Brefi, a good mile distant and the "local" village served.

The Manchester and Milford took on a suddenly dramatic character beyond Pont Llanio as it crossed and recrossed the Teifi. The river in this area had gouged a horseshoe bend deep into the surrounding land and the builders of the M. & M., rather than tunnel to the west, had been obliged to bridge the water by means of two high lattice girder spans, each of 60ft. length, and separated by a considerable embankment. A further crossing was called for half a mile before Tregaron, this time by means of a single span of 77ft. 6in., before the short sharp climb into the station.

Tregaron, population 1,500, was another centre noted for its fairs and as a base for cattle and horse dealing. It could also be described as a gateway to the east, since a rough road beginning in Tregaron led over a pass through the Cambrian Mountains to Abergwesyn, from where it was an easy journey to the three "Wells" of Llanwrtyd, Builth and Llandrindrod. Like many a "frontier town", such beauty as Tregaron possessed it acquired from the magnificent mountain backdrop, but for all that its commerce brought useful traffic onto the railway, which passed by to the west. The station did nothing to heighten the architectural pretensions of the place, being one of the M. & M.'s by now all-too-familiar shacks. There were, however, two platforms, although passengers on the Down side were without any form of shelter until around the time of the Great Western takeover, when a small wooden waiting room was erected opposite the main building.

The track layout at Tregaron was a little more complex than those usually found on the M. & M. by virtue of the considerable length of the passing loop. This extended the full distance along the platforms and roughly as far again towards Pencader. The goods facilities were arranged on the southeast or town side, and were connected into the Up line near the Pencader end of the main loop and with the Down line midway along, near the start of the platform, and right by the 22¼ mile post. In this way facing points were avoided at the cost of a fixed crossing laid in over the Up line. Three sidings trailed off the goods refuge back towards the passenger station, the first of which was equipped with cattle pens and a goods shed. There was also a headshunt.

In the early years of the present century and at the time of our journey over the line, the signal box with its 12-lever frame was to be found by the Up platform, where a distant watch could be kept on the level crossing located beyond the station at the Aberystwyth end. Shortly afterwards, it was moved to a position just past the opposite end of the other platform by the point giving access from the goods sidings. As well as the usual combination of fixed distant, home and starter for each direction, Tregaron boasted an outer starter for Up trains, and in later years needed four subsidiary signals and a further starter for control of shunting movements. Four levers operated the passing loop and point locks and two more, the connections for the goods yard. This made for a total of 16 levers from the latter-day 24-lever frame. A seventeenth locked the gates where the Tregaron-Aberystwyth road crossed.

Once over this crossing, Tregaron was left behind and the way led alongside the road towards Pontrhydfendigaid as far as Alltddu, a place noteworthy in the annals of the railway as the point at which the route deviated from the early plans. Alltddu could thus be said to mark the beginning of the "northern" section, although there was little there other than a farmhouse, for the benefit of whose inhabitants and any chance passers-by a halt was subsequently built. This stood on the Up side and consisted of a short, raised, wooden platform, primitive shelter, nameboard and lamp column. The line took on a new direction at Alltddu. The course of the railway had lain in a north-easterly direction up to this point, but here it struck north, preparatory to turning again towards Aberystwyth. Alltddu also marked the beginning of the most spectacular part of the trip. For the last two miles, the Bog of Tregaron had stretched out to the west. Cors Goch Glan Teifi — the red bog on the banks of the Teifi — was a great natural wilderness of peat and sedges, harbouring countless species of birds, and deriving its name from the colour of the vegetation as it died away in autumn. Once, only the Teifi divided this marshy expanse, situated some 500ft. above sea level. Now, the railway strode across it on a causeway, stretching in a straight line for almost two miles, and broken only by bridges over the Fflur and — for the last time — the Teifi, by means of twin 40ft. plate girder spans.

Strata Florida station, 27¼ miles from the start, marked the passing of the bog and the end of the straight. The site was once intended to be a junction, and the station was laid out on a bend of around 15 chains radius, originally planned as the south-to-west curve of the triangle. There were two platforms but little in the way of facilities for passengers: just the usual squat buildings on the Carmarthen platform huddled next to the goods shed, which was again of noticeably sturdier stone construction. Even the signal box, next to the goods shed at the Carmarthen end and of a neat standard design, looked more sanitary and appealing than the passenger accommodation. Nor was Strata Florida without its passengers. The nearby village of Ystrad Meurig boasted a well-known grammar school, which would have meant some coming and going. A mile and a half distant lay Pontrhydfendigaid, a village of far from negligible size by the standards of the area. A mile further afield stood the ruined Cistercian Abbey of Strata Florida, the name a latinised version of Ystrad Fflur, or plain of the River Fflur, on which the abbey stood. This 12th century foundation, amongst the best preserved of its type in the Principality, was already starting to attract numbers of tourists.

Goods traffic was catered for with two sidings trailing in on the Up side and a short lay-back beyond the Aberystwyth end of the Up platform. Beside one siding stood a store for lead, a reminder that Strata Florida was one of the collection points for the mines further up in the hills around Pontrhydygroes. The yard was also equipped with crane, end-loading bank and weighbridge — used mainly by the Cardiganshire Coal Co. who were for many years the principal coal traders along the railway. The station was also one at which engines often took on water, and large tanks were provided at the appropriate end of each platform for that purpose. In Great Western days these were replaced by water columns fed from a standard pattern tank on a tall pedestal.

The approach to Strata Florida across the bog had been all but level, and provided the engine crews with a welcome breather before the heavy work ahead. No sooner had the Manchester and Milford's train restarted into the cutting at the Aberystwyth end of the station on a gradient of 1 in 79 than this steepened to 1 in 53 and 1 in 44. The climb continued for a mile before the summit was reached near the 28½ mile post, 670ft. above sea level. Corporation Siding, a line about ¼ mile long leading to

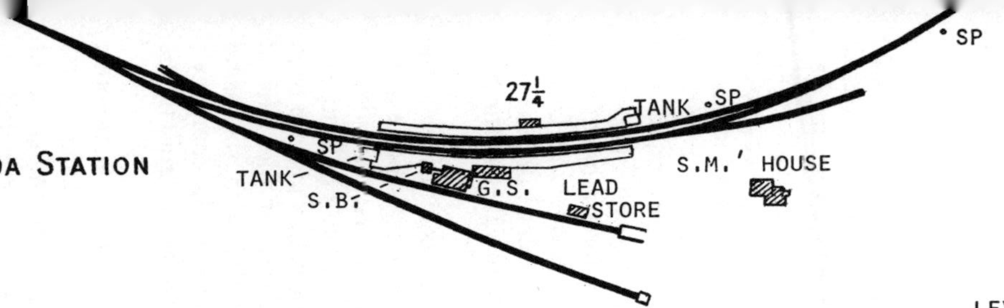

STRATA FLORIDA STATION

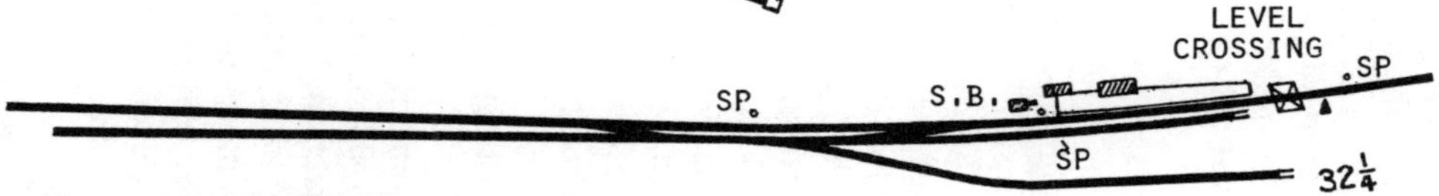

TRAWSCOED STATION

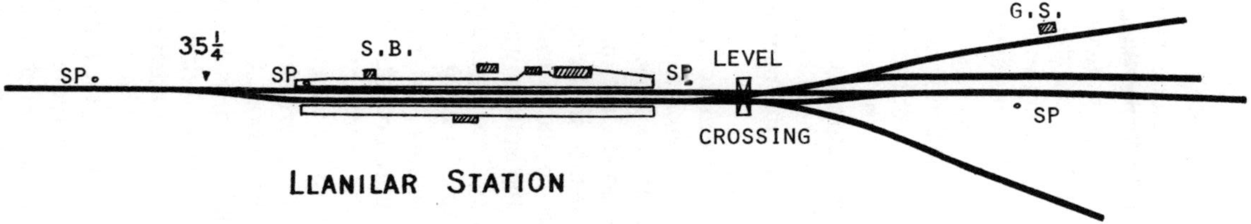

LLANILAR STATION

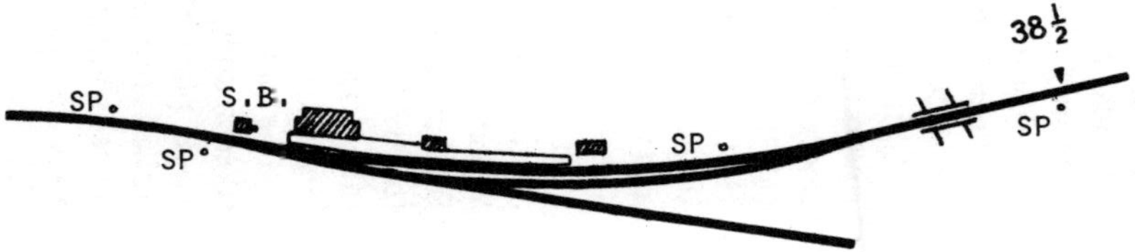

LLANRHYSTYD RD. STATION

the Ystrad Meurig quarry, was to be found here. The connection was trailing for Aberystwyth-bound trains — the direction in which loaded wagons were mostly required — and was once controlled from a primitive signal cabin. The long descent of Trawscoed Bank began immediately beyond this point, its 4½ miles — by now marked at between 1 in 41 and 1 in 51 — interrupted only by a short respite for Trawscoed station.

Gaining speed the while, the carriages can be visualised lurching round the bends as the line followed the contours high above the valley floor; first into a cutting, then through the 100 yard-long Tanycraig tunnel, then immediately afterwards past the point where Caradog Falls Halt was later built, in the shape of a 70ft. platform and small wooden shelter on the Up side, almost a mile past the summit. Deep rock cuttings and wooded embankments came one after the other in rapid succession. The hillside rose steeply to the south-west, while on the other side, the land fell towards a new river valley, that of the Ystwyth. At first, the river could only be seen intermittently through the dense foliage of Pen-y-Bont Wood; for this part of the valley had escaped the deforestation of areas further upstream, stripped to provide charcoal for ore smelting. Only as the train rounded a sharp bend a mile before Trawscoed did the true magnificence of the vistas open up across the Ystwyth valley to the hills beyond.

The halt at Trawscoed would no doubt have been accomplished to the screech and pungent aroma of hot brakes. Trawscoed station possessed a single platform on the Down side beyond the crossovers. Two sidings trailed into the goods line on the Up side opposite the platform and a headshunt extended in the other direction. Little seems to have been done to pander to the considerable local influence of the Earl of Lisburne, and the station was once more provided with the usual M. & M. building. Sharing the platform was another of the company's neat signal boxes, its eight — later eleven — levers controlling the minimal requirements of signals and points.

The descent continued after Trawscoed, but now through more open countryside down towards river level. The gradient finally slackened off by the 33 mile post, by which point the line occupied an embankment alongside the river. Shortly after came the site of Felin Duffryn Halt, on the river side of the railway. Constructed by the GWR in 1935, it was the last of the five halts towards Aberystwyth and, like Alltddu, consisted of a wooden platform with shelter, supported on an open framework. The other three halts had a rather more permanent appearance by dint of their solid platforms.

For the next two miles the railway followed a straight cut of the river, no more than a few feet above its height and directly alongside. It was this stretch which caused so much trouble with flooding. Llanilar station was reached towards the end of the straight, 35¼ miles out from Pencader

Junction. By the time of our tour it sported two platforms, facing one another across the loop, but it was probably not always thus. The Up platform, besides the Ystwyth, and a siding which trailed into the Up line at the Aberystwyth end appear to have been fairly recent additions. The waiting shelter on this platform was quite an elaborate affair, though still of wood. The main station building was also rather better than the norm, although it is difficult to imagine that the station ever attracted enough passengers to justify the favour shown to them.

Goods traffic was catered for by two sidings on the Down side, but with buffers towards Aberystwyth. The connection to them crossed directly over the Down line in order to trail into the Up, an arrangement which was later simplified by the substitution of a facing point into the Up line and removal of the crossing. Signals and points were controlled from a cabin on the platform used by Aberystwyth trains. The usual arrangements were afterwards augmented by an outer starter for Carmarthen trains, while a two-arm bracket signal substituted the starter for the other direction.

A ford was marked across the Ystwyth by the platform end at Llanilar, although it would be a brave soul who used it in all but the driest weather. There was also a footbridge a little way upstream which was swept away on more than one occasion and just as often replaced. If its recent appearance was anything to judge by, its use would also call for either courage or dire necessity. At the turn of the century, a fall in the river was to be avoided for, however sparkling its demeanour as it tumbled over the stones, it was laden with effluent from the lead workings.

The journey continued alongside the Ystwyth on gently falling gradients across the flat meadowlands left by the river, whose course had been diverted in order to minimise engineering works. Nonetheless, a crossing was inevitable if Aberystwyth was to be reached, and this was executed barely two miles from Llanilar by a single 58ft. 6in. lattice girder construction carried between substantial stone pillars and abutments. A mile and half of generally adverse gradients was then encountered before the last true Manchester and Milford station, Llanrhystyd Road.

Llanrhystyd Road was, as its name suggested, a station serving nowhere in particular but with aspirations towards a great many places. It was in fact located 38½ miles from the junction at Pencader and immediately before a bridge over the main coast road south from Aberystwyth. As such it was a potential interchange for anyone wishing to travel by road to Aberayron, New Quay or Cardigan. Whether many people would wish to travel very far on the M. & M. in order to make such a tour is a moot point, since all of these places had omnibus connections from elsewhere. Not surprisingly, therefore, the station was provided with a minimum of facilities. The platform was arranged on the Down side of a short loop, from which a single siding projected back towards

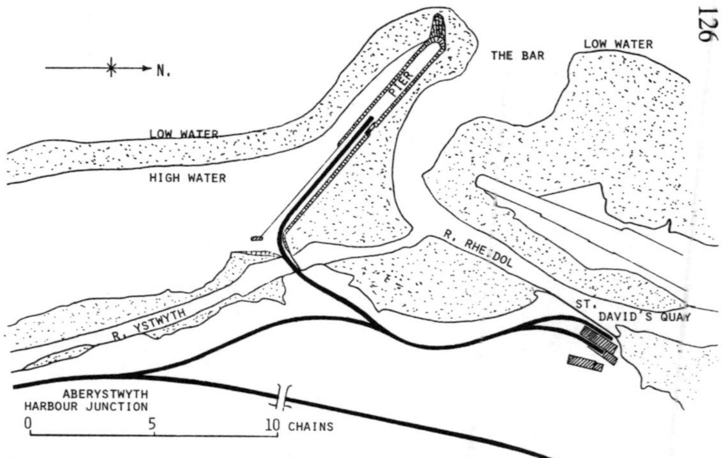

Track Arrangements at Aberystwyth Harbour as they were believed to exist Pre-1900.

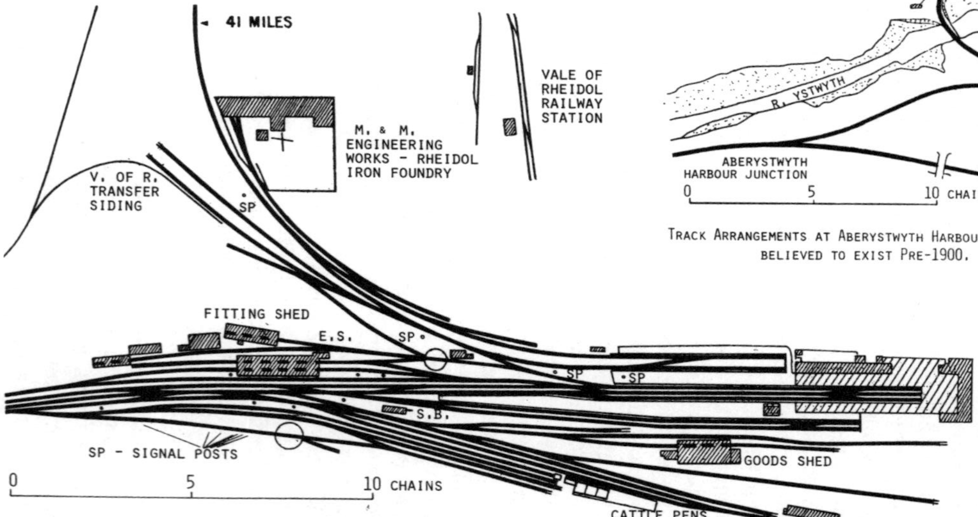

Aberystwyth Station

Aberystwyth. For all that, the station building was ultimately almost double the usual size, and the Great Western, when replacing the M. & M.'s signal cabin in May 1916 with one of its own structures further along the platform, employed a design of quite unnecessarily large dimensions.

It might be imagined that all the interesting scenery now lay behind; but far from it. From Llanrhystyd Road there was another sharp and winding descent, much of it at 1 in 42, down towards the Ystwyth once more. Soon after, the railway rounded the slopes of Pen Dinas, a curiously shaped hill some 400 feet high overlooking Aberystwyth, and suddenly a superb view over the Bay of Cardigan opened out. The line was now perched on a ledge below Pen Dinas — once the site of an Iron Age fort and now commemorating the Iron Duke with a column in the shape of a cannon — and above the Ystwyth, whose outlet to the sea was delayed by a long tongue of land terminating in Aberystwyth harbour bar. At an earlier date, there had been a facing junction for a line to the harbour from a point just before the 40½ mile post. The Manchester and Milford's harbour branch once headed northwards past a goods station and into the narrow strip of land between the main line and the landward side of the tidal basin, and terminated in two sidings either side of a warehouse on St. David's Wharf. There had also been a spur curving across the Ystwyth to the harbour bar, although this was probably very lightly laid and made use of an existing bridge. No doubt it was formerly a place of no little activity, but by the date of our tour it was moribund and the junction had been removed; a victim of the general decline in coastwise shipping.

The sea was left behind as the M. & M. swung east, completing a virtual half circuit of Pen Dinas. The main road south from Aberystwyth was bridged once more, giving views of the town close by on the left. Then — almost 41 miles out from the start of the railway — came a girder bridge over the Afon Rheidol, its 128ft. length comprising two main and two subsidiary spans. The main pair, each of 45ft., bridged the river. A third of 18ft. span was used to cross the Vale of Rheidol's line, which at that date pursued a highly circuitous course into Aberystwyth along the bank of the Rheidol before turning around to terminate at right angles to the Cambrian's station.

The Manchester and Milford's rails meanwhile curved sharply back towards the north, passing the company's engineering works on the left and the interchange sidings with the Vale of Rheidol Railway and the locomotive depot on the right, before terminating in the bay platform, number 5, at Aberystwyth. Our passenger could finally alight in order to sample the town's healthy air and seaside pleasures; travel-weary but hopefully invigorated by the sights and experiences of the trip.

GRADIENT PROFILE FOR THE MANCHESTER AND MILFORD LINE

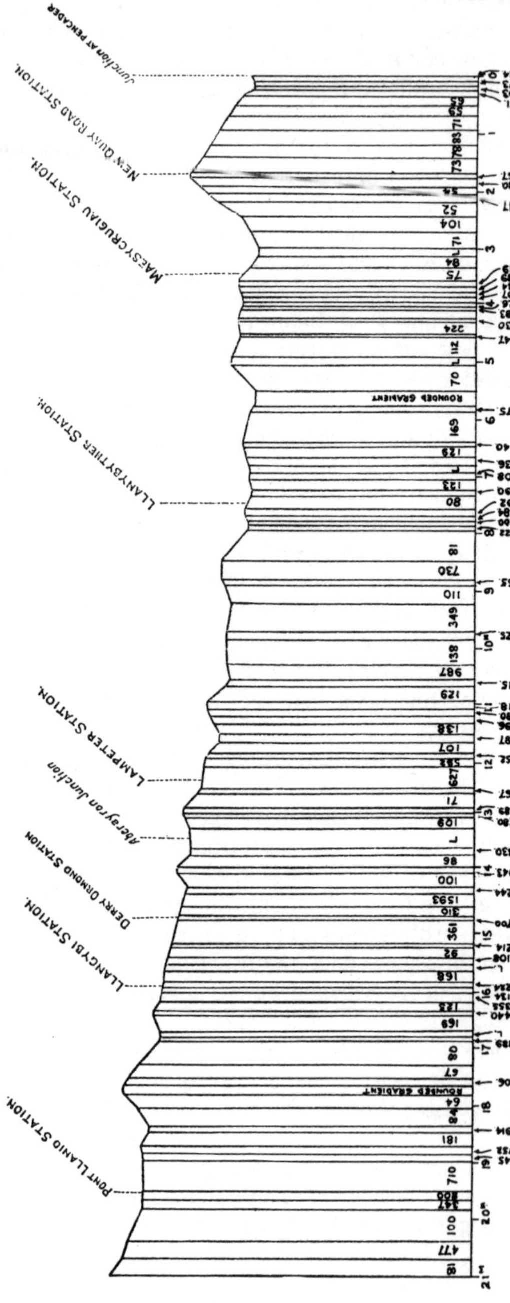

GRADIENT PROFILE FOR THE MANCHESTER AND MILFORD LINE

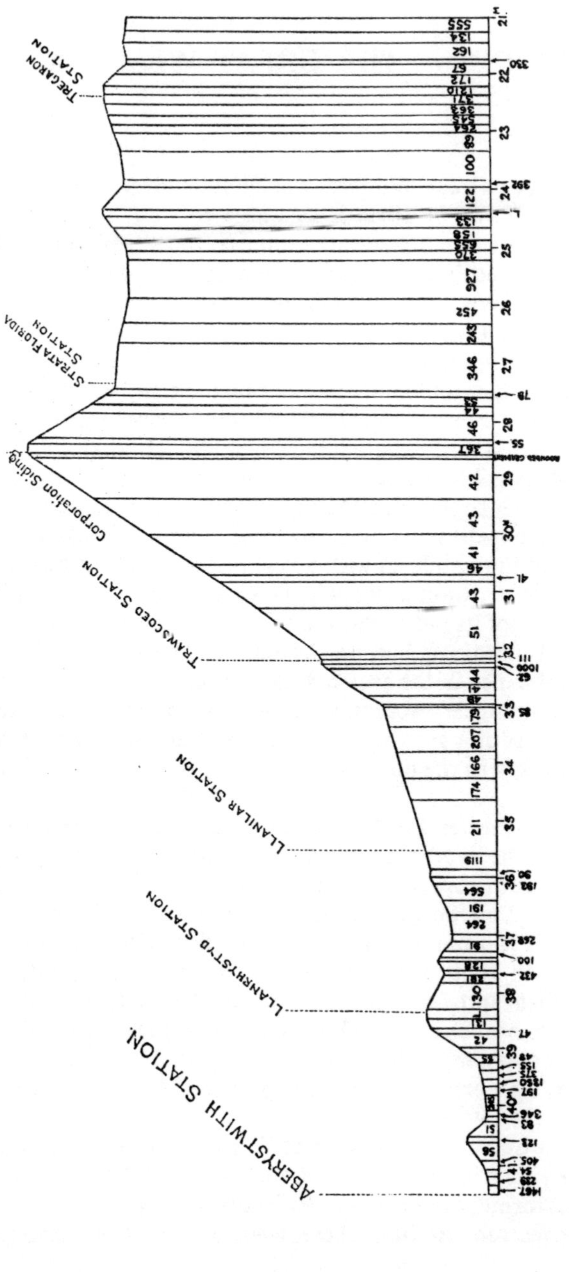

CHAPTER 8

POSTSCRIPT — THE GREAT WESTERN PERIOD AND AFTER

When the Great Western finally took over the Manchester an Milford Railway in 1911, it was able to view its new acquisition i circumstances far different from those under which the line's form proprietors had been obliged to operate. Whether the price paid wa cheap or otherwise is an open question. In relation to the railway original cost, it was of course a bargain. In relation to the likely futu earnings, set against the investment needed on structures, permane way and stock, it could not really be said to be any sort of a bargain at a The Great Western itself almost certainly never viewed the matter such terms. It had secured the M. & M. at what was probably th cheapest possible price, unencumbered — and here lay the re advantage — by the debilitating effects of accrued debt: not for th GWR the hopelessness faced by the Barrows, Russell and the rest, ever-mounting liabilities with no chance whatever of liquidating them But most of all, the new owner had secured an advance into mid-Wales the expense of its old rivals, the Cambrian and the London and Nor Western Railways. It had won an entry to Aberystwyth, the only town any significance in the area not already served by the encircling Gre Western network. Aberystwyth, as an administrative and cultur centre, heart of a growing tourist trade, and a university town of 8,0 inhabitants, was the one source of traffic which was worth the effort exploiting.

The Manchester and Milford line was largely, therefore, a strateg addition to the Paddington empire. The local traffic receipts would mo or less cover the operating costs, if not much of the outlay on renewal with through traffic giving a welcome bonus whose benefit would be fe both south and north of Pencader Junction. Under its new owner, th Aberystwyth route logically became the main line, with the form Carmarthen and Cardigan line to Llandyssul and Newcastle Emly demoted to branch status. This was a noticeable reversal of the situatic of former years, when the C. & C.'s stranglehold on Carmarthen and th M. & M.'s poverty contributed to give the M. & M. much the inferi status of the two.

The line quickly took on a Great Western appearance, with little mo than the persisting mediocrity of much of the station accommodation betray its former ownership. GWR stock was soon drafted in, and GW locomotives too. At first, these seem to have been largely the Dea tandard goods class, which had already established its suitability, but ter, many types found their way onto the Manchester and Milford ection. Early arrivals were the "Duke" and "3521" outside-framed -4-0 classes. After the Grouping came the large 0-6-0s of the Cambrian's 89" class, and Collett's modern 2251 series, then "43xx" 2-6-0s and the ebuilt 4-4-0s known as the "Dukedogs". Finally in Great Western days, ie versatile "Manor" class 4-6-0s appeared together with "Aberdare" utside-framed 2-6-0s, the latter on heavy munitions trains operated uring the Second World War between Llandeilo and Saltney, near hester, but routed over the former M. & M. The "Aberdares" were elatively heavy machines, and their use serves to indicate that weight estrictions were rather less severe than on many of the Great Western's econdary routes in Wales. Originally classified as "yellow", the line's atus was enhanced to "blue" in mid-1939, and all engines with ppropriate route availability were allowed with the exception of the 28xx" 2-8-0s, which were excluded on clearance grounds.

Despite the predominance of tender types in Great Western days, tank ngines were to be seen between Carmarthen and Aberystwyth. A variety f vintage four-coupled machines, superceded by the familiar pannier inks, worked the Newcastle Emlyn and Aberayron branches and made ccasional forays onto the main line, where the larger "prairie" engines ere also tried. Most of the route, to south of Bryn Teifi — as New Quay oad was renamed in October 1916 — came within the Oswestry entral Wales) Division after the Grouping, with the remainder coming nder Swansea.

With a countryside as sparsely populated as that through which the rmer Manchester and Milford passed, there was very little potential for creased local traffic. Events at large did not help. The Great War rought restrictions and a massive increase in costs. Then followed dustrial unrest, the general strike and the depression. By the time the onomic climate had once more begun to improve, the motorbus had tablished itself as a cheaper and more convenient alternative in untry areas. The Second World War brought new difficulties, and the ost-war period saw private car ownership on a large scale. Small wonder en that passenger traffic remained light, as a glance at the passenger unts will show. The daily average for southbound trains during a week January 1920 amounted to the following:

epartures from Aberystwyth	*7.00 a.m.*	*9.40 a.m.*	*12.15 p.m.*	*4.50 p.m.*
ssengers at Aberystwyth	13	27	36	98
" " Llanilar	20	29	30	59
" " Tregaron	13	31	19	35
" " Lampeter	29	46	38	37
" " Bryn Teifi	39	54	35	41
" " Pencader	56	79	55	72

In the reverse direction, the figures were:

Departures from Carmarthen	*7.30 a.m.*	*10.15 a.m.*	*2.30 p.m.*	*5.50 p.m.*
Passengers at Pencader	17	44	50	54
,, ,, Llanybyther	12	39	48	44
,, ,, Lampeter	17	27	62	32
,, ,, Tregaron	18	20	38	17
,, ,, Trawscoed	39	27	29	14
,, ,, Llanrhystyd Road	48	41	42	35

The early morning trains were both particularly badly patronised, a least until they neared their destinations. It will be seen that there was regular flow of passengers by the morning trains into Aberystwyth fro the nearby villages along the Ystwyth valley, returning by the 4.50 p.n Yet only rarely were more than 100 passengers to be found on individu trains as they arrived or departed from Aberystwyth. All the Carmarthe bound trains saw over 100 passengers on at least one day of the week i question, but only over the last stretch south from Pencader, where a least half of those travelling by the best-used services began the journeys. On no train did the number of passengers travelling first cla exceed eight, or the week's average four. Totals were broadly maintaine through to the end of the 1920's, although there were then addition services. By the outbreak of war in 1939, the rot had begun.

There was little that the Great Western could do. The train servic could hardly be expanded as a means of attracting new customers whe the numbers carried were so few. With the possible exception of Strat Florida, none of the Manchester and Milford's stations was particular badly located for the community it purported to serve. Even so, five hal were introduced for the convenience of the local pupulation. The firs was Olmarch, opened at the end of 1929 and mid-way between Derr Ormond and Pont Llanio, followed by Pencarreg, one mile north o Llanybyther, in June 1930; then Caradog Falls, a mile down Trawscoe Bank and immediately north of the second of the line's two short tunnel dating from September 1932. The last two were, as previously note Felin Duffryn, mid-way between Trawscoed and Llanilar, and Alltdd where the line started out across the Bog of Tregaron, brought into use i June and September 1935 respectively.

Otherwise, the only major change in station facilities, apart fro lengthening of many of the crossing loops, took place at Aberystwyt which was extensively remodelled in 1925. This, however, had little to d with promoting local traffic. A new frontage was built, through whic access was gained to a large glass-roofed circulating area, and muc extended platforms. The new platforms necessitated the removal of locomotive turntable, and a spur was constructed between the forme Cambrian and Manchester and Milford lines which completed th triangle, so engines could henceforth be turned in this way. The spur wa not used for any traffic which might want to avoid Aberystwyth station.

The regular passenger service comprised four trains each way for much of the Great Western period, although there were timetables when this total was increased, for example 1928. In later years, the service once more reverted to a morning, midday and afternoon train in both directions, a foretaste of which was given by the timetable operated during the 1920 miners' strike. For an example of Great Western operation, the 1915 service might be quoted as typical. Towards Aberystwyth, the following trains were run:

M. Ch. from *Carmarthen*			*Pass.*	*Goods*	*Goods*	*Pass.*	*Goods*	*Goods*	*Pass.*	*Pass.*
15.31.	Pencader	arr.	6.14	—	8.25	10.46	11.15	12.40	2.16	5.46
		dep.	6.40	7.20	9.00	10.50	11.40	12.45	2.21	6.00
15.65	Pencader Jc.	pass	6.42	7.25		10.52	11.45	12.50	2.23	6.02
17.38.	New Quay	arr.		7.30		10.55	11.50	12.55		
	Road	dep.	6.48	7.35		10.58	12.00	1.05	2.28	6.06
19.17.	Maesycrugiau	arr.		7.40		11.02	12.10	1.15		
		dep.	6.54	7.45		11.07	12.15	1.26	2.32	6.10
23.16	Llanybyther	arr.	7.04	7.55		11.15	12.25	1.30	2.39	6.18
		dep.	7.07	8.26		11.18	12.40	1.50	2.43	6.21
28.12.	Lampeter	arr.	7.19	8.36	9.43	11.27	12.50	2.00	2.52	6.30
		dep.	7.24	10.15	11.00	11.32	1.10	3.05	3.02	6.35
30.37.	Derry	arr.						3.12		
	Ormond	dep.	7.31		11.07	11.38		3.15	3.08	6.41
31.57.	Llangybi	dep.	7.35		—	11.42		—	3.13	6.45
35.33.	Pont	arr.						3.25		
	Llanio	dep.	7.42		11.19	11.50		3.40	3.22	6.53
38.10.	Tregaron	arr.	7.46		11.27	11.55		3.50	3.27	6.58
		dep.	7.50		11.45	11.57		4.25	3.37	7.00
43.05.	Strata	arr.	7.59		11.55	12.06		4.35	3.47	7.09
	Florida	dep.	8.02		12.22	12.08		4.42	3.54	7.11
48.05.	Trawscoed	arr.			12.40			5.00		
		dep.	8.16		12.55	12.22		5.10	4.08	7.25
51.10.	Llanilar	arr.			1.05			5.20		
		dep.	8.23		1.25	12.29		5.35	4.15	7.31
54.16.	Llanrhystyd Rd.	arr.			1.35	12.35		5.45		
		dep.	8.30		1.50	12.40		5.55	4.24	7.39
56.67.	Aberystwyth	arr.	8.37		2.00	12.47		6.05	4.31	7.46

The 7.20 a.m. goods ex-Pencader could be extended to Tregaron if necessary for the cattle traffic; and to Aberystwyth on the first Monday of the month only. There was also a cattle working in connection with Tregaron market, on the Tuesday preceding the first Wednesday in the month. Empties left Aberystwyth at 7.00 a.m. and were booked to reach Tregaron at 8.10. The special then left Tregaron at 3.30 p.m. and, with allowances of twenty minutes at each of the three stations Strata Florida, Trawscoed and Llanilar, was due back at Aberystwyth at 5.22.

The service of trains towards Carmarthen in 1915 balanced with that already given for Pencader to Aberystwyth, with one exception: the early morning goods from Aberystwyth ran only as far as Lampeter, the engine presumably working back double-headed on the 9.00 a.m. goods ex-Pencader. This apart, there were four passengers trains and one goods in each direction over the whole line, and two goods services running Pencader-Lampeter-Pencader. Arrival times have been indicated in the last table, and in that which follows, only when station stops exceeded two minutes.

Towards *Carmarthen*		*Pass.*	*Goods*	*Goods*	*Goods*	*Pass.*	*Goods*	*Pass.*	*Pass.*
Aberystwyth	dep.	7.00		7.15	8.50	9.35		3.10	6.22
Llanrhystyd Rd.	arr.			7.25	9.00				
	dep.	7.08		7.30	9.10	9.43		3.18	6.30
Llanilar	arr.			7.38	9.18			3.25	6.36
	dep.	7.15		7.48	10.15	9.50		3.30	6.40
Trawscoed	arr.			7.56	10.23				
	dep.	7.23		8.15	10.40	9.58		3.38	6.48
Strata	arr.				11.10			3.53	7.03
Florida	dep.	7.39		8.38	11.28	10.14		3.57	7.10
Tregaron	arr.			8.45	11.38			4.06	
	dep.	7.49		8.55	11.56	10.24		4.13	7.21
Pont	arr.			9.05	12.02				
Llanio	dep.	7.55		9.15	12.05	10.30		4.19	7.27
Llangybi	dep.	8.03		9.21	—	10.38		4.27	7.35
Derry	arr.				12.16				
Ormond	dep.	8.09		9.27	12.30	10.42		4.33	7.40
Lampeter	arr.	8.12	8.36	9.43	12.36	10.46	12.50	4.38	7.45
	dep.	8.15	10.15	11.00	1.36	10.49	1.10	4.43	7.48
Llanybyther	arr.		10.27		1.47		1.20		
	dep.	8.25	11.30		1.58	10.59	1.35	4.54	7.58
Maesycrugiau	arr.		11.41		2.08		1.45		
	dep.	8.33	11.50		3.05	11.07	1.50	5.02	8.06
New Quay	arr.		12.00		3.15	11.12	—		
Road	dep.	8.40	12.05		3.20	11.16	—	5.09	8.13
Pencader Jc.	pass	8.43	12.10		3.25	11.19	2.00	5.12	8.16
Pencader	arr.	8.45	12.15		3.30	11.21	2.05	5.14	8.18
	dep.	8.50	12.53		3.45	11.27	2.25	5.27	8.22

At this period, passenger trains were barred from crossing at Derry Ormond, Pont Llanio, Trawscoed or Llanrhystyd Road; New Quay Road being a surprising omission from this list. Passenger trains could cross goods trains at these stations, the latter being admitted to the loop to leave the main line clear. The "loop" at Trawscoed was not long enough for this purpose — or designation — so use had to be made of a siding, and crossing trains were not allowed to leave either Strata Florida or Llanilar until the goods was safely isolated in this way. Signal boxes were in use at all eleven former Manchester and Milford stations between Pencader Junction Box, which was closed in July 1929, and Aberystwyth Junction Box, located north of the Rheidol on the approach to Aberystwyth station. The total of eleven excluded Llangybi which, being without sidings, had more in common with the halts on the line. There was also a signal box controlling Aberayron Junction until August 1929, and another so-called, but in fact no more than a ground frame, at Corporation Siding. Aberystwyth Harbour Junction had long since been taken out. Speed limits over the route were fairly severe with no more than 40 m.p.h. maximum, several intervening 25 and 30 m.p.h. sections, and 15 m.p.h. through many of the stations. Four auto-trains were shown each way on the Aberayron branch, taking 50 minutes for the 13½ miles between Lampeter and Aberayron. There was also a solitary goods working out and back along this branch.

The second half-century of the former M. & M. line's existence was comparatively uneventful. The emphasis was very much on consolidating the limited traffic which the region was able to offer, rather than on any thought of development. It is therefore remarkable that during the Great War, of all times, a proposal to resuscitate the line to Llangurig was aired before the Cambrian, and enthusiastically taken up by Llanidloes Town Council and sundry local newspapers. Revival of agriculture and reopening of the lead mines beyond Llangurig were the expressed aims, and prisoner-of-war labour the intended means. The Cambrian seems to have taken the proposal more or less seriously, but replied that there were no prospects of reconstructing the Llangurig branch while the war continued, and suggested that the scheme should be put to the government after hostilities ceased. A report indicated that Llangurig had a population of no more than 200-300, from which possibly 50-70 passengers a week might be expected. The lead mines four miles further up the valley had produced 90 tons in 1912 and 140 tons in 1913, while lime and coal requirements around Llangurig were estimated at respectively 150 and 300 tons a year. With sheep and cattle traffic also taken into the reckoning, total annual revenue might amount to around £300. Operating costs would, however, be three times this figure, so the Cambrian naturally steered clear of any commitment.

A further proposal had been to revive the mountain line to Strata Florida, a proposal which the Cambrian considered equally unrealistic. The distance from Llanidloes to Aberystwyth would be 37 miles by the suggested route via Strata Florida, as against 51 miles via Moat Lane, so the main impact of such a scheme was felt to be to pull traffic rates down. For traffic to and from the north, the projected route would actually be at a two mile disadvantage between Moat Lane and Aberystwyth compared with the existing Cambrian line through Machynlleth. A letter in a local newspaper hit the nail on the head. It suggested that to carry the branch over sparsely populated country, through deep cuttings and extensive tunnels, merely as a short cut into Cardiganshire, would be costly out of all proportion to the revenue it could command, and unwarranted by public need. The Cambrian could be expected to be opposed to the Strata Florida scheme, and the Great Western, who still owned the old earthworks, would probably not be interested in either this or the simpler proposal covering opening to Llangurig only. The most that might be hoped for would be for the Cambrian to build a light railway to the village making use of the existing alignment.

The prelude to Nationalisation came in the form of a severe snowstorm, which interrupted traffic for several days in the harsh winter of 1947. The 5.30 p.m. ex-Carmarthen, hauled by a "Duke" 4-4-0, stuck in drifts at Lampeter. Two locomotives were sent to the rescue from Aberystwyth, but they also became embedded some miles from their objective. It finally took a further four engines before the track was cleared.

Operations, following Nationalisation, appeared to continue much as before, but the underlying economics became more and more enfeebled, as for so many other secondary routes and branch lines up and down and country. It was the same old story of rising costs and flagging traffic, compounded in this case by the economic stagnation of the region. British Railways introduced new colour schemes and new locomotive types, and 75xxx 4-6-0s, 78xxx 2-6-0s and 80xxx 2-6-4 tank engines saw service over the line. A sight which would have made John Barrow sit up and take note was the appearance of a pair of Stanier 2-8-0 heavy goods engines, Nos. 48309 and 48728, to haul the royal train from Milford Haven to Aberystwyth and back in August 1956. In anticipation of this visit, a number of bridges were strengthened and a considerable amount of track relayed; an intriguing if indirect application of royal patronage! The growl of diesels was first heard in 1963, when "Hymeks" and type 37 machines began to operate.

The Beeching Report, published in March 1963, could have surprised no one when it recommended closure between Carmarthen and Aberystwyth, together with many other routes in the Principality. Here was a classic case for the combatants in the public transport debate. In purely economic terms, there was no doubt that the line should close. Yet there was equally no question that it filled a social need for which — cynicism about such services aside — the substitution of buses and commercial carriers was not wholly adequate compensation. Local roads were too primitive for the traffic from the milk factories at Green Grove, near Felin Fach on the Aberayron branch, and at Pont Llanio on the main line. The feeling that was uppermost amongst local spokesmen was that here was a region in need of development, yet the infrastructure which was necessary for that development to take place was being dismantled. Beeching was concerned with trying to make the railways pay. Since then, the political pendulum has swung towards a greater concern for the social implications and costs. So it is an area for speculation — assuming that the line had survived intact for a few more years — whether it would then have been allowed to close, or whether it would have remained among the ranks of those whose future appears forever uncertain.

In fact, closure of the former Manchester and Milford route was a long drawn-out affair in which the forces of nature played a major role. Withdrawal of goods facilities had begun in December 1963 at Bryn Teifi, Derry Ormond, Trawscoed, Llanilar and Llanrhystyd Road, followed in March 1964 by those at Pont Llanio, apart from the milk factory siding, Tregaron and Strata Florida. Then, on December 14th 1964, the railway was severed by floods at that old trouble spot, Llanilar. Trains from Carmarthen were thereupon terminated at Strata Florida, and a bus service was substituted to maintain the connection with Aberystwyth. The line north of Strata Florida was closed immediately, as goods facilities at all stations on this section had already been withdrawn. Official closure came on February 22nd 1965, when passenger services over the remainder of the line were withdrawn, and the northern section offered for sale. The furthest point of working then became the station limits at Pcnt Llanio, just under 20 miles from Pencader.

Goods facilities at Pencader, Maesycrugiau and Llanybyther had been withdrawn in September 1965, leaving Lampeter as the railhead for general freight and Pont Llanio and Green Grove siding on the Aberayron branch as the points from which milk traffic was operated: passenger services on the Aberayron branch had ceased in mid-1951, and goods facilities, ultimately at Aberayron and Felin Fach only, went in April 1965. Milk workings from Pont Llanio survived until mid-1970, and closure between Pont Llanio and Aberayron Junction took place at the beginning of October that year. This left Green Grove, which lasted until the end of September 1973, when the remainder of the line was closed. Track was, however, still in situ to just north of Aberayron Junction in the summer of 1974, as were sidings at Lampeter which had been in use for goods traffic until the previous September.

Dates at which sidings were taken out of use, usually shortly after the withdrawal of goods facilities, and at which signal boxes closed were:

	Sidings	*Signal Box*
Llanrhystyd Road	15 April 1964	(To ground frame ca. 1931)
Llanilar	15 April 1964	28 September 1964
Trawscoed	15 April 1964	28 September 1964
Strata Florida	15 April 1964	28 September 1964
Tregaron	3 August 1964	22 February 1965
Pont Llanio	1 October 1970	22 February 1965
Derry Ormond	15 April 1964	28 September 1964
Lampeter	1 October 1973	2 January 1966
Llanybyther	28 September 1964	28 September 1964
Maesycrugiau	22 February 1965	22 February 1965
Bryn Teifi	2 December 1963	28 September 1964
Pencader	13 July 1967	13 July 1967

It will be many years before all trace of the railway is lost. Closed lines in more populated areas have often been obliterated by housing, roads or industrial use, but the pace of change in mid-Wales is unlikely to disturb most of the station sites, let alone the testament of earthworks in open countryside. Many structures still stand, although the larger bridges have been dismantled with the exception of that across the Teifi at Strata Florida. The girder bridge here survives in most unsafe-looking condition for access over the old trackbed to a bird sanctuary, which has thoughtfully been created along the Bog of Tregaron. Much of the course of the Llangurig Branch can still be followed, from its junction at Penpontbren to the station site and beyond at Llangurig: a remarkable situation for a route which was left to the ravages of nature so many years ago. Indeed, the exact point at which work stopped in a field west of Llangurig could, until very recently, be clearly detected. Here, perhaps, is where we should leave the Manchester and Milford Railway, looking towards the mountains which were to be the frustration of the company's hopes.

ACKNOWLEDGMENTS

The author wishes to thank the following organisations for the use of research facilities or illustrative material, and for all the assistance so freely given at a personal level:

— The British Transport Historical Records section of the Public Record Office.
— The Map Room of the British Library.
— The National Library of Wales.
— Dyfed Archives, formerly the County Record Offices for Carmarthen and Pembrokeshire.
— The Public Relations Department of British Railways, Western Region.
— The Reference Library, Birmingham Public Libraries, for material on Metropolitan Carriage and Wagon Co. rolling stock.
— Hunslet Holdings Ltd., for material on Manning Wardle engines.
— Kidderminster Art Gallery and Museum, for the photograph of Pencader Station from the Chambers Collection.

Thanks are also due to L. T. George, J. L. Smith, and Ian Allan for the use of photographs from the L. & G.R.P., Lens of Sutton, and L.P.C. collections respectively; to M. Hale and C. C. Green for the use of photographs, also Colin Judge, Roy Miller and Harold Morgan. I am particularly indebted to Jack Slinn for information on M. & M.R. carriage stock in the GWR period, to Martin Connop Price for much valuable guidance and material on the M. & M.'s relations with the Pembroke and Tenby Railway, and to Tony Cooke for details of track layouts and alterations, closure dates, and many helpful suggestions on the chapters covering the post-M. & M. period.

Lastly, I must record my gratitude to the "family firm": my brother James, who did much of the research, and my wife Pam, who participated in many areas of the book's preparation, and encouraged me through the five years it took to complete. Without their support, this history of the Manchester and Milford Railway would not have been written.

APPENDIX I

£000s

Capital Account & General Balance to:	End-1868	Mid-1875	End-1880	End-1888	End-1893	End-1899	Mid-1906	Mid-1911	Note
Share Receipts	521.6	513.3	513.3	513.3	513.3	513.3	513.3	513.3	1.
Forfeited Shares	0.4	-	-	-	-	-	-	-	
Loans	170.4	164.2	164.2	163.7	165.2	174.8	175.2	175.2	2.
Capitalised Rent Charges	24.7	24.7	24.7	24.7	24.7	24.7	24.7	24.7	
Total Receipts	717.1	702.2	702.2	701.7	703.2	712.8	713.2	713.2	
Total Expenditure	741.1	750.7	751.5	752.2	753.8	763.9	764.3	764.3	
Balance on Capital Account	(24.0)	(48.5)	(49.3)	(50.5)	(50.6)	(51.1)	(51.1)	(51.1)	
Cumulative Balance on Revenue A/C	(6.9)	(63.1)	(111.3)	(203.0)	(260.6)	(328.5)	(355.3)	(398.9)	
Deficit on Capital & Revenue A/C	30.9	111.6	160.6	253.5	311.2	379.6	406.4	450.0	
Cash-in-Hand and Debtors	1.5	3.6	11.0	11.8	11.7	10.5	5.4	-	
	32.4	115.2	171.6	265.3	322.9	390.1	411.8	450.0	3.
Financed by:									
Unpaid Rent Charges	1.9	6.4	14.6	2.3	-	-	-	-	
Unpaid Debenture Interest	11.5	62.6	107.5	169.6	209.5	249.6	306.5	344.2	
Unpaid Rent etc.	-	-	-	22.2	31.8	45.8	-	-	
Temporary Loans	12.0	40.2	40.9	62.0	73.0	83.3	94.4	105.8	4.
Sundry Creditors	7.0	6.0	8.6	9.2	8.6	11.4	10.9	-	
	32.4	115.2	171.6	265.3	322.9	390.1	411.8	450.0	5.
Residual Borrowing Powers:	44.4	34.4	33.6	8.2	21.3	11.2	10.8	10.8	6.
Revenue Account, Annual Average for:	1868	1869-1875	1875-1880	1881-1888	1889-1893	1894-1899	1900-1906	1906-1911	7.
Traffic Receipts	13.9	16.1	17.3	18.4	20.2	22.3	24.9	5.2	8.
Costs of Working	9.5	13.3	15.9	14.6	18.0	19.1	23.9	1.6	
Profit on Operating Account	4.4	2.8	1.4	3.8	2.2	3.2	1.0	3.6	
Rent Charges & Debenture Interest	10.1	11.2	10.1	10.0	10.2	10.4	10.5	10.6	9.
Rent on Llanidloes Line & Station	-	0.2	-	2.6	1.9	2.4	(7.1)	-	10.
Interest on Temporary Loans	-	-	-	2.6	1.6	1.7	1.7	1.7	
Balance on Revenue Account	(5.7)	(8.6)	(8.7)	(11.4)	(11.5)	(11.3)	(4.1)	(8.7)	

Mileage Statement, Annual Average:

Notes.

1. £555,000 in ordinary shares were created by the 1860 Act, of which £175,000 was cancelled and replaced by preference shares in 1865. A further £15,300 in preference shares was authorised by the 1865 Act for a total of £570,300. £57,000 of the ordinary shares remained unissued for all but the first years of the company's life.
2. Loans of £185,000 were authorised by the 1860 Act. A further £5,100 was authorised in 1865 but not created until 1872, and never taken up. New borrowing powers were created by the Board of Trade certificates issued under the Regulation of Railways Act 1889 for expenditure on signalling and train braking. Certificates were for £9,289 in 1892 and £5,411 in 1893, although the money was raised only slowly over a period of years.
3. The general balance sheet can be interpreted as matching the money owed by third parties and by the business itself - since costs exceeded revenue and more money had been spent than raised as shares etc. - with money owed to third parties. The M. & M. was financing its deficit by not paying bills and defaulting on liabilities, notably on the interest due on loans.
4. The sudden increase in temporary loans recorded in 1875 can be seen as an indication of the crisis which overwhelmed the company that year, following two years of particularly poor operating results. The increase was, however, largely attributable to an attempt to get past receipts and expenditure properly recorded.
5. The accounts conclude with the note that interest and loans to the amount of £450,000 were cancelled under the Vesting Act of 1911.
6. Residual borrowing powers during the period 1868-1880 were calculated as the total of unissued shares and loans, less the over-spending on capital account. From 1881 - Russell's first full year at the helm - they were corrected to show the capitalised rent charges as part of the statutory borrowing powers, and not as additional to these.
7. The revenue account and mileage statement for 1868 are also quoted on the "annual average" basis, although the figures are derived from the July to December period only: no accounts appear to have survived for the first half-year.
8. Traffic receipts as such ceased to be shown from mid-1906, when they were taken over by the Great Western under the leasing arrangements. Operating profit in subsequent years corresponded roughly with the minima provided for in the lease.
9. Included under the average rent charge and interest heading for 1869-1875 is a payment of £6,300 to John Barrow for the cumulative hire costs for engines from 1868.
10. Liabilities for the costs of the Llanidloes joint line and station had been accruing since 1872, and for interest on temporary loans, since the line opened. Yet somehow they escaped attention until 1884, when it became necessary to incorporate the unpaid backlog - all but £28,000 - as a charge on the revenue account. This sum is included with the 1881-1888 average. The GWR, on leasing the M. & M. in 1906, made a settlement with the Cambrian for all the outstanding debt for the Llanidloes joint line and station, and this debt was "written off" by means of a credit to the revenue account.
11. All train mileage was shown as mixed until mid-1897, when seperate totals for mixed, passenger, and goods workings were kept for the first time. From then until mid-1906, some 37% of the total was mixed, 35% passenger, and 28% by goods train.

Descriptive List of Engines taken over by the Great Western Railway, June 1906. Appendix II

Type	Number	Started	Reb'lt	Maker	Weight in W'k Order	Cylinders	Whl. Dia.	W'base	Boiler Length	Boiler O/S Dia	Firebox Length Outside	Firebox Length Inside
0-6-0	1 1338	1904	-	L&NWR	29t.11cwt	17"by24"	4'3"	15' 6"	9'10"	4' 0"	6' 0"	4' 8½"
2-4-2T	2 1304	(1866)	(1891)	Sharp Stewart	45t. 5cwt	17"by22"	(3'6") (5'6")	20' 8"	9' 8"	4' 3"	4'10"	4' 1"
2-4-0	3 1305	1866	1891	Sharp Stewart	25t.10cwt	16"by20"	(3'6") (5'6")	14' 4½"	9' 8"	4' 4"	4'10"	4' 1"
0-6-0	4 1339	1868	1898	M.W'dle	30t. 0cwt	17"by24"	4'6"	14'10½"	10' 1"	4' 5"	5' 6"	4' 9"
0-6-0	5 1340	1870	1891	S.St'rt	26t.10cwt	16"by24"	4'6"	14'10"	10' 4"	4' 2"	5' 1½"	4' 4"
2-4-2T	6 1306	1896	-	Sharp Stewart	47t. 0cwt	17"by22"	(3'6") (5'6")	21' 5"	9' 7"	4' 4"	5' 5½"	4'10½"
0-6-0	7 1341	1902	-	L&NWR	29t.10cwt	17"by24"	4'3"	15' 6"	9'10"	4' 0"	6' 0"	4' 8½"

Firebox Width	Firebox Depth	Tubes No.	Tubes Length	O/S Dia	Tubes manf.	Boil. Pres.	Tender in W'k Order	Tender wheels No.	Tender wheels Dia	Tender wheels W'base	Tank(s) (gall.)	Remarks
4'0½"	5'6½"	194	10' 4"	2"	Steel	150lb	25t. 0cwt	6	3'6	12' 0"	1,800	New copper firebox in 1904
3'9"	5'3"	168	10' 1"	2"	Brass	140lb	-	-	-	-	1,000	New copper firebox in 1903
3'8"	5'3"	168	9'10½"	2"	Brass	140lb	17t.18cwt	4	3'6	9' 7"	1,200	New copper firebox in 1904
4'0"	5'3"	171	10' 6"	2"	Brass	160lb	24t. 0cwt	6	3'6	11' 1"	1,600	Not working order. To repair
4'1"	5'3"	172	10' 9"	2"	Brass	140lb	17t.18cwt	4	3'6	9' 7"	1,200	New copper firebox in 1902
3'7½"	5'3"	179	10' 0"	2"	Brass	140lb	-	-	-	-	1,290	Based Pencader. New f/b 1905
4'0½"	5'6½"	194	10' 4"	2"	Steel	140lb	25t. 0cwt	6	3'6	12' 0"	1,800	

Notes.

1. Wheel diameters have been corrected. Other dimensions are unchanged from the original list and are thus not altogether to be relied on. - Refer to Chapter 6.
2. Dates for no.2 are shown in parenthesis, since the first refers to the original no.2, "Carmarthen", and the second to the construction of the new no.2, "Plynlimmon".

Descriptive List of Passenger Stock taken over by the Great Western Railway, June 1906. **Appendix III**

Number M&M	Number GWR	Class, and (No. compts.)	Over Mouldings Length	Over Mouldings Width	Inside Height	Wheels No.	Wheels W'base	Builder	Date	Cost
2	3976	Third (5)	25' 8"	8' 0"	6' 8"	4	14' 7"	?	?	?
3	3977	Third (5)	25'10"	8'1½"	7' 1"	"	14' 6"	Ashbury	1890	£ 333
4	3978	Third (5)	25' 9"	8' 0"	7' 0"	"	14' 7"	"	"	"
5	3979	Third (5)	25'10"	8'1½"	7' 1"	"	14' 6"	"	"	"
6	1421	(Pass. Lugg.) (& Brake Van)	23' 2"	(9' 2") (7'11")	6' 8"	"	13' 7"	?	?	?
18	1422	(Pass. Lugg.) (& Brake Van)	"	(9' 2") (7'11")	"	"	"	"	"	"
19	7895	First/Sec'd (2) / (2)	25' 9"	8' 0"	7' 0"	"	14' 6"	Ashbury	1890	"
20	7896	First/Sec'd (2) / (2)	"	"	"	"	"	"	"	"
8	7897	1st/2nd/3rd (1)/(1)/(5)	38' 3"	8' 1"	6' 9"	6	28' 0"	Met.C&W	1883	£ 498
10	3980	Third (8)	42' 3"	8' 2"	7' 4"	8	35' 8"	"	1895	£1231
11	3981	Third (8)	"	"	"	"	"	"	"	"
12	7898	1st/2nd/3rd (2)/(2)/(3)	41' 2"	8' 0"	7' 0"	"	33' 9"	Ashbury	"	£1496
13	7899	1st/2nd/3rd (2)/(2)/(3)	"	"	"	"	"	"	"	"
14	7900	(1st/lav/2nd) (saloon & bk)	43' 2"	"	"	"	35' 9"	"	"	£ 740
15	3982	(Third/Lugg.) (Brake (3))	37'10"	(8'11") (8' 0")	"	"	27'10"	"	1892	£ 800
1	841	Horse Box	15' 6"	7' 2"	7' 7"	4	10' 1"	?	?	?

Notes.

1. Dimensions are quoted unchanged from the original list, regardless of inaccuracies. Thus the lengths indicated above for nos.10-13 and no.15 are almost certainly wrong. - Refer to Chapter 6.
2. The building date for nos.3-5 relates to rebuilding, and not new construction. - Refer again to Chapter 6.
3. All vehicles had laminated springs to buffing and drawgear, except for no.8, and all apart from the horsebox were equipped with automatic vacuum brake; the four-wheeled brake vans also had hand brakes. Eight-wheeled vehicles had steel frames; the remainder had frames of wood.
4. An alternative source shows the same dimensions, apart from length, for no.4 and no.5, i.e. width 8' 0", height 7' 0", wheelbase 14' 7".

Descriptive List of Goods Stock taken over by the Great Western Railway, June 1906.

Appendix IV

	Number			Tare Wt			Internal Dimensions					
Type	M&M	GWR	S	T.	Cwt.	Q	Length	Width	Height	W'base	Builder	Buffers
Ballast	5	14922	S	4	4	2	15' 3"	7' 1"	1' [illegible]"	9' 0"	M. & M.	Dead
"	7	3	S		?		"	"	"	"	"	"
"	9	4			?		"	"	"	"	"	"
"	11	5		4	0	0	"	"	"	"	"	"
"	17	6		4	4	0	"	"	"	"	"	"
"	22	7		4	0	0	"	"	"	"	"	"
"	27	8			?		"	"	"	"	"	"
Mineral	6	74826			?		15' 2"	7' 0"	1' 4"	9' 4"	"	"
"	8	7		4	4	1	"	"	"	"	"	"
"	10	8		4	4	1	"	"	"	"	"	"
"	12	9		4	8	0	"	"	"	"	"	"
"	13	74830	S	4	5	1	"	"	"	"	"	"
"	14	1		4	4	0	"	"	"	"	"	"
"	15	2		4	4	1	"	"	"	"	"	"
"	18	3		4	6	2	"	"	"	"	"	"
"	19	4		4	4	1	"	"	"	"	"	"
"	20	5	S	4	3	2	"	"	"	"	"	"
"	23	6	S	4	5	0	"	"	"	"	"	"
"	24	7		4	8	0	"	"	"	"	"	"
"	26	8		4	3	1	"	"	"	"	"	"
"	28	9		4	7	0	"	"	"	"	"	"
"	29	74840		4	6	2	"	"	"	"	"	"
"	30	1	S	4	3	0	"	"	"	"	"	"
"	31	2			?		"	"	"	"	"	"
Coal/Goods	32	3		4	15	0	"	"	2' 3"	9' 0"	"	"
Loco coal	33	33911	S	4	10	0	"	"	"	"	"	"
Coal/Goods	35	74844		4	17	0	"	"	3' 0"	"	"	"
"	36	5		4	12	0	"	"	2' 3"	"	"	"
"	37	6		4	11	0	"	"	"	"	"	"
"	38	7	S	4	14	0	"	"	"	"	"	"
"	39	8		4	15	0	"	"	"	"	"	"
"	40	9		4	10	0	"	"	"	"	"	"
Loco coal	41	33912	S	4	8	0	"	"	"	"	"	"
Coal/Goods	42	74850	S	4	13	2	"	"	3' 0"	"	"	"
"	43	1		4	7	2	"	"	2' 3"	"	"	"
"	44	2		4	10	0	"	"	"	"	"	"
"	45	3	S	4	9	0	"	"	"	"	"	"
"	47	4	S	4	12	0	"	"	"	"	"	"
"	49	5		4	17	0	"	"	"	"	"	"
"	50	6		4	15	0	"	"	"	"	"	"
"	52	7		4	18	0	"	"	3' 0"	"	"	"
Loco coal	53	33913		4	14	0	"	"	2' 3"	"	"	"
"	54	4		4	12	0	"	"	"	"	"	"
"	55	5	S	4	15	2	"	"	"	"	"	"
"	56	6	S	4	1	3	"	"	"	"	"	"
"	57	7	S	4	12	0	"	"	"	"	"	"
Coal/Goods	58	74858	S	4	13	0	"	"	"	"	"	"
"	59	9	S	4	14	2	"	"	"	"	"	"
"	60	74860		4	6	0	"	"	"	"	"	"
"	61	1			?		"	"	"	"	"	"
"	63	2		4	8	2	"	"	"	"	"	"
Loco coal	64	33918	S	4	9	0	"	"	"	"	"	"
Coal/Goods	65	74863		4	12	1	"	"	"	"	"	"
"	102	4		4	15	0	"	"	3' 0"	"	"	"
Loco coal	103	33919		4	11	1	"	"	?	"	"	"
Coal/Goods	104	74865		4	12	0	"	"	2' 3"	"	"	"
Loco coal	105	33920	S	4	10	0	"	"	"	"	"	"
Coal/Goods	106	74866	S	4	10	0	"	"	"	"	"	"
"	107	7		4	15	0	"	"	"	"	"	"

Type	M&M	GWR	S	T.Cwt.Q	Length	Width	Height	W'base	Builder	Buffers
Coal/Goods	108	74868		4 16 1	15' 2"	7' 0"	2' 3"	9' 0"	M. & M.	Dead
"	110	9		4 11 0	"	"	"	"	"	"
"	111	74870	S	4 10 0	"	"	"	"	"	"
Loco coal	112	33921		4 8 0	"	"	"	"	"	"
Coal/Goods	113	74871		4 16 0	"	"	"	"	"	"
Loco coal	114	33922	S	4 14 0	"	"	"	"	"	"
Coal/Goods	115	74872		4 18 0	"	"	"	"	"	Volute
"	116	3		4 12 2	"	"	"	"	"	Dead
"	117	4	S	4 13 2	"	"	"	"	"	"
"	118	5		4 12 1	"	"	"	"	"	"
"	137	6		4 13 0	"	"	3' 0"	"	"	"
Goods Van	67	79591		5 17 2	14' 4"	7' 3"	6' 8"	"	Met.C&W	Spring
" "	68	2		6 4 0	"	"	"	"	"	"
" "	69	3		6 1 0	"	"	"	"	"	"
" "	70	4		5 15 1	"	"	"	"	"	"
" "	71	5		4 11 0	16' 3"	6'10"	6' 3"	9'11"	M. & M.	S/Cont.
" "	72	6		5 4 0	"	"	"	"	"	"
" "	73	7		5 0 2	"	"	"	"	"	"
" "	74	8		5 7 2	"	"	"	"	"	"
" "	75	9		4 17 1	"	"	"	"	"	"
" "	76	79600	S	5 4 2	"	"	"	"	"	"
" "	77	1		5 7 0	"	"	"	"	"	"
" "	78	2		5 2 0	"	"	"	"	"	Volute
" "	79	3	S	5 3 0	"	"	"	"	"	"
" "	80	4		5 5 0	"	"	"	"	"	"
Cattle "	119	68982		?	15' 4"	7' 3"	6' 9"	10' 0"	"	"
" "	120	3		?	"	"	"	"	"	"
" "	121	4		?	18' 3"	"	6' 8"	10' 6"	Met.C&W	Spring
" "	122	5		?	"	"	"	"	"	"
" "	123	6		?	"	"	"	"	"	"
" "	124	7		?	"	"	"	"	"	"
" "	125	8		?	15' 7"	"	6' 9"	10' 0"	M. & M.	Volute
" "	128	9		?	"	"	"	"	"	"
" "	129	68990		?	"	"	"	"	"	"
" "	131	1		6 8 2	18' 6"	"	6' 8"	"	"	"
Timber	133	70919		4 16 0	14' 7"	6'10"	3"	8'10"	"	Dead
"	134	70920		4 15 0	"	"	"	"	"	"
"	135	1		4 15 2	"	"	"	"	"	"
"	136	2		4 13 0	"	"	"	"	"	"
Brake Van	81	56481		10 2 1	16' 6"	6' 8"	6'10"	9' 6"	Met.C&W	Spring
Breakdown	138	14929	S	?	14'11"	7' 0"	6' 7"	"	Ashbury	Volute

Notes.

1. Dimensions are quotes unchanged from the original list, regardless of inaccuracies: "repeat" data is the most suspect.
2. All vehicles had four wheels of nominal 3ft. diameter, and wood frames and bodies. "S" indicates probable early scrapping by the GWR.
3. All M. & M.-built vehicles had india-rubber drawgear springing, dead or volute or self-contained spring buffers as indicated, and double - i.e. two block - brakes. They were of 7 tons capacity.
4. Metropolitan C. & W. goods and cattle vans had laminated spring buffing and drawgear, and double brakes. They were built in 1898 and delivered in 1899.
5. The Metropolitan C. & W. brake van was as above, except for four-block brakes operated by shaft and screw.
6. The Ashbury vehicle was described as a P. W. breakdown van. Both buffing and drawgear had volute springs. Braking was by shaft and screw operating on four blocks.
7. The Manchester and Milford Railway possessed 36 wagon sheets, numbered 1-24 and 132-143, of which no.9 was destroyed by fire.

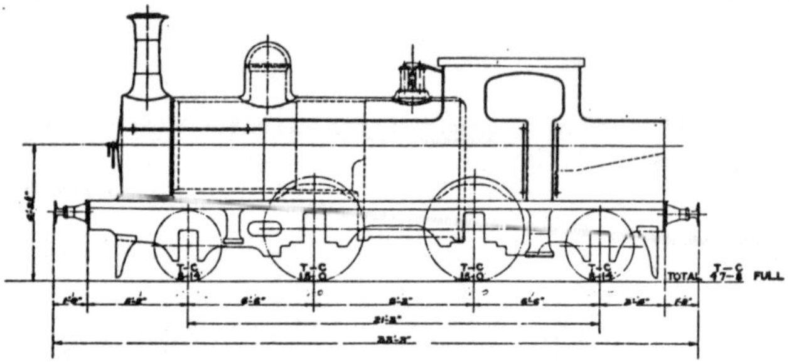

— DESCRIPTION —

CYLINDERS	DIAR 17 IN STROKE 22 IN STEAM PORTS 14½ IN X 1 IN EXHAUST 14½ IN X 3½ IN
BOILER	BARREL 9 FT - 7 INS DIAR OUTS 4 FT - 4 INS & 4 FT - 3 INS
FIREBOX	OUTS 5 FT - 6 INS X 3 FT - 8 INS INS 4 FT - 10½ INS X 3 FT - 1½ INS HEIGHT 5 FT - 2½ INS
TUBES	Nº 179 DIAR 2 IN LENGTH 9 FT - 10½ INS
HEATING SURFACE	TUBES 923 SQ FT FIREBOX 91·5 SQ FT TOTAL 1014·5 SQ FT
AREA OF FIREGRATE	15·25 SQ FT
WHEELS	LEADING 3 FT - 6 INS DRIVING 5 FT - 2 INS INTERMEDIATE 5 FT - 2 INS TRAILING 3 FT - 6 INS
WATER CAPACITY OF TANKS	1290 GALLONS
WORKING PRESSURE	140 LBS
TRACTIVE EFFORT	12921 LBS

— ENGINE Nº 1306 —

— SCALE ⅛ IN = 1 FOOT — — CLASS - 2-4-2 T —

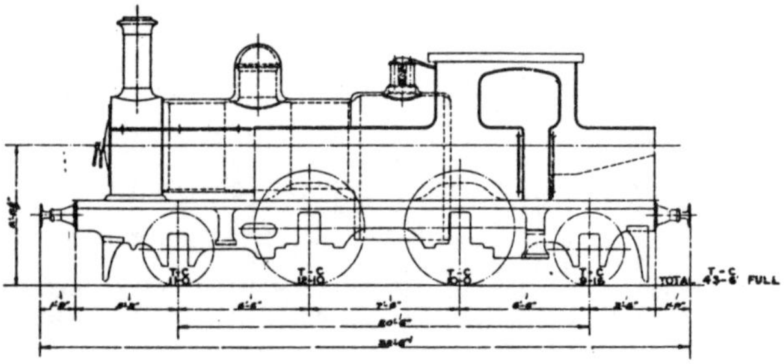

— DESCRIPTION —

CYLINDERS	DIAR 17 IN STROKE 22 IN STEAM PORTS IN X IN EXHAUST IN X IN
BOILER	BARREL 9 FT - 7 INS DIAR OUTS 4 FT - 2 INS & 4 FT - 1 INS
FIREBOX	OUTS 4 FT - 9 INS X 3 FT - 8 INS INS 4 FT - 1½ INS X 3 FT - 1½ INS HEIGHT 5 FT - 2½ INS
TUBES	Nº 163 DIAR 2 IN LENGTH 9 FT - 10½ INS
HEATING SURFACE	TUBES 866·33 SQ FT FIREBOX 82·31 SQ FT TOTAL 948·64 SQ FT
AREA OF FIREGRATE	12·88 SQ FT
WHEELS	LEADING 3 FT - 9 INS DRIVING 5 FT - 6 INS INTERMEDIATE 5 FT - 6 INS TRAILING 3 FT - 6 INS
WATER CAPACITY OF TANKS	1000 GALLONS
WORKING PRESSURE	140 LBS
TRACTIVE EFFORT	12138 LBS

— ENGINE Nº 1304 —

— SCALE ⅛ IN = 1 FOOT — — CLASS - 2-4-2 T —

GWR diagrams for the two former Manchester & Milford Railway tank engines, "Cader Idris" (above) and "Plynlimmon" (below).

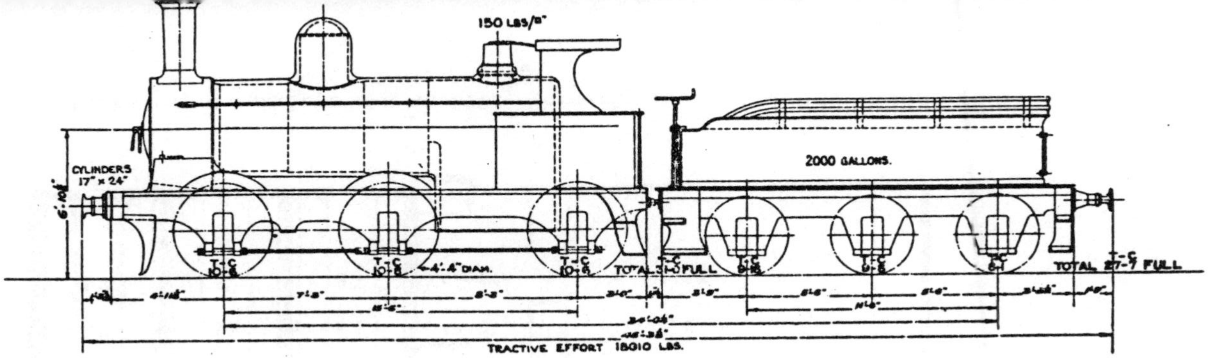

— DESCRIPTION —

Cylinders	DIAR 17 IN STROKE 24 IN STEAM PORTS 12¼ IN × 1½ IN EXHAUST 12¼ IN × 5¼ IN
Boiler	BARREL 9 FT - 9¾ INS DIAR OUTS 4 FT - 2 INS & 4 FT - 0 INS
Firebox	OUTS 5 FT - 5¼ INS × 4 FT - 0¾ INS INS 4 FT - 9⅛ INS × 3 FT - 5½ INS HEIGHT 5 FT - 7 INS
Tubes	Nº 194 DIAR 1¾ IN LENGTH 10 FT - 0⅜ INS
Heating Surface	TUBES 960·2 SQ FT FIREBOX 94·6 SQ FT TOTAL 1054·8 SQ FT
Area of Firegrate	17·1 SQ FT
Wheels	LEADING 4 FT - 4 INS DRIVING 4 FT - 4 INS TRAILING 4 FT - 4 INS
Water Capacity of Tender	2000 GALLONS
Working Pressure	150 LBS
Tractive Effort	18010 LBS

— ENGINE Nº 1338 —

— CLASS 0-6-0 —

— SCALE ⅜ IN = 1 FOOT —

GWR diagram for the ex-LNWR goods engine, M. & M.R. no.1

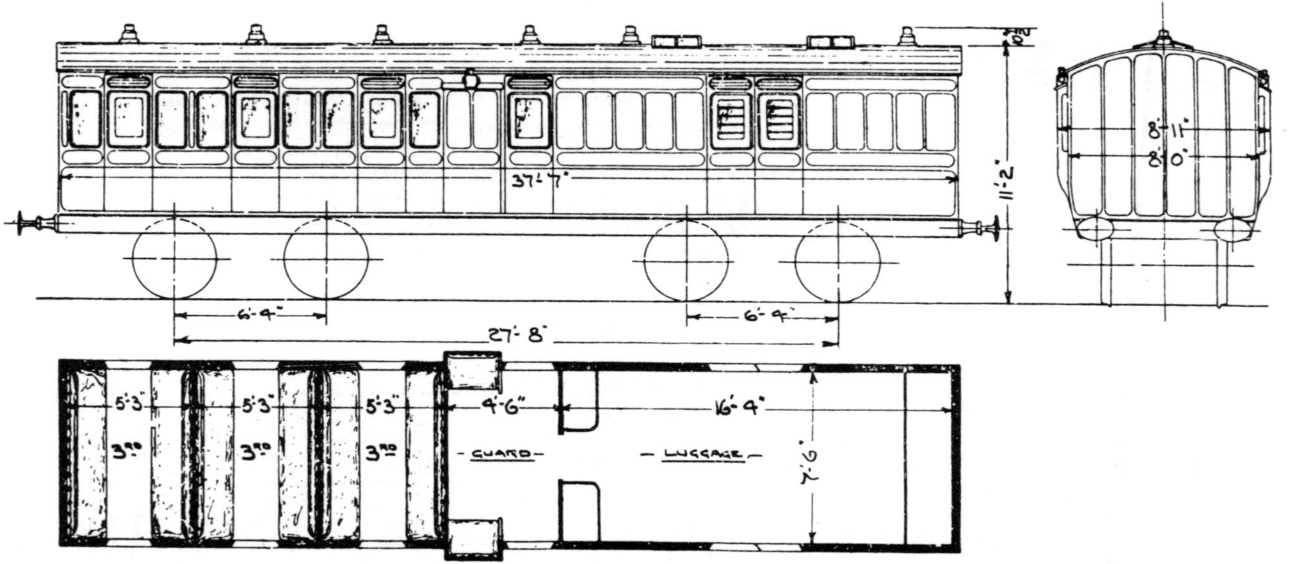

Brake third carriage GWR no.3982, formerly M. & M. no.15.

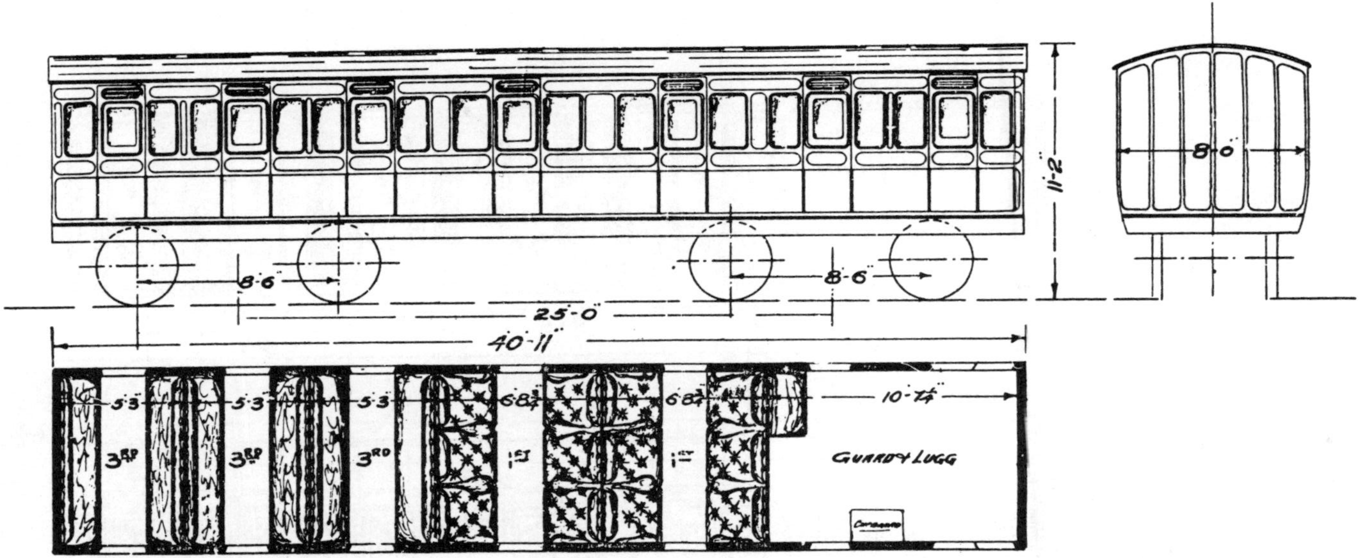

Brake composite carriage GWR no.7898, formerly M. & M. tricomposite no.12, later GWR brake third no.657.

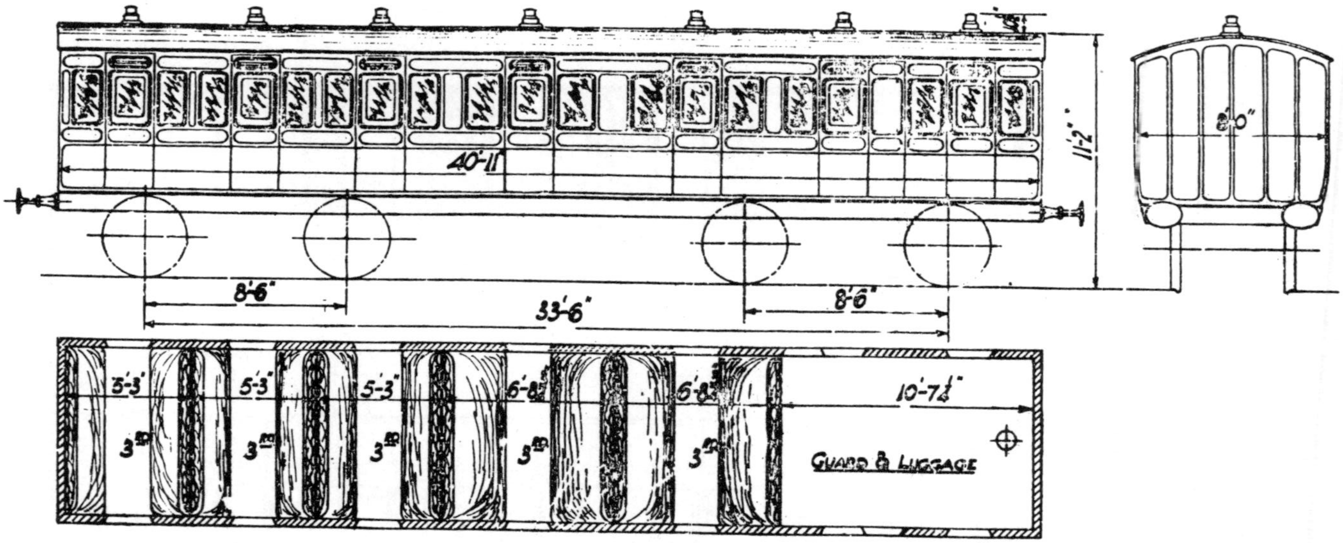

Brake third no.606, ex brake composite no.7899, formerly M. & M. tricomposite no.13, showing differences in brake end arrangement compared with no.7898.

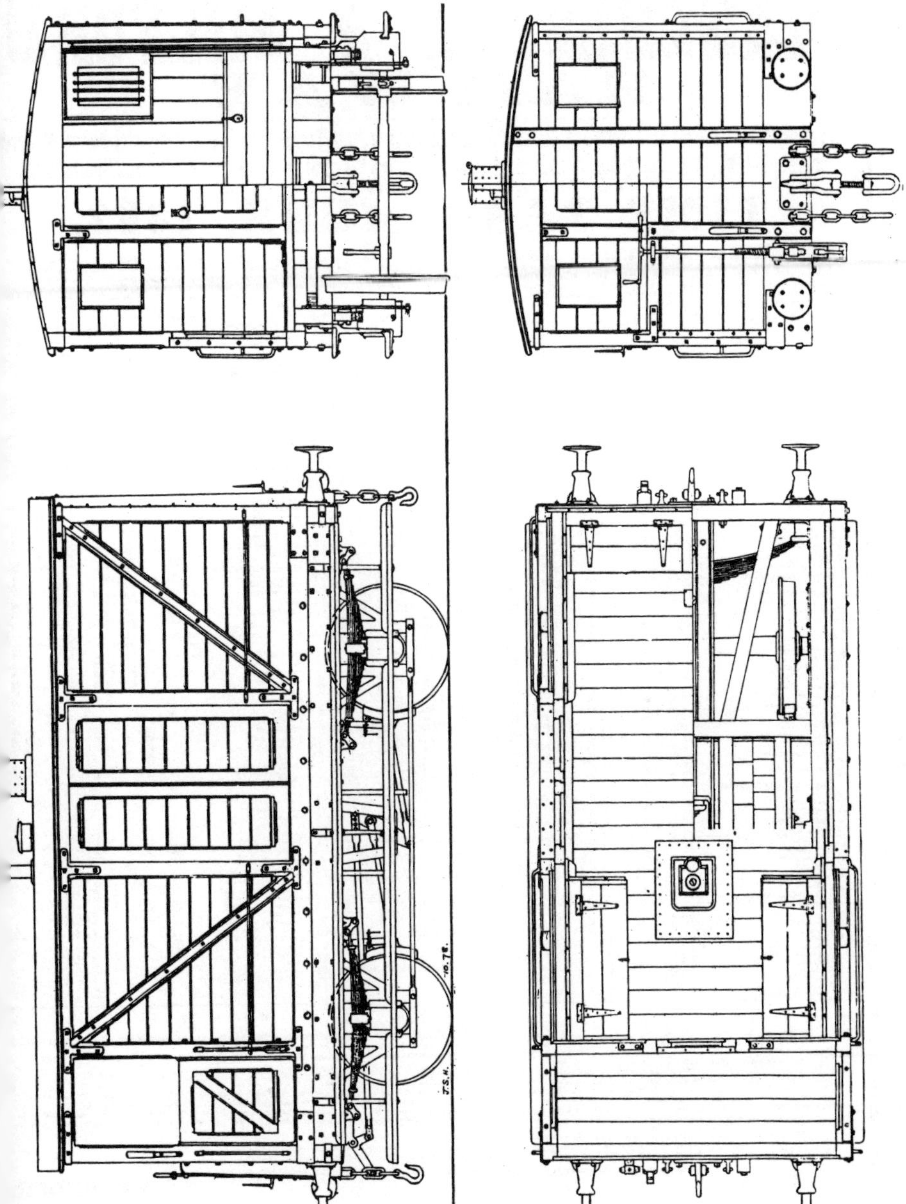

Goods brake van no.81, GWR no.56481, built by Metropolitan C. & W. Co. 1898, into stock, 1899.

ABERAYRON—A Four-horse Coach leaves Aberayron daily, arr. at Lampeter in time for the 10.14 a.m. Up Train. Returning after the arrival of the Down Train, due at Lampeter at 4.24 p.m.
NEW-QUAY—A covered Spring Van leaves New-Quay daily at 6.0 a.m., arr. at New-Quay Road at 10.20 a.m. Returning at 4.1 p.m., arriving in New-Quay about 8 p.m.

MANCHESTER & MILFORD RAILWAY.

Forming the shortest route between Aberystwyth and Carmarthen, Tenby, Pembroke, Haverfordwest, Milford Haven, Llanelly, Swansea, Cardiff, Newport, Bristol, and the West of England, Gloucester and Cheltenham.

TIME TABLE--JUNE, 1882.

[AND UNTIL FURTHER NOTICE.]

Passengers, to ensure being Booked, should be at the Stations Five Minutes before the time fixed for the Departure of the Trains. The times shown on this Bill are the times at which the Trains are intended to arrive at, and depart from, the several Stations, but the Company cannot guarantee these times being kept, under any circumstances, nor will they be responsible for delay. The times of other Railways, and Coaches, are inserted for the convenience of the Public, but the Company do not guarantee their correctness. NOTE.—The Station Clocks are set to Greenwich Time, and are faster by eleven minutes than the true time of the District. Granting Tickets to Passengers to places off this Company's Line is an arrangement made for the greater convenience of the Public, but the Company do not hold themselves responsible for any delay, detention, or other loss or injury arising off their Line, or from the acts or default of other parties, or for the correctness of the times over other Lines or Companies, or of Coaches, or for the arrival of this Company's Trains in time for the nominally corresponding Train or Coach, of any other Company or Party.—When their Trains do not arrive in time, such Tickets will be available onward by the first practicable Train, and the Tickets are issued subject to this understanding and proviso.

UP.

Railway	STATIONS	WEEK DAYS 1	2		3		4
G. W. Ry.	MANCHESTER (Victoria Station) dep.	...	...	...	a.m. 6 20	...	a.m. 10 5
	Warrington „	...	...	...	7 18	...	10 53
	LIVERPOOL (Landing Stage) „	...	...	...	8 10	...	11 30
	Birkenhead „	...	...	...	8 26	...	11 45
	Chester „	...	...	...	9 5	...	12 30
	Wrexham „	...	...	...	9 31	...	12 56
	Ruabon „	...	...	...	9 42	...	1 11
	OSWESTRY (G. W.) arr.	...	...	...	10 16	...	1 38
L. & N. W. Ry.	LONDON (Euston Square) dep.	...	...	...	5 15	...	9 0
	Birmingham (New Street.) „	...	...	...	7 20	...	11 20
	Liverpool (Lime Street) „	...	...	...	7 20	...	12 0
	Shrewsbury „	...	...	...	10 30	...	2 20
	Welshpool (S. & W'pool.) arr.	...	...	...	11 15	...	3 10
	Leeds dep.	...	...	...	...	...	9 25
	Manchester (London Road.) „	...	...	...	7 15	...	11 45
	Preston „	...	...	...	5 50	...	11 25
	Crewe „	...	...	...	8 40	...	1 7
	Whitchurch arr.	...	...	...	9 14	...	1 28
Cambrian Railway. DOWN	Whitchurch dep.	...	a.m.	...	9 50	...	1 40
	Oswestry „	...	3 0	...	10 40	...	2 25p
	Welshpool „	...	4 40	...	11 30	...	3 15p
	Newtown „	...	5 16	...	12 7	...	3 50
	Moat Lane Junction „	...	5 30	...	12 19	...	4 5
	Machynlleth „	...	6 35	...	1 28	...	5 3
	Borth „	...	7 4	...	2 0	...	5 35
	Aberystwyth arr.	...	7 25	...	2 27	...	5 57
	Classes...(Manchester & Milford Railway.)	1 2 3	1 2 gov.		1 2 3		1 2 3
Manchester & Milford Railway.	ABERYSTWYTH dep.	a.m. ..	a.m. 8 30	..	p.m. 2 35	..	p.m. 6 15
	Llanrhystyd Road „	...	8 40	..	2 43	..	6 28
	Llanilar „	..	8 48	..	2 50	..	6 39
	Trawscoed „	..	8 58	..	2 59	..	6 57
	Strata Florida „	..	9 29	..	3 25	...	7 33
	TREGARON „	..	9 44	..	3 35	..	7 48
	Pont-Llanio „	..	9 53	..	3 41	..	7 57
	Llangybi „	.. (Signal)	A	.. (Signal)	..	.. (Signal)	A
	Derry Ormond „	..	10 6	..	3 52	..	8 9
	LAMPETER „	8 5	10 19	..	4 0	..	8 19
	Llanybyther „	8 20	10 35	..	4 13	..	8 32
	Maesycrugiau „	8 30	10 44	..	4 20	..	8 44
	New-Quay Road „	8 40	10 50	..	4 27	..	8 54
	PENCADER arr.	8 50	10 58	..	4 33	..	9 0
Great Western Railway.	Pencader dep.	8 55	11 3	..	5 0	..	9 10
	Llanpumpsaint „	9 15	11 19	..	5 16	..	9 26
	Conwil „	9 26	11 29	..	5 26	..	9 37
	Bronwydd Arms „	9 40	11 43	..	5 41	..	9 49
	CARMARTHEN arr.	9 51	11 55	..	5 54	..	10 2
	CARMARTHEN dep.	9 55	12 0	..	6 15	..	...
	CARMARTHEN JUNCTION arr.	9 59	12 5	..	6 19	..	...
	CARMARTHEN JUNCTION dep.	11 20	2 39	..	6 30	..	..
	St Clears „	11 36	2 55	..	6 47	..	..
	WHITLAND arr.	11 47	3 7	..	6 58	..	..
	Haverfordwest dep.	12 30	3 50	..	7 43	..	..
	NEW MILFORD arr.	12 55	4 15	..	8 10	..	..
Pem. & Tenby R. DOWN	Whitland dep.	12 0	3 25	..	7 20	..	..
	NARBERTH „	12 15	3 40	..	7 36	..	..
	Saundersfoot „	12 35	4 5	..	7 55	..	...
	TENBY „	12 50	4 20	..	8 30	..	..
	Manorbier „	1 2	4 51	..	8 45	..	...
	PEMBROKE „	1 15	5 5	..	9 5	..	..
	PEMBROKE DOCK arr.	1 25	5 15	..	9 15	..	..
Great Western Railway.	CARMARTHEN JUNCTION dep.	10 15	12 19	...	6 30	...	...
	Llanelly „	10 50	1 8	...	7 4	...	...
	SWANSEA arr.	11 25	1 55	...	7 45	...	...
	Neath dep.	11 35	2 7	...	7 36	...	...
	Cardiff arr.	12 40	3 55	...	9 5	...	...
	Newport dep.	1 5	4 20	...	9 30	...	...
	Portskewet Junction „	1 35	4 56	...	...	...	...
	BRISTOL „	3 10	6 45	...	...	...	...
	Chepstow „	1 35	5 12	...	10 0	...	...
	GLOUCESTER „	2 20	6 20	...	10 47	...	...
	Cheltenham „	2 55	6 55	...	11 35	...	...
	PADDINGTON „	5 45	10 20	...	4 35	...	...

FARES.

	RETURN. 1st	2nd	3rd	SINGLE. 1st	2nd	3rd	Gov.
ABERYSTWITH TO	s. d.	s. d.	s. d.	s. d.	s. d.	s. d.	s. d.
Llanrhystyd Road	[illegible]	[illegible]	[illegible]	[illegible]	[illegible]	[illegible]	[illegible]
Llanilar	[illegible]	[illegible]	[illegible]	[illegible]	[illegible]	[illegible]	[illegible]
Trawscoed	[illegible]	[illegible]	[illegible]	[illegible]	[illegible]	[illegible]	[illegible]
Strata Florida	[illegible]	[illegible]	[illegible]	[illegible]	[illegible]	[illegible]	[illegible]
Tregaron	[illegible]	[illegible]	[illegible]	[illegible]	[illegible]	[illegible]	[illegible]
Pont Llanio	[illegible]	[illegible]	[illegible]	[illegible]	[illegible]	[illegible]	[illegible]
Derry Ormond	[illegible]	[illegible]	[illegible]	[illegible]	[illegible]	[illegible]	[illegible]
Lampeter	[illegible]	[illegible]	[illegible]	[illegible]	[illegible]	[illegible]	[illegible]
Llanybyther	[illegible]	[illegible]	[illegible]	[illegible]	[illegible]	[illegible]	[illegible]
Maesycrugiau	[illegible]	[illegible]	[illegible]	[illegible]	[illegible]	[illegible]	[illegible]
New-Quay Road	[illegible]	[illegible]	[illegible]	[illegible]	[illegible]	[illegible]	[illegible]
Pencader	[illegible]	[illegible]		[illegible]	[illegible]	[illegible]	[illegible]
Carmarthen	[illegible]	[illegible]	[illegible]	[illegible]	[illegible]	[illegible]	[illegible]
STRATA FLORIDA TO	1st	2nd	3rd	1st	2nd	3rd	Gov.
Aberystwith	[illegible]	[illegible]	[illegible]	[illegible]	[illegible]	[illegible]	[illegible]
Tregaron	[illegible]	[illegible]	[illegible]	[illegible]	[illegible]	[illegible]	[illegible]
Lampeter	[illegible]	[illegible]	[illegible]	[illegible]	[illegible]	[illegible]	[illegible]
Llanybyther	[illegible]	[illegible]	[illegible]	[illegible]	[illegible]	[illegible]	[illegible]
New-Quay Road	[illegible]	[illegible]	[illegible]	[illegible]	[illegible]	[illegible]	[illegible]
Pencader	[illegible]	[illegible]		[illegible]	[illegible]	[illegible]	[illegible]
TREGARON TO	1st	2nd	3rd	1st	2nd	3rd	Gov.
Aberystwith	[illegible]	[illegible]	[illegible]	[illegible]	[illegible]	[illegible]	[illegible]
Strata Florida	[illegible]	[illegible]	[illegible]	[illegible]	[illegible]	[illegible]	[illegible]
Lampeter	[illegible]	[illegible]	[illegible]	[illegible]	[illegible]	[illegible]	[illegible]
Llanybyther	[illegible]	[illegible]	[illegible]	[illegible]	[illegible]	[illegible]	[illegible]
New-Quay Road	[illegible]	[illegible]	[illegible]	[illegible]	[illegible]	[illegible]	[illegible]
Pencader	[illegible]	[illegible]	[illegible]	[illegible]	[illegible]	[illegible]	[illegible]
Carmarthen	[illegible]	[illegible]	[illegible]	[illegible]	[illegible]	[illegible]	[illegible]
LAMPETER TO	1st	2nd	3rd	1st	2nd	3rd	Gov.
Aberystwith	[illegible]	[illegible]	[illegible]	[illegible]	[illegible]	[illegible]	[illegible]
Llanrhystyd Road	[illegible]	[illegible]	[illegible]	[illegible]	[illegible]	[illegible]	[illegible]
Llanilar	[illegible]	[illegible]	[illegible]	[illegible]	[illegible]	[illegible]	[illegible]
Trawscoed	[illegible]	[illegible]	[illegible]	[illegible]	[illegible]	[illegible]	[illegible]
Strata Florida	[illegible]	[illegible]	[illegible]	[illegible]	[illegible]	[illegible]	[illegible]
Tregaron	[illegible]	[illegible]	[illegible]	[illegible]	[illegible]	[illegible]	[illegible]
Pont Llanio	[illegible]	[illegible]	[illegible]	[illegible]	[illegible]	[illegible]	[illegible]
Derry Ormond	[illegible]	[illegible]	[illegible]	[illegible]	[illegible]	[illegible]	[illegible]
Llanybyther	[illegible]	[illegible]	[illegible]	[illegible]	[illegible]	[illegible]	[illegible]
Maesycrugiau	[illegible]	[illegible]	[illegible]	[illegible]	[illegible]	[illegible]	[illegible]
New-Quay Road	[illegible]	[illegible]	[illegible]	[illegible]	[illegible]	[illegible]	[illegible]
Pencader	[illegible]	[illegible]	[illegible]	[illegible]	[illegible]	[illegible]	[illegible]
Carmarthen	[illegible]	[illegible]	[illegible]	[illegible]	[illegible]	[illegible]	[illegible]
LLANYBYTHER TO	1st	2nd	3rd	1st	2nd	3rd	Gov.
Aberystwith	[illegible]	[illegible]	[illegible]	[illegible]	[illegible]	[illegible]	[illegible]
Strata Florida	[illegible]	[illegible]	[illegible]	[illegible]	[illegible]	[illegible]	[illegible]
Tregaron	[illegible]	[illegible]	[illegible]	[illegible]	[illegible]	[illegible]	[illegible]
Lampeter	[illegible]	[illegible]	[illegible]	[illegible]	[illegible]	[illegible]	[illegible]
New-Quay Road	[illegible]	[illegible]	[illegible]	[illegible]	[illegible]	[illegible]	[illegible]
Pencader	[illegible]	[illegible]	[illegible]	[illegible]	[illegible]	[illegible]	[illegible]
Carmarthen	[illegible]	[illegible]	[illegible]	[illegible]	[illegible]	[illegible]	[illegible]
NEW-QUAY RD. TO	1st	2nd	3rd	1st	2nd	3rd	Gov.
Aberystwith	[illegible]	[illegible]	[illegible]	[illegible]	[illegible]	[illegible]	[illegible]
Strata Florida	[illegible]	[illegible]	[illegible]	[illegible]	[illegible]	[illegible]	[illegible]
Tregaron	[illegible]	[illegible]	[illegible]	[illegible]	[illegible]	[illegible]	[illegible]
Lampeter	[illegible]	[illegible]	[illegible]	[illegible]	[illegible]	[illegible]	[illegible]
Llanybyther	[illegible]	[illegible]	[illegible]	[illegible]	[illegible]	[illegible]	[illegible]
Pencader	[illegible]	[illegible]	[illegible]	[illegible]	[illegible]	[illegible]	[illegible]
Carmarthen	[illegible]	[illegible]	[illegible]	[illegible]	[illegible]	[illegible]	[illegible]
PENCADER TO	1st	2nd	3rd	1st	2nd	3rd	Gov.
New-Quay Road	[illegible]	[illegible]	[illegible]	[illegible]	[illegible]	[illegible]	[illegible]
Maesycrugiau	[illegible]	[illegible]	[illegible]	[illegible]	[illegible]	[illegible]	[illegible]
Llanybyther	[illegible]	[illegible]	[illegible]	[illegible]	[illegible]	[illegible]	[illegible]
Lampeter	[illegible]	[illegible]	[illegible]	[illegible]	[illegible]	[illegible]	[illegible]
Derry Ormond	[illegible]	[illegible]	[illegible]	[illegible]	[illegible]	[illegible]	[illegible]
Pont Llanio	[illegible]	[illegible]	[illegible]	[illegible]	[illegible]	[illegible]	[illegible]
Tregaron	[illegible]	[illegible]	[illegible]	[illegible]	[illegible]	[illegible]	[illegible]
Strata Florida	[illegible]	[illegible]	[illegible]	[illegible]	[illegible]	[illegible]	[illegible]
Trawscoed	[illegible]	[illegible]	[illegible]	[illegible]	[illegible]	[illegible]	[illegible]
Llanilar	[illegible]	[illegible]	[illegible]	[illegible]	[illegible]	[illegible]	[illegible]
Llanrhystyd Road	[illegible]	[illegible]	[illegible]	[illegible]	[illegible]	[illegible]	[illegible]
Aberystwith	[illegible]	[illegible]	[illegible]	[illegible]	[illegible]	[illegible]	[illegible]

NO SUNDAY TRAINS ON THIS LINE.

DOWN.

Railway	Miles	STATIONS	WEEK DAYS 1	2	3	4		5
Great Western Railway.		PADDINGTON dep.	...	p.m. 8 10	a.m.	a.m. 5 30	p.m. ...	a.m. 10 20
		Cheltenham „	...	11 55	...	8 40	...	1 10
		GLOUCESTER „	...	12 50	...	9 15	...	1 40
		Chepstow „	...	1 40	...	10 19	...	2 23
		BRISTOL „	...	...	...	9 0	...	12 45
		Portskewet Junction „	...	...	...	10 32	...	2 15
		Newport „	...	2 13	...	11 0	...	2 55
		Cardiff „	...	2 38	...	11 26	...	3 18
		Neath „	...	3 55	7 5	12 52	...	4 30
		SWANSEA „	...	4 5	7 20	1 0	...	4 35
		Llanelly „	...	4 44	8 4	1 47	...	5 15
		CARMARTHEN JUNCTION arr.	...	5 16	9 11	2 30	...	5 45
Pem. & Tenby Ry. UP		PEMBROKE DOCK dep.	..	..	..	10 0	..	4 30
		PEMBROKE „	..	..	..	10 8	..	4 38
		Manorbier „	..	..	..	10 22	..	4 51
		TENBY „	..	..	..	10 40	12 55	5 7
		Saundersfoot „	..	..	..	10 49	1 10	5 16
		NARBERTH „	..	..	..	11 10	1 35	5 35
		WHITLAND arr.	..	..	..	11 20	1 50	5 50
Great Western Railway.		NEW MILFORD dep.	..	2 45	6 45	10 35	1 0	5 0
		Haverfordwest „	..	..	7 9	10 57	1 24	5 24
		WHITLAND „	..	..	7 51	11 39	2 5	6 0
		St. Clears „	..	..	8 3	11 55	2 18	..
		CARMARTHEN JUNCTION arr.	..	3 48	8 20	12 11	2 33	6 25
		CARMARTHEN JUNCTION dep.	..	5 26	9 0	2 45		6 35
		CARMARTHEN „	..	5 45	9 7	2 55		7 0
		Bronwydd Arms „	..	5 56	9 18	3 6		7 11
		Conwil „	..	6 10	9 31	3 16		7 22
		Llanpumpsaint „	..	6 21	9 43	3 27		7 36
		Pencader arr.	..	6 40	10 4	3 47		7 56
	Mls.	Classes...(Manchester & Milford Railway).	1 2 3	1 2 3	1 2 gov	1 2 3		1 2 3
Manchester & Milford Railway.	—	PENCADER dep.	a.m. On Mondays only.	a.m. 6 45	a.m. 10 10	p.m. 3 54	...	p.m. 8 5
	2	New-Quay Road „		7 0	10 16	4 1	...	8 12
	4	Maesycrugiau „		7 10	10 25	4 6	...	8 18
	8	Llanybyther „		7 30	10 35	4 15	...	8 32
	13	LAMPETER „	...	7 45	10 53	4 26	...	8 47
	15	Derry Ormond „	...	...	10 59	4 30	...	8 54
	16	Llangybi „	... (Signal)	...	A	(Signal)	... (Signal)	A
	20	Pont-Llanio „	...	...	11 13	4 41	...	9 8
	23	TREGARON „	9 10	...	11 22	4 48	...	9 16
	26	Strata-Florida „	9 26	...	11 37	5 0	...	9 29
	33	Trawscoed „	9 47	...	11 57	5 20	...	9 52
	36	Llanilar „	9 53	...	12 6	5 27	...	10 0
	38	Llanrhystyd Road „	10 5	...	12 15	5 37	...	10 9
	42	ABERYSTWYTH arr.	10 15	...	12 25	5 45	...	10 20
Cambrian Railway. UP		ABERYSTWYTH dep.	...	...	12 50	6 0	...	...
		Borth arr.	...	...	1 11	6 28	...	...
		Machynlleth „			1 50	6 56	...	...
		Moat Lane Junction „			3 5	8 1	...	
		Newtown „			3 12	8 15	...	...
		Welshpool „			3 47	8 50	...	...
		Oswestry „			4 48	9 28	...	
		Whitchurch „			5 45	10 15	...	
L. & N. W. Ry.		Whitchurch dep.		...	6 20	10 58	...	...
		Crewe arr.		...	7 0	11 25	...	...
		Warrington „	...	...	8 20	1 34	...	...
		Liverpool (Lime Street) „	...	...	8 20	3 0	...	...
		Preston „	...	...	9 20	1 58	...	...
		Manchester (London Road) „	...	...	8 20	12 50	...	...
		Leeds „	...	...	11 30	...	...	
		Welshpool (S. & W'pool) dep.	..	...	3 55	9 0	...	
		Shrewsbury „	..	...	5 35	10 20	...	
		Birmingham (New Street) arr.	..	...	8 0	2 10	...	...
		LONDON (Euston Square) „	..	...	10 0	4 30	...	...
G. W. Ry.		OSWESTRY (G. W.) dep.			5 35	11 45	...	...
		Ruabon arr.		...	6 10	12 18	...	...
		Wrexham „	...	...	6 22	12 22	...	...
		Chester „	...	...	6 55	12 45	...	...
		Birkenhead „	...	...	7 47	3 5	...	...
		LIVERPOOL (Landing Stage) „	...	...	8 5	3 40	...	
		Warrington „	...	...	8 48	...	...	...
		MANCHESTER (Victoria Station) „	...	...	9 40	...	...	...

NOTICES, &c.

LLANGYBI:—For the convenience of parties attending the Aberystwith Market a Train will call at 11.3, and for the Tregaron Market the First Down Train will call at 11.3 a.m., and the Return Train in the Evening at 8.3 p.m.; also on Fridays for Lampeter Market at 10.1 a.m., and the Return Train at 8.56 p.m. The same arrangements will be in operation on Fair days.
MARKET TICKETS will be issued from all Stations to Aberystwith, Llanilar, Strata Florida, Tregaron, Lampeter, Llanybyther, New Quay Road, and Carmarthen, on Market and Fair Days, available for Return by the last Up and Down Trains only.
HOLDERS OF SEASON TICKETS are subject to the same Rules and Regulations as Ordinary Passengers.
CHILDREN'S TICKETS—Children under three years of age are Conveyed Free; and those above three and under twelve at half price.
DAY TICKETS—[not Transferable] issued on Saturdays will be available for return on the day they are issued or on the Monday following. Passengers taking Day Tickets and getting out of the Train at any Station otherwise than the one mentioned on the Ticket will not be allowed to re-enter the Train without re-booking. No Tickets will be issued after a Train is in sight at an intermediate Station.
PASSENGERS' LUGGAGE—The Company are not responsible for Luggage unless it is booked and paid for according to its value. Each first class Passenger is allowed 112lbs.; each second class Passenger 100lbs., and each third class Passenger 60lbs. weight of Luggage free of charge, the same not being MERCHANDISE or other articles carried for HIRE or PROFIT. Any Passenger carrying more than the above weight will be charged for the excess.
GRATUITIES—The receiving of gratuities by any of the Company's servants will be followed by dismissal.
SMOKING—Smoking in the Carriages, except those provided with Smoking Compartments, or at the Stations, is strictly prohibited, under a penalty of Forty Shillings.
HORSE BOXES, CARRIAGE TRUCKS, AND CATTLE WAGGONS—Twelve hours notice must be given when either of these Vehicles are required.

THERE IS A REFRESHMENT ROOM AT THE LAMPETER STATION.

General Manager's Office,
Aberystwyth, May 24th, 1882.

BY ORDER.

JOHN MORGAN, STEAM PRINTER, OBSERVER OFFICE, 1, NORTH PARADE, ABERYSTWYTH.

Typical Manchester & Milford Rly. sheet timetable displayed at the company's stations.